Corp

CORPS COMMANDER

Lieut.-General Sir Brian Horrocks

with Eversley Belfield and
Major-General H. Essame

LUME BOOKS

LUME BOOKS

First published by Sidgwick and Jackson Limited in 1977

Copyright © Sir Brian Horrocks, Eversley Belfield and Major-General H. Essame 1977

This edition published in 2023 by Lume Books

The right of Sir Brian Horrocks, Eversley Belfield and Major-General H. Essame to be identified as the authors of this work has been asserted by them in accordance with the Copyright, Design and Patents Act, 1988.

All rights reserved. No part of this publication may be reproduced, stored in a retrieval system, or transmitted in photocopying, recording or otherwise, without the prior permission of the copyright owner.

www.lumebooks.co.uk

Contents

List of Maps		vii
Brief Chronology		viii
Operation Code-Names		x
Introduction		1
1.	Back to the War	7
2.	Taking Over XXX Corps	32
3.	The Falaise Pocket	55
	i) Introduction	55
4.	Crossing the Seine	82
	i) The Crossing at Vernon	82
	ii) The Canadian Advance at Elbeuf	92
5.	The Advance to Brussels and Antwerp	96
6.	The Battle for the Arnhem Start Line	119
7.	The Arnhem Spearhead	129
	i) Montgomery's Instructions and My Orders to XXX Corps	129
	ii) Break-Out	139
	iii) The Other Side of the Hill	143
	iv) The Battle of Arnhem and the Advance to Nijmegen	148
	v) Fighting on the Island	159
8.	The Coastal Flank and the Opening of Antwerp	171
9.	The November Offensive Geilenkirchen	196
10.	The Ardennes Battle	209
	i) Introduction	209

	ii)	The Battle	215
	iii)	The Air in the Ardennes	222
	iv)	Goring's Last Fling	223
11.	The Battle for the Lower Rhine Bridgehead		231
	i)	Operation 'Veritable'	231
	ii)	The Canadian Corps in the Second Stage of the Battle	247
	iii)	Summary	254
12.	The Rhine Crossing and the Advance to the Elbe		255
13.	The Final Liberation of the Netherlands		274
	i)	Introduction	274

Postscript - Germany after V-E Day   286

British and German Artillery   291

British and Canadian Divisional Organization   293

Authors' Acknowledgements   304

List of Maps

The Falaise Pocket	72
The Crossing of the Seine and the Advance into Northern France	80
'Market Garden' Operation: The advance to Nijmegen and Arnhem, 17-26 September 1944	
The Arnhem-Nijmegen Battle	131
The Clearance of the Approaches to Antwerp and the Advance to the Maas, October-November 1944	147
The Ardennes Counter-Offensive	184
The Battles for the Banks of the Rhine, February-March 1944 and the Rhine Crossings	228
North-West Europe	296
Normandy Battle Front: The position on 1 and 16 August 1944	298
Forward Lines on 1, 15 and 30 September, and on 15 December 1944	300
The Final Advance into Germany and Holland, April-May 1945	302

Brief Chronology

1944

6 June	D-Day
9 July	Caen captured
25 July	Americans begin break-out from Normandy
6–8 August	German counter-attack at Mortain
8 August	Le Mans captured by Patton
15 August	Allied landings in the south of France
16–20 August	Climax of the Battle of the Falaise Gap
19 August	American forces gain bridgehead over the Seine
25–27 August	Second British Army cross the Seine
3 September	Brussels captured
4 September	Port of Antwerp captured intact
12 September	Le Havre captured, badly damaged
17–26 September	'Market Garden', Arnhem operation
22 September	Boulogne captured, badly damaged
1 October	Calais captured, badly damaged
6 October–8 November	Battles for the clearance of the Scheldt Estuary
28 November	Port of Antwerp opened
16 December	German counter-offensive in the Ardennes started

1945

22 February–10 March	Battles for the Lower Rhineland
7 March	Patton seizes the Remagen bridge across the Rhine

23–24 March	Rhine crossings made by the Twenty first Army Group
14 April	Arnhem captured
26 April	Bremen captured
4 May	German surrender to Montgomery

Note: The distance from Bayeux to Brussels is about 360 miles or 480 kilometres.

Operation Code-Names

BODENPLATTE:	Luftwaffe air attack on Allied airfields in Holland and Belgium, 1 January 1945
COBRA:	American break-out near St Lô, 25–29 July 1944
FORTITUDE:	Cover plan for 'Overlord'
MARKET GARDEN:	Second Army and airborne operations to seize bridge at Nijmegen and Arnhem, 17–26 September 1944
OVERLORD:	Allied campaign in north-west Europe, 1944–45
TOTALIZE:	Phase I of the First Canadian Army's attack towards Falaise, 8–11 August 1944
TRACTABLE:	Phase II of the First Canadian Army's attack towards Falaise, 14–16 August 1944
VERITABLE:	First Canadian Army's Rhineland attack, 8 February–10 March 1945

Introduction

SIR BRIAN HORROCKS

A Corps is the highest formation in the British Army which fights the day to day tactical battles. The Corps Commander is therefore in a unique position. He must obey the Commanders above him, and my immediate boss was General M. C. Dempsey, M.C., Commander of the Second Army, who issued my orders for the forthcoming battle, but in addition I was often visited by Montgomery, the Army Group Commander, and even by General Eisenhower, the Supreme Commander himself. Thus I was also more or less *au fait* with the strategical situation.

Unlike a Division, which always has its own troops under command, a Corps consists only of a permanent H.Q. staff, certain administrative echelons and usually some Corps Artillery Regiments consisting of heavier guns than those normally handled by Divisions. My superior commanders allotted me the divisions and specialist arms which, in their opinion, were required for the forthcoming battle.

For instance, XXX Corps was 200,000 strong during the Battle of the Reichswald, but after Alamein it consisted of only a few hundred men belonging to a salvage unit, because it was left behind to clear up the battlefield while the rest of the Eighth Army set off in hot pursuit of Rommel's defeated army.

My task as a Corps Commander was to plan the battle with the forces at my disposal, issue the orders, and then spend the greater part of every day going round the front – 'smelling the battlefield', as I used to call it – normally returning to my H.Q. at night.

When planning this book, my first inclination was to write it with the assistance of Brigadier Essame alone, as he was not only an extremely gallant infantry leader, one of the best if not the best in that famous West Country Division, the 43rd, which served throughout in XXX Corps, but also an historian in his own right. The difficulty which faced us was how to make this a straightforward account which would be understood by a wide public, many of whom would know little of military matters. If we stuck to our original brief inherent in the title, *Corps Commander*, the story would be limited almost entirely to the battles fought by my XXX Corps, operating on a comparatively narrow front, often only some twenty-five miles in width, and therefore occupying a very small slice of the vast canvas of Western Europe on which the war was being waged.

Then Essame had a brilliant idea and introduced me to a third prospective author in the shape of Eversley Belfield. It would be impossible to imagine anyone better qualified for this task; for over twenty-five years he has been on the staff of Southampton University, where he is the Senior Lecturer in Military History in the Adult Education Department, and has written several books on his own account, notably *The Boer War*, in the 'Concise Campaigns' series published by Leo Cooper. But, far more important from my point of view, he served throughout the war with the Royal Artillery and was an Air Observation Pilot with the Canadian Army, which included the Polish Division and was operating on the left flank of the Twenty-first Army Group. His official title was 'Air Observation Post Pilot with the Canadian Army', which meant in simple terms two things. Firstly, that, flying above the battle in a very small aircraft on his own, he reported back the fall of shot fired by the British and Canadian Army Group Royal Artillery (AGRA) which consisted of their medium and heavy guns. Secondly, good Air Observation Pilots were in short supply, and played such an important and dangerous part in the battle that they were privileged people and welcome to attend conferences at all levels. They therefore had an almost unique opportunity of viewing and understanding the battle as a whole.

Looking back, I realize now that I was so involved with XXX Corps battles that I literally knew nothing about the operations of the Canadians, Poles and certain other British Corps which fought from time to time in the Canadian Army on our left flank. My only contact with them came during the first phase of the Battle of the Reichswald, when I was under Canadian command. Belfield has described with simplicity – always the hallmark of a good writer – the vitally important campaign fought by the Canadians and Poles on our left flank in the clearance of the German troops holding the Pas de Calais area, and incidentally he also mentions the destruction of the VI site from which those horrible missiles were being launched and doing so much damage to the south of England. He also describes the battle for the different ports so badly needed as administrative bases by the Twenty-first Army Group, the capture of the Channel Ports, and the eventual opening of the Scheldt Estuary, so that Antwerp could become our main forward administrative base. Fortunately, contrary to the strictest orders (which he claims were unknown to him), Belfield kept and carried with him a diary, so his account is probably unique in the history of the European Campaign, and completely accurate. His chapters are so valuable that they must appear under his own name, as otherwise readers may be confused; moreover, in those chapters in which we both describe separate operations each part will bear the name of its author.

This is not a military history, giving detailed accounts of the various battles. There are plenty of these available, some good, some bad. I have tried to make this story primarily, but not exclusively, a personal account of the trials, tribulations and very occasional triumphs of one man during the long advance from Normandy to the Baltic. Hence the title, *Corps Commander*.

Unfortunately, and most unexpectedly, Essame died half-way through his contribution to the book. As I have therefore had to write the bulk of the chapters dealing with XXX Corps operations, Belfield very generously offered to take over the role of editor-in-chief. I will therefore end this Introduction by saying simply, 'Thank you, Eversley; you have saved a *Corps Commander* from the waste-paper basket!!'

Fig 1. General Horrocks, September 1944.
(*Sir Brian's private collection*)

Fig 2. General Horrocks receiving the C.B. from King George VI in 1944.
(Sir Brian's private collection)

Chapter 1
Back to the War
SIR BRIAN HORROCKS

On 3 August 1944 I took off from Northolt in General Montgomery's personal aircraft in order to fly out to Normandy and take over command of the veteran XXX Corps. At the beginning of June 1943 I had been wounded in North Africa and had spent the last fourteen months in a hospital backwater, remote from the strains and stresses of war. Now I was on my way back once more into the main stream of battle.

As we flew in a south-easterly direction I thought of many things. This was the third time in thirty years that I had crossed the Channel to France, in order to fight against the Germans. The first was in August 1914 when, at the age of eighteen, I was placed in charge of ninety-six Reservists – the first reinforcements for my Regiment, the 1st Battalion Middlesex Regiment, then fighting in France – and as I marched through cheering crowds to Chatham Station at the head of my draft, I felt a king among men. This was, I suppose, the last time that any glamour was attached to war. I lasted for exactly six weeks before being wounded and taken prisoner, which was three weeks longer than the average life of a subaltern in the 1914 war.

The second occasion was in May 1940. I was then an Instructor at the Staff College, Camberley, where I received a telephone call to the effect that I had been given command of the 2nd Battalion, Middlesex Regiment which, with the rest of the British Expeditionary Force (B.E.F.), was moving up to the line of the River Dyle in Belgium to meet the German army which had just invaded the Netherlands. Although I had no written orders, I managed to get on a boat sailing from Southampton and, on arrival in France, I sat on my valise at the side of the road up which the B.E.F. was advancing into Belgium. Eventually, a kindly Dental Officer gave me a lift in his truck which was taking up stores to a forward Casualty Clearing Station. I remember thinking at the time that Commanders in the past had entered battle in many different ways, but I was probably the first to do so in a dental truck. I arrived just in time, as we had our first clash with the Germans on the next day.

On this third occasion I was arriving in a much grander fashion, in the Dakota aircraft belonging to the Commander-in-Chief himself. I only hoped that I would prove worthy of such a distinguished entry into battle.

On 8 June, two days after D-Day, I had visited General Eisenhower in his U.K. Headquarters in Bushey Park, where I had been given a personal briefing by Bedell Smith, Eisenhower's extremely efficient Chief of Staff, on the situation in Normandy. This had enabled me to follow in outline the Battle of the Build-up as best I could from the newspaper reports. Although the initial landing had been successful, subsequent progress seemed to me to have been painfully slow, and the press obviously thought likewise. I knew enough about war to realize that some very bitter fighting must be taking place in the thick Normandy Bocage, as the beachhead was slowly being expanded. Could the Germans concentrate troops in Normandy faster than we could land on the beaches? The success of the whole operation depended on this simple question. I realized, moreover, that the storm which had lasted from 19 to 21 June must have seriously interfered with the intricate landing tables for both men and stores.

The initial landing on D-Day of this vast force had obviously been a triumph of naval planning and seamanship, organized by that great sailor, Admiral Sir Bertram Ramsay, an old friend from the days when he had been Flag Officer Dover. Fortunately, the air effort provided by the U.S. and R.A.F. was on an unprecedented scale, and Göring's Luftwaffe had been literally shot out of the sky.

Suddenly, we were over the beachhead. I don't know what I had expected to see, but certainly nothing comparable to the astonishing scenes of military activity which lay below. Offshore there was intense maritime activity, ships at anchor, unloading at the monstrous Mulberry Harbours – monstrous that man should have had the impertinence to throw down such a challenge to the sea and construct in a few days his own artificial harbour where none had existed before. It had been a truly Churchillian conception, and here it was, working away below me, playing a vital role in the Battle of the Build-up.

Small boats were darting about and hundreds of DUKWs (amphibious lorries) were driving backwards and forwards between the sea and the beachhead. The area inland from the beaches looked just like a dusty ant-heap, with stores, troops and vehicles moving about in every direction, and all the time aircraft were taking off and landing on strips which had been hewn out of the Normandy countryside. If it hadn't been for them, none of this would have existed at all. Without almost complete air superiority we would never have dared to risk such a concentration of men and materials as I saw below me.

Glancing to the east, I could see the eastern end of the bridgehead and the mouths of the River Orne and the Caen Canal. About five miles upstream lay the bridges at Bénouville which the 6th Airborne Division had captured on D-Day, landing in the dark and then pushing on north-east of Caen to the densely wooded ridge just west of the River Dives. This excellent defensive position I could faintly discern in the far distance.

In the bright sunlight the great sprawling city of Caen, with its many churches, dominated this flank. Neither was there any mistaking the huge steelworks of Colombelles in the northern suburbs west of the Orne, which had held up our advance for so long. Between Caen and Bayeux small compact villages dotted the countryside, now yellow with ripe corn. Looking inland to the south, I caught a glimpse in the dim distance of the belt of high ground which sprawls across the Cotentin peninsula, rising in places to a thousand feet or more, intersected by steep valleys and cut by streams and small rivers. Looking west for a brief moment, my eye was caught by the high cliffs on either side of the little harbour of Port-en-Bessin. This had been the point of junction between the British and American Armies on D-Day and the scene of the magnificent exploit of the 47th Royal Marine Commando supported by the Royal Navy and the R.A.F.

Today, of course, a combined operation on this scale would be far too vulnerable to nuclear attack, and we shall probably never see anything like it again.

A jeep was waiting to take me to Montgomery's Headquarters. At that time he had a dual role, C.-in-C. Twenty-first Army Group, and Commander of all the Ground Forces in Normandy. Though Eisenhower had come over to

Normandy two days before, his Supreme Headquarters was still in process of being established.

I entered the endless stream of vehicles moving through clouds of swirling dust along a road battered by the traffic of the past eight weeks. The air was sickly with the vapour of petrol and hot rubber. I caught sight of a 'brewed up' (burnt out) tank which had come to grief in the original landing. Beside the roads there were endless dumps of ammunition and rations. Some farm buildings had been completely obliterated. Others were pock-marked with the scars of machine-gun fire and shelling. Near the coast I caught sight of notice boards marked 'Danger – Mines' and 'Achtung – Minen' A few French peasants gazed glumly at the never-ending traffic with apparent indifference. Their corn, now yellow, lay uncut and trampled down in the fields.

As I drove through this scene of intense military activity, I had two main worries. Fourteen months was a long time to be out of action, and many things would have changed. I felt rather out of touch. Moreover, all my friends must surely still be in the Middle East or Italy and I would be very much a stranger.

On this score, however, I was soon set at ease, for as we approached Twenty-first Army Group Tactical Headquarters I recognized more and more old faces from Africa. It was uncanny how the same people always seemed to turn up in the battle zone, wherever it might be. Far from feeling a stranger, I began to feel that I belonged to the most exclusive club in the world.

Montgomery's Tactical Headquarters were in an orchard at Creully, a small village a few miles east of Bayeux. Apart from some heavily camouflaged lorries and caravans under the trees, there was little to connect this peaceful place with the war going on all around, still less to suggest that here was the nerve centre of a battle front stretching a hundred miles in which 1,580,000 troops were involved.

Montgomery always fought his battles from a very small, unostentatious tactical headquarters, where, in comparative peace, he was able to relax and, above all, think. He usually lived there, with half a dozen liaison officers, or 'gallopers' – tough young men of considerable tactical ability, whom he dispatched daily to key areas in the battle, with orders to report back to him each evening. He was thus always completely up to date with what was happening. As a Corps Commander I used to welcome their visits, and I gave orders that they must see me personally before departure. By this means I was able to ensure that the stresses and strains on my front were appreciated correctly at the highest level, and this often meant that reinforcements of men and material, if available, would be sent to me as required. Unfortunately, the American Commanders usually regarded them as Montgomery's British spies, and it was often made difficult for them to obtain accurate information of the battle on the U.S. sector.

Montgomery loathed visitors, unless they had come with a definite purpose. Members of Parliament were a particular nuisance – shoals of them seemed to arrive almost all the time. Lord Alanbrooke, who was Churchill's Chief of Staff, told me how one evening he was rung up at his flat in London by his very irate master, who said, '*Your Montgomery*' – he always started in this way when Montgomery had irritated him particularly – 'has issued an instruction that he will see no more visitors at his H.Q. in Normandy. This is an impertinence. Does he meant that I, the Prime Minister, cannot visit one of my Army Commanders?' Alanbrooke did his best to calm him down. In any case, he was flying over next day to visit Montgomery and he took him to task for this last unfortunate instruction. Lord Alanbrooke, incidentally, was the only person from whom Montgomery would always take a reprimand. 'I didn't mean to stop the Prime Minister coming', said Montgomery. 'All right,' said Alanbrooke, 'send him this wire.' He then dictated to Montgomery a conciliatory message, which was to be sent off at once, to the effect that a visit from Churchill would always be very welcome at any time, etc. That night, back again in his London flat, the telephone rang once more. It was Churchill, who said, in a very different tone of voice, 'I have received a very nice message from Monty, which has altered the whole situation.' He then happily read out the message which Alanbrooke had dictated to Montgomery that morning.

Unfortunately, criticism was mounting about Montgomery's handling of the Normandy battle. The British press claimed that he was over-cautious, and cited as an example that his offensive towards Caen had been launched with considerable publicity and then had been allowed to grind to a halt through lack of drive.

In addition, there was a section of Eisenhower's H.Q. headed by Air-Marshal Tedder, the Deputy Commander-in-Chief, and including several other British officers, which was definitely hostile to Montgomery and was constantly trying to influence Eisenhower to replace him. Tedder and Montgomery had never seen eye to eye since Alamein. Fortunately, however, at this time Montgomery was meticulous in his dealings with General Omar Bradley, the Commander of the U.S. Assault Forces. Throughout the battle of the beachhead, relations between the two were very close. Their headquarters were within easy reach of each other. All Montgomery's directives were issued after discussion with Bradley. Since D-Day Bradley had had as tough an assignment as any Allied general in the Second World War. First there had been the shambles of Omaha, then all the exasperations of the advance to Cherbourg, and finally the long battle of attrition, lasting three weeks in the hedgerows, leading up to the capture of St Lô on 18 July and the breakout at Avranches on 30 July. This had cost the Americans 40,000 casualties, 90 per cent of which were infantry. No one understood what Bradley and his troops had had to endure better than Montgomery. After the war Bradley wrote, 'During the operations in the lodgement area, Montgomery bossed First U.S. Army as part of the Twenty-first Army Group and exercised his allied authority with wisdom, forbearance and restraint. I could not have wanted a more tolerant and judicious Commander.' So far, so good. Regrettably, relations with the celebrated 'Blood and Guts' George Patton, commanding the Third U.S. Army, now bursting out on the western flank, fell below this level. Patton in fact had developed an almost pathological aversion to Montgomery from the very moment when they first met in Tripoli at a conference held by Montgomery to demonstrate the tactics he had employed in the victorious advance of the Eighth Army from Alamein to Tunis. Probably the clash of personalities was inevitable. Both were very high-grade professional military commanders. Both were intensely ambitious and both were showmen at heart, equally determined to hold the centre of the stage and take the plaudits of the crowd. Both were playing a part and dressing for it – the one the reincarnation of Cromwell, the Lord Protector, and the other resembling Murat, the great cavalry leader and the most flashy of Napoleon's marshals, up-dated by Hollywood in an American setting. Each saw, or probably thought he saw in the other the qualities he personally found offensive. Moreover, neither of them knew when to keep his mouth shut. Patton's worst gaffes were behind him; Montgomery's were still to come.

Suddenly it seemed to me as though Montgomery had hostile critics and enemies on every side, ready to pounce on any mistake he might make. The last time I had seen him in action was after the German and Italian forces had capitulated in North Africa. There had been no criticism then. He was the great Commander who had turned the tide of defeat into victory in the Middle East and the Eighth Army worshipped him. As an example of this, I remembered well, when a high-level concert party arrived in Tripoli to entertain the troops, the theatre was packed and, as Montgomery entered his box in the centre of the dress circle, the whole audience, without any prompting, rose to their feet, turned their backs on the stage, and clapped and cheered for several minutes. Every soldier in the Eighth Army felt that he knew Montgomery personally, but the Twenty-first Army Group was too large to become almost his own personal army.

On the Command level, even in the Middle East, he had always been a little prickly. There was a famous story to the effect that, when he was summoned to General Eisenhower's H.Q. in Algiers to explain why he had altered the plan for the invasion of Sicily, he said, on arriving at the airport, to General Bedell Smith, who was there to meet him, 'I expect I am a bit unpopular up here.' Bedell Smith looked at him sadly and replied, 'To serve under you would be a privilege, alongside you would not be too bad, but to serve over you is hell!' All men who rise to command great armies in war must be tough, resolute characters and therefore hell to serve over. Would all this have affected his morale, I wondered. I was soon to find out.

I had arrived at Creully to find Montgomery and Eisenhower in conference. Eisenhower himself gave me a characteristically warm welcome. I had hardly expected him to recognize me after all this time, but his friendliness immediately made me feel that I was back where I belonged.

People have often asked me whether Eisenhower was a great Commander. In the strictly military sense, the answer must be No. The first time I had met him in Africa, when he had been appointed our Commander-in-Chief, he was only a full Colonel in the American Army, yet twenty-three months later he was a 5-star General, which I believe is the fastest promotion ever known in the United States Army – so he lacked the battle experience of many of those serving under him; but he had other qualities which more than made up for this, and the greatest was his complete selflessness. Eisenhower did not count with him at all. All he was concerned with was winning the war; moreover, he was a 'soldier's General' who really cared for the men under his command.

Unfortunately, when Commanders rise to dizzy heights, they sometimes tend to forget that it is men who win wars. No matter what sophisticated ironmongery is available, it is men who have to handle this equipment, so they are the basis of the whole thing. Eisenhower never forgot this. He always had a deep feeling for the men under his command and, curiously enough, this seeped down very rapidly to the troops in the front line. As a rule, the British soldier does not like top brass, particularly if it is foreign top brass, but they all liked Eisenhower and they called him Ike – though of course not to his face. He was also a very shrewd man, who had no intention whatever of allowing any inter-Allied friction, which was all the greater risk in this case as both sides spoke approximately the same language. Nevertheless, thanks to his influence, there was no doubt that on the whole we got on very well with the Americans. Eisenhower was also a superb co-ordinator, or chairman of committees, and he had some pretty difficult people under him. I do not believe that anyone else in the world could have succeeded in driving that difficult team to the end of the road – people like Montgomery, Patton, Mark Clark, Bradley and so on. He always insisted on having a completely integrated staff, composed mainly of American and British officers, and he had every intention of seeing that this staff worked amicably together; which it did. It was a known fact in the Middle East, throughout the whole of his H.Q., that he did not mind an American Staff Officer calling his opposite number a bastard, but if he called him a British bastard he would be on his way back to America the next morning and, in view of the U-boat menace, he would probably be travelling by slow convoy without escort. I have always reckoned that his staff, composed of officers from different nations, could not possibly have got on better – and remember that you could not be in the Eisenhower entourage for long without developing a deep affection for him.

There is one last quality, however, without which no one can hope to be a successful Commander – the power to take decisions. I once asked General Eisenhower which was his worst moment during the war. He replied that it was the launching of the 82nd and 101st U.S. Airborne Divisions prior to the D-Day landings from the sea. Their role was to drop inland from the Utah Beaches and it was terribly important that they did, in fact, drop there, because the Germans had flooded considerable areas close to Utah Beach, on which the 4th U.S. Infantry Division was due to land. Behind the beach defences there was a mile-wide lagoon, crossed by only five causeways, and there was a grave danger that if these were not secured by our airborne troops, the seaborne forces would not be able to penetrate inland. Leigh-Mallory, the Air Force Commander, was bitterly opposed to this landing, and warned General Eisenhower that this area was thick with flak guns and searchlights. Moreover, the only open space where the gliders could land had been heavily obstructed. In fact, he said that casualties would probably be as high as 70 per cent and that the Supreme Commander was sending two superb Divisions to almost certain destruction. This was a terribly difficult decision for the Commander to take. Eisenhower went off for a short walk by himself to think it out. On his return he came into the Operations Room and said that the 82nd and 101st Airborne Divisions would fly as planned. As it turned out. the operation was completely successful and the casualties were not nearly as high as had been predicted. But, being Eisenhower, what did he do? He went down to the airfield from which the 101st Airborne Division would take off, and he told me how all the men gathered round him, patting him on the back, and kept on saying that it would be all right and that he was not to worry – they would do the job for him, and so on. He then said, 'As I stood there and saw their aircraft disappearing into the darkening sky, I felt like a murderer.' Decisions on the level of an Army Group Commander are terribly difficult to take, but Eisenhower never shirked them. He may not have been a great strategist like, shall we say, Marlborough, but he was a superb co-ordinator of Allied armies and on this count alone he deserves an honoured place among the great captains of war.

After he had departed, Montgomery took me into his map lorry, where I underwent a minute scrutiny, which I felt concerned my physical fitness. Had I really recovered sufficiently to be entrusted with the command of a Corps in battle? This was what he was considering and, knowing how shrewd he was, I felt uneasy, because every now and then I still had bouts of high temperature combined with sickness. I was afraid that if he discovered this I should be on the next aircraft back to England. I must have passed the test, for he turned to the map, to give me one of those brilliant military appreciations which I had come to know so well. It was soon obvious that he was in top form. He might be tactless and difficult, but there could be no doubt at all that he was a great Commander in the field, whose nerve was not readily shaken. During a longish briefing he put me completely in the picture about the Normandy situation.

As Montgomery talked to me I began to feel more and more guilty at ever having doubted his capacity to shrug off criticism like water from a duck's back. He was, of course, fortunate that at a difficult time like this he had the backing of some very powerful people. First of all, from Lord Alanbrooke, whose contribution to victory in the last war has never been fully recognized. Although on several occasions he had taken Montgomery to task for tactlessness, he never once questioned his fine military qualities. Thanks to his influence, the powerful figure of Churchill himself stood solidly behind the Commander of the Twenty-first Army Group. Ever since Montgomery had been appointed to take over the Eighth Army in the desert, there had developed a curious love-hate relationship between them. Montgomery refused to be hustled into launching attacks before he was ready and this irritated

Churchill; on the other hand, Montgomery was always victorious. The most valuable support of all, however, came from Sir James Grigg, Churchill's able and tough War Minister, who frequently visited the front. He once said to me, later in the campaign, 'Montgomery is the greatest British Commander in the field since Wellington', and I heartily agreed with him.

By now, of course, I knew Montgomery well, as every battle in which I had fought, with the exception of Tunis, had been under his command. The withdrawal to Dunkirk had been my first introduction to the Montgomery technique of making war and although this retreat was on a more modest scale, it was a far more nerve-shattering experience than the vast battle in Normandy. Although only a Lieutenant-Colonel, I had, as the Commander of the Machine-Gun Battalion in his 3rd Division, attended all his conferences and seen him almost every day, and the more I studied him the more I came to admire his superb control. Throughout the whole of the Dunkirk retreat he had remained calm and confident, and had always insisted on having his meals at regular hours. He went to bed early and slept peacefully all night, with the result that he had arrived back at Dunkirk as fresh as when he had started. He had never hesitated to take the most difficult decisions, and as a result the 3rd Division was completely successful in that most difficult of all military operations, a fighting withdrawal.

But, to return to his caravan in Normandy: when I asked him why the D-Day landings had been so successful, he replied that there were several reasons. Firstly, the success of the cover plan, which was given the code-name of 'Fortitude' The Germans had always believed that the invasion would come in the Pas de Calais area, where the sea voyage was shortest and where most of their V-bomb launching sites were located; they were still hoping to win the war with these weapons. Most Germans have card-index minds, and our Intelligence Service skilfully played on this and released the right sort of information in the right quarter. The Reserve Divisions of the British Liberation Army (B.L.A.), which could not be landed early in the assault, were concentrated in camps in the Dover area, while an elaborate dummy Combined Operations H.Q. was also constructed there. Dummy landing-craft were assembled in the Thames Estuary, dummy gliders appeared on the airfields in Kent. Though Montgomery's H.Q. was close to Portsmouth, all messages, orders, etc., were conveyed by land lines to Kent and then transmitted by radio from the dummy H.Q. Special precautions were also taken to limit all contact with Eire, which was a nest-bed of German spies, and in April a belt ten miles wide round the east and west coasts of the U.K. was closed to all visitors.

It was hoped that 'Fortitude' would not only deceive the Germans as to where the main landings were to take place, but also lead them to think that the landings in Normandy were not the main invasion but a deception calculated to make them retain their forces in the Pas de Calais area. From the German point of view this was understandable, for it would take seven weeks before all the thirty-seven Divisions under Eisenhower could be transported to Normandy, while von Rundstedt, the German C.-in-C., had some sixty Divisions at his disposal, strung out all along the coast from the Zuider Zee to Normandy.

Montgomery then told me that the Germans had fallen for this deception, hook, line and sinker; although we were well ashore in Normandy and the build-up of our forces was proceeding according to plan, von Rundstedt had still got an army of a quarter of a million men, sitting on their backsides doing nothing, between Antwerp and Le Havre, awaiting our main assault. Our Air Forces probably made the greatest contribution of all to the success of 'Fortitude' Twice the air effort was concentrated on the Pas de Calais area; for every ton of bombs dropped on coastal defences west of Le Havre, two tons were put down in Normandy. In order to prevent movement by the Germans out of the Pas de Calais area, railway yards, rail junctions, traffic centres and bridges were consistently attacked and destroyed. By D-Day only one bridge over the Seine west of Paris was still intact. As a final gesture of deception the Germans had been led to believe that the two 'follow-up' Armies, constituting our main assault force (First Canadian and Third American) were destined to land in the Pas de Calais area under the command of Lieut.-Gen. George S. Patton, the most publicized American General, whose name was widely known to the Germans. Montgomery then added that he had dealt with the main points of 'Fortitude' in considerable detail because this was, in his opinion, the most carefully prepared and completely successful cover plan in the history of war.

The weather, of course, had also helped to achieve surprise. After some very good weather in May, when the Germans expected our invasion almost daily, it had deteriorated badly at the beginning of June. In order to meet the requirements of all three Services, only three days in each month were possible, and 5 June had been originally selected as D-Day. Fortunately, Eisenhower's Meteorological Adviser, Group Captain J. M. Stagg of the R.A.F., whom Admiral Ramsay's Chief of Staff, Admiral Creasy, described as 'six foot two of Stagg and six foot one of gloom', was a strong, decisive character and a scientist to his finger-tips. On his shoulders lay the intolerable burden of the lives of millions of men and many months of detailed training. The conferences, attended by all the Commanders, at Southwick House near Portsmouth, were some of the most dramatic ever held. It was impossible, owing to bad weather, to launch the invasion on 5 June, but, as Montgomery explained, to defer it after the 6th would have meant a postponement of two weeks, and this was virtually impossible as the troops could not be cooped up in their camps for much longer. They had now all been briefed and somebody was certain to talk; in which case, all the elaborate painstaking build-up of 'Fortitude' would be wasted.

It was decided to take the final decision at a conference to be held on Sunday 4 June at 9 p.m. As the Commanders gathered, the winds were howling through the trees and understandably the atmosphere was very, very gloomy, as this was the final and most important meeting. To everyone's surprise, in spite of the appalling weather conditions outside, Stagg predicted a period of better weather on the 6th for some thirty-six hours – far from perfect, windy, with rough seas, but just possible. He could not, however, predict whether this was likely to continue for long. 'I felt very sorry for Eisenhower,' said Montgomery, 'because he and he alone had to make the final decision, and if, after the leading troops got ashore, another prolonged period of gales and high seas had developed, the follow-up formations and vital stores could not possibly have got ashore, and the leading troops would have been isolated and open to counter-attack by superior German forces. All the same, I felt that this was a risk we simply had to take. Eisenhower turned to me, and I said "Go!" After pacing backwards and forwards in deep thought for a minute or so, he turned to us and said, "O.K. We'll go!" – possibly the most momentous decision ever taken.'

As it turned out, the bad weather was all to our advantage. The German forces, which had been at a state of 'immediate alert' during the fine weather, did not believe that we would risk a landing under the existing conditions, as quite high seas were still running. The immediate alert was cancelled and everyone relaxed. Even the indefatigable Rommel went on leave to visit his family back in Germany. He was our chief opponent, as his command stretched from the Zuider Zee to the River Loire and consisted of the LXXVIII Corps in Holland, the Fifteenth Army from Antwerp to the Orne and the Seventh Army from the Orne to the Loire.

It must have come as a terrible shock to the German sentries when they saw the immense Allied Armada approaching the Normandy coast at first light on D-Day, 6 June. Two other factors which contributed to our success were the jealousies and quarrels in the German High Command. Rommel we all knew well. He was determined to halt the invasion on the beaches, because of the superiority we enjoyed in the air. He quite rightly believed that all movement of German reinforcements by day to the beachhead area would be impossible, and that they were bound, therefore, to lose the Battle of the Build-up once we were firmly established ashore. Until his arrival, the Normandy beaches were sparsely manned with most inadequate defences. This he proceeded to rectify with his usual energy and all sorts of horrors began to appear on the beaches – iron stakes, minefields, batches of powerful guns in concrete emplacements, to mention only a few. He had arrived to take over his new command in February 1943 and it was lucky for us he had not come earlier – otherwise the beaches might have become almost impregnable.

Montgomery spoke almost with affection of his old opponent in the desert. He added that Rommel had been badly wounded during the Caen offensive on 17 July. As he talked, I could not help comparing in my mind these two famous Generals. Rommel was probably the best Armoured Corps Commander who served in the last war, and when battle was joined he was usually to be found, almost in the front line, picking up mines, possibly, with his own hands, or taking command of leading units, but often out of touch with his Main Headquarters.

Montgomery, on the other hand, would probably be already planning the next battle or even the next but one. Although he frequently visited the front, he never allowed himself to be embroiled in the hurly-burly of the tactical battle. He was, therefore, in my opinion, the better Army or Army Group Commander of the two.

Von Rundstedt, the C.-in-C. West, and Rommel's superior, did not agree with the latter's conception of the forthcoming battle. He wished to stand back from the beaches and group his forces, particularly his tanks, at strategic centres, from which he could launch powerful counter-attacks before we were firmly established in the beachheads and drive us back into the sea. When our D-Day landings were launched, the German forces were deployed half-way between these two conceptions.

Von Rundstedt was one of Germany's most successful Commanders, who had led the Panzer Blitz through the Ardennes in 1940 and had never been defeated. He was now, however, in Montgomery's opinion, too old to control a battle of this magnitude.

I met von Rundstedt several times after the war, when he was an inmate of a prisoner-of-war camp earmarked for high-level German Generals in Western Command, of which I was then the General Officer Commanding. Usually we discussed old battles, but one day I said to him, 'We are both professional soldiers. Is there anything I can do to improve your lot?' He replied, 'Yes, General, there are many people in this camp who call themselves Generals but are not real generals at all. Could you have them removed elsewhere, please?' 'To whom are you alluding?' I asked. He replied, 'There are General Doctors, General Engineers, Administrative Generals. It is most unpleasant for us, of the old German General Staff, to consort with such people.' I could hardly believe my ears, but this was typical of the pre-war German Army, in which the great General Staff, particularly if they were Guardsmen like von Rundstedt, considered themselves the élite and had a complete contempt for the common herd.

On only one point were they all agreed – on their hatred for Hitler. Von Rundstedt said bitterly, 'After you landed I rang up Hitler and asked for permission to attack with my Panzer Reserves. Although his Headquarters were in East Prussia and he could not possibly know accurately what was going on in the west, he refused. We continued to ring up every few hours, but when we did get permission you were firmly established ashore, with your anti-tank guns and tanks. It was then too late. I practically had to ask Hitler,' he added, 'through his lackeys, Keitel and Jodl, for permission to move a sentry from the front to the rear of my Headquarters.' There is no doubt that behind this bitter, exaggerated comment lay one of the main reasons why Germany lost the war. Hitler would by this time never listen to his military experts, particularly after the attempt on his life. He, and he alone, directed the war. Churchill, on the other hand, never once in the course of the whole war overrode the advice of his military advisers. He would protest and argue, but ultimately he would always give way to their expert opinions. Churchill's only failure was that he loved to become involved in the tactical battle and was never happier than when he had escaped from Whitehall to the sharp end of the battle, where his presence had a wonderful effect on the morale of the troops, but where he was a perfect nuisance to their immediate Commanders, because he never seemed to realize that tactical methods had changed somewhat since he had charged, most gallantly, with the 21st Lancers during the Battle of Omdurman. However, at his level, it was the strategical decisions which counted, and fortunately he and Roosevelt always saw eye to eye. Churchill very wisely frequently emphasized the fact that his mother had been an American.

Montgomery then went on to say that in spite of all the careful planning beforehand, he doubted whether our landings would have been successful if it had not been for the intense period of training which had gone on before them. This was originally organized by General Sir Bernard Paget, the C.-in-C. Home Forces, who was a tireless worker and a master of detail. So the framework was there when he himself arrived from Italy and all he had to do was to carry on the good work. I was secretly amused; having commanded a Division under Montgomery in South Eastern Command before he went to the Middle East, I could just imagine that his arrival must have been equivalent to the explosion of a very large bomb in Military Headquarters in the U.K. I wondered whether he had again insisted on all his staff officers going for weekly cross-country runs.

During the last week in May, the assault forces were sealed off in their camps and the process of briefing began. Every possible aid was used – projectors, models, large-scale maps – and suddenly the troops realized that the strongpoint which they had attacked so often during training was a copy of the one they would have to capture in Normandy. They were shown the support which they would get during the landing from the air, and from naval gunfire, but more important than anything else was the close support which would be provided by the tanks of the famous 79th Armoured Division, commanded by General Sir Percy Hobart, the original Commander of the 7th Armoured Division in Egypt. Hobo, as he was called affectionately by his many admirers, always spoke his mind, and for a short period in 1940 he had been prematurely retired, owing to his outspoken criticism of the lack of imagination displayed by those in high places regarding armoured warfare. For a short period he became a Corporal in the Home Guard. Fortunately he was rescued by Churchill in 1943 and was given command of the 79th Armoured Division, where his inventive genius came into full play.

After the disastrous raid on Dieppe in July 1942, it was realized that, in the face of modern weapons, barbed wire, mines, etc., the assaulting infantry must be given close armoured support. Every time our remarkable Intelligence Service reported the presence of some new horror on the beaches, Hobo was asked to produce the antidote in tank form, and this he did. They became known throughout the Army as the 'Funnies' – there were flail tanks to beat passages through minefields, bulldozer tanks to clear away mined obstacles, tanks which spouted flame to deal with German concrete emplacements, and above all, the D.D. tanks (amphibious

Sherman tanks), which would swim ashore with the assaulting craft and give immediate support on the beaches.

Hobo's technicians devised a method by which tanks could be sealed and made to float, complete with crew and armaments, propelled mechanically; they were really large armoured motor boats, and probably the most vital arm in the whole of the landings. As all this was explained to the troops, their morale rose; it seemed that every conceivable detail had been thought out beforehand.

So it was a highly trained force, confident of victory, which assaulted the Normandy beaches through stormy seas in the early hours of 6 June. Had the troops not been physically fit and trained to the last ounce, they would never have succeeded in landing. Many of them had been cooped up in ships and landing-craft for a long period, and nearly all of them had suffered severely from sea-sickness. The beaches on which the Americans landed were the roughest of all.

The landing on Omaha Beach in particular had been a nightmare – the landing-craft cast off from the mother ships too soon, twelve miles out to sea, the loss of twenty-seven out of thirty-two of their D.D. tanks and all their close-support artillery in their approach to land, the chaotic battle on the beaches, made all the more costly by the lack of adequate support from the sea and the air, the frightful congestion on the beaches, the wrecked landing-craft, the burning vehicles and the maze of mines. They had, in fact, come up against, not the second-category coast defence troops they had expected, but a good German division which knew its job and did its grim duty. Nevertheless, the American commanders had the situation, ghastly though it was, well under control by mid-day. Montgomery added that, although the Americans could make as many mistakes as ourselves, they had a remarkable aptitude for quickly re-adjusting themselves, often with great ingenuity, to an unanticipated reverse. Like us they had had their teething troubles with some of their troops in action for the first time: their sector had contained the very worst Bocage in Normandy, much of it marshy, blind and overgrown with rank vegetation. They had now, thanks largely to the firm and intelligent leadership of Bradley, Hodges, Collins and others, overcome these troubles and their morale was high. Patton and the Third Army, who had missed the strain and frustration of the Battle of the Hedgerows, were well launched for the pursuit due east; it could not be in better hands.

So much for the landings. This was unquestionably the longest briefing I had ever received from Montgomery, and he now finished by bringing me up to date with a brief account of the fighting in the beachhead. The battle, he insisted, was working out perfectly, in accordance with the orders which he had issued prior to D-Day at his H.Q. in St Paul's School (his old school). By attacking continuously in a southern direction, the Twenty-first Army Group had tied down the bulk of the German forces and in particular their Panzers on the British front. At present, fourteen British and Canadian Divisions were opposed by fourteen German Divisions and 600 tanks, while nineteen U.S. Divisions had opposite them only nine German Divisions and 110 tanks. He remarked that I had arrived at the right moment, since the gruelling Battle of the Bocage was almost over and the U.S. forces were breaking out in a westerly direction, which would enable them to capture Brest. He concluded, 'As you have probably realized from the congestion in the beachhead, we want a port badly, the Mulberries have done magnificently and, without them, the build-up would have been impossible, but you cannot continue to supply an expeditionary force of this size without a suitable base port. The U.S. forces will subsequently wheel round in an easterly direction and the bulk of the German Army will be trapped. The key tactical feature now in our advance is Mont Pinçon, which dominates the surrounding country and must be captured as soon as possible. It is on XXX Corps' front, so that will be your first major problem.'

Chapter 2
Taking Over XXX Corps
SIR BRIAN HORROCKS

As I left Montgomery's orchard and drove to Second Army H.Q., my mind switched to the man I was about to meet, Dempsey, Commander of the British Second Army, who would be my immediate chief and under whom, although of course I did not know it at the time, I was destined to fight every battle, with the exception of the Battle of the Reichswald, right up to the end of the war.

I had first seen his name on my arrival as a new boy at the Staff College, Camberley, in 1931 Captain M. C. Dempsey, M.C., of the Berkshire Regiment, was a member of the Senior Division; in those days, he was chiefly renowned as being a very good cricketer and a keen horseman, but rather reserved and difficult to get to know. No other student of either of the two divisions then at the Staff College was to rise to such heights as he did during the 1939–45 war.

I realize now how very fortunate I was to have scraped, after five years' unavailing attempts, into the Staff College at this particular time; the standard of instruction was very good, and a high proportion of the students subsequently distinguished themselves during the Second World War. This made for good co-operation, as most of us spoke the same language and had a similar approach to military problems, having almost certainly worked together in the same syndicates while at Camberley. As an example of this, during the final stages of the war in North Africa, there was no love lost between the First and Eighth Armies. The First Army had been fighting hard against very tough opposition in the mountainous country of North Africa, without much public recognition, while the Eighth Army, under Montgomery, had been sailing along happily and had captured all the headlines. The first units to make personal contact between the First and Eighth Armies were the 6th Armoured Division (in the First) and my X Corps (in the Eighth). I went over in an armoured car to meet Charles Keightley (subsequently Gen. Sir Charles Keightley), the Commander of the Armoured Division. Immediately all friction vanished as we had been Instructors together at the Staff College and were very good friends.

The Commandant of the Staff College was then General Sir John Dill, a highly intelligent man who also had great personal charm. He commanded I Corps in 1939, was then appointed Chief of the General Staff and subsequently sent to be the Senior British Officer in the U.S.A. General Marshall, head of the U.S. Army, and the most powerful military figure in America, soon came to realize his brilliant qualities and they became great friends. It is almost impossible to exaggerate the importance of this from the British point of view. Dill died on 4 November 1944 and was buried in Arlington Cemetery – an honour reserved in the U.S.A. only for those who rise to the highest pinnacle of military or political fame. It was largely thanks to the modern methods of training which he introduced, such as the tutorial system, and imaginative testing exercises, plays and war games, that the standard of staff work in the upper echelons of the British Army was, generally speaking, so high.

I shall, of course, be accused of exaggeration, but the first Staff Course held at Camberley after the outbreak of war in 1939 was attended by some of the best brains in Britain – young, progressive men, drawn from many walks of life, as for instance Captain J. S. B. Lloyd, now Lord Selwyn-Lloyd, subsequently Foreign Secretary and Speaker in the House of Commons; also D. C. Walker-Smith, who became Minister of Health. At the end of the course all these bright young men, without exception, paid high tribute to the standard of instruction which they had received at Camberley.

But to return to Dempsey: in some curious way he has remained a somewhat shadowy figure, and a General almost completely unknown to the public. This was due primarily to the fact that he loathed any kind of publicity. It was also partly owing to the large size of the Second Army, which never therefore captured the imagination of the public as the smaller Eighth Army had. I was lucky in that I knew him better than most, for on leaving the Staff College I had taken over his staff appointment in the War Office and had then succeeded him as Brigade Major of the 5th Infantry Brigade at Aldershot, which formed part of the embryo Expeditionary Force. Subsequently we were two of the first infantry men to be given command of an Armoured Division. Then finally, in the desert he had taken over XIII Corps from me, when I had been moved to command X Corps. Our paths had therefore crossed frequently and I knew him to be one of the ablest soldiers in the British Army. He was very shrewd, he never flapped, and consequently his Second Army H.Q. was highly efficient and devoted to their Commander. I doubt whether anyone else could have worked so harmoniously and successfully with Montgomery as his immediate boss. The two were complementary – Montgomery the extrovert, who loved the headlines; Dempsey the introvert, who shunned publicity but got on with the job efficiently and without any fuss. Montgomery was not at his best with Allies; Dempsey went out of his way to iron out the friction so often caused by the other's tactlessness. Early in 1940 he was Brigadier General Staff (B.G.S.) to McNaughton, who commanded the Canadians in the U.K., and became very friendly with Simonds, their outstanding Corps Commander. This no doubt helped to foster good relations between the two Armies in Normandy.

I have often been asked whether Dempsey was much involved in the higher planning of the Normandy campaign. I don't think so. Where the higher strategical issues were concerned, Montgomery relied almost entirely on his own judgement. The only person he would occasionally consult was Lord Alanbrooke, though his Chief of Staff, 'Freddie' de Guingand, was never afraid to speak his mind to his master, particularly when the staff duties aspect was concerned.

I, of course, was no more than a Corps Commander, but I can only recall one instance when Montgomery ever consulted me about future operations. It was after the Battle of Arnhem, when he called at my H.Q. and asked me, if an attack was launched in a south-easterly direction, between the Rivers Meuse and Rhine, how many Divisions I would require. I replied, 'Six.' He then said he was on his way to Eisenhower's H.Q. for a conference to discuss the future conduct of the campaign. This attack subsequently became known as the Battle of the Reichswald, but it did not take place until February 1945, owing to the surprise offensive launched by the Germans in the Ardennes. During the Battle of the Reichswald, Second Army H.Q. was not involved, and Dempsey was able to plan the crossing of the Rhine, which took place afterwards and went like clockwork; this, of course, did not involve high-level strategy.

One last point – Dempsey was much tougher than he appeared at first sight. On one occasion during our advance towards Belgium he arrived at my Command Post, calm and collected as usual. He gave me my orders with his usual clarity, then, sitting in my caravan, he confirmed them briefly in writing (he always wrote with his left hand), and it was only after his departure that I learned that the small Auster aircraft in which he always travelled had been forced to make a crash landing and had turned completely over. He must have been badly shaken, yet he never even mentioned it to me. This was the man whom I came to admire more and more as the war progressed.

On my arrival at Second Army H.Q., which was close to Montgomery's, Dempsey described to me briefly his experiences during the D-Day landings and the subsequent fighting in the beachhead. Turning to the map, he said, 'When all did so well it is rather invidious to pick out anyone for special mention, but the two outstanding examples of initiative and the value of tough individual training were on my right and left flanks, carried out by the 47th Royal Marine Commando and the 6th Airborne Division respectively.' He then dealt first with the right flank. The capture of Port-en-Bessin had been vital for two reasons: firstly, it formed a junction point between the British right flank on Gold Beach and the American V Corps, landing on Omaha; secondly, it was essential as the main terminal for our petrol supplies, petrol being the life-blood of a modern mechanized army. The Germans had turned the place into a veritable fortress, dominated by two high hills, one on either side, honeycombed with trenches. To all intents and purposes it was impregnable by any attack launched from the sea. So it was decided to land the 47th Royal Marine Commando (420 men, commanded by Col. Phillips) on Gold Beach after it had been captured. They would then move across country, and attack and capture Port-en-Bessin from the rear.

But far from its being the peaceful landing which had been expected, while still some distance from the beach they had come under heavy fire, some landing-craft were sunk and many Marines had to swim ashore, losing all their arms and equipment in the process. They were also scattered along the beach and it took Col. Phillips several hours to collect them. So instead of a fresh, fully-armed unit, he had a force of tired, wet, bedraggled men, many of whom were without some garment or other – quite a number had no boots and others had lost their trousers. Sixty men had been killed or wounded, and only half the force which remained was still armed. It would be difficult to imagine a worse start to an extremely hazardous operation which involved a 15-mile march across enemy-occupied territory. But, undaunted, they set off with the armed Marines in front. They came across numerous German defensive positions, each of which they attacked and overran, capturing the weapons for their own use. Thus, by the time they arrived close to the port, many were re-equipped with German arms. Their first objective was one of the strongly occupied hills, but by now the men were pretty exhausted, which was hardly surprising after their extremely rough crossing and their swimming ashore, followed by a strenuous cross-country march and a series of small but fierce engagements. They were therefore given a two-hour rest, while a patrol was sent off to try to contact the Americans, who were to supply the artillery support for their attack on the town. But the U.S. forces had also had difficulty in landing, and no artillery support was forthcoming. To make matters worse, none of their wireless sets would work and as they were completely cut off from all Allied forces, the situation must have seemed pretty desperate.

However, they managed to get one set working and made contact with the Navy, who promised naval gunfire support and low-flying attacks from the air. Both these took place that afternoon and the Marines launched their attack on the town, clearing it house by house; but the Germans counter-attacked and overran their rear Administrative H.Q., which was very sparsely protected, as they could not afford to leave more men in a purely defensive role. Nevertheless, they went straight on and cleared the town; but Port-en-Bessin could not be held until the two high hills on either side had been captured. Their attack on the first was beaten back. They then made two further unsuccessful attempts to capture the second, all the time suffering heavy casualties. A young Captain called Cousins, who had taken part in the unsuccessful attempts to capture the second hill, had noticed a zig-zag path leading to the top, which seemed to be undefended. When it was dark he collected every available man and made a last desperate attack up the path. This time they were successful, though Cousins was killed by a grenade just as they reached the top. But with one of the hills in their possession, as so often happens in war, the German defences suddenly collapsed, and the Marines held Port-en-Bessin for two days until they were relieved. It is doubtful whether, in their long, distinguished history, the Royal Marines had ever achieved anything finer. It was not generally appreciated what a vital role they had played in 'Operation Overlord' No less than 17,500 were involved, including five Commandos, a high proportion of the crews manning the assault boats and half of the men engaged in the highly dangerous task of clearing mine obstructions on the beaches, plus, of course, Marine detachments in the naval bombarding ships.

'It is an interesting fact which nobody seems to have realized', said General Dempsey, 'that Montgomery unquestionably won the last battle that he fought against his old desert opponent, Rommel.' Rommel had been very active ever since his arrival, strengthening the defences on all the beaches where our invasion might come. He was firmly convinced that our landing would be made at high tide, so his main belts of mined barbed wire, etc. were sited from this point of view. Each possible beach was also protected by a number of guns encased in thick concrete bunkers, with their weapons so sited that they could fire in echelon along the obstacles where, in his opinion, our assaulting troops would be held up. As a result, however, the bulk of the German guns could not fire out to sea, but were protected against the fire of our warships by specially fixed concrete walls. The initial landings had therefore to take place at half-tide when our leading waves of troops would be out of range of the German guns, and they would be, of course, also accompanied by their D.D. tanks, capable of destroying the German gun emplacements, and it was for this reason that only three days in each month were considered to be possible for our invasion. On the eventful day this was one of the main reasons why the casualties among our leading waves of troops were much lower than had been expected.

Prior to the assault the warships of the British Navy had started a heavy bombardment of the German defences, which had already been subjected to repeated attacks by Bomber Command. In fact, on Gold Beach where the troops from

XXX Corps landed, the only hostile gunfire encountered was from four 6-inch guns at Longues, north of Bayeux. Their first salvo straddled the ship carrying the Sector H.Q. and the Commander of XXX Corps. The guns of H.M.S. *Ajax* were at once brought to bear and within twenty minutes the German guns were silenced. The British naval gunfire was so accurate that two British shells actually penetrated the narrow embrasures of the pillboxes, destroying everything inside.

Dempsey emphasized that his greatest anxiety concerned the left flank, where the 3rd Division was landing on Sword Beach, just west of the River Orne. The German Armoured Divisions had been located in the area Chartres–Paris–Amiens–Rouen, and were led by the 21st Panzer Division which had recently moved into the area between Caen and Falaise, and there was great concern lest they should launch an attack from the east before our beachhead could be firmly established. This would have meant complete disaster and the whole front, including the American sector, might have been rolled up by armoured formations. So the 6th Airborne Division was allotted the important and very onerous task of protecting this open flank.

Richard Gale, the Divisional Commander, was given the following objectives for the period between midnight and dawn on D-Day: firstly, to capture, intact if possible, the bridges over the canal which ran parallel to the River Orne from the sea to Caen, and to seize and destroy five bridges in the flooded valley of the River Dives, some six miles east of the Orne; further, to capture and hold the high wooded ground between the two rivers; finally, and perhaps most important of all, to destroy the coastal battery at Merville, which was capable of firing in echelon right along Sword Beach.

Major-General Gale decided that these initial objectives were to be secured by the 3rd and 5th Parachute Brigades, plus a small glider-borne force; but that, for the subsequent defence of the area, he would be reinforced during the middle of D-Day by Commandos of the 1st Special Service Brigade, who would land on Sword Beach and fight their way through to join him. In the evening of D-Day the remainder of his Division, consisting of the 6th Air Landing Brigade, were to arrive in 250 gliders. This was a difficult enough task if carried out in perfect weather and if everything went well, but it took more than a dangerous operation like this to daunt Richard Gale, one of the greatest Airborne Commanders to emerge during the last war. I knew Gale well and his red face, with his bushy white moustache, belied his brilliant, original brain and exceptional qualities of leadership. Fortunately, he was also a first-class trainer. Before D-Day, every man in the Division was briefed personally and knew exactly what to do on landing, even if things went wrong. This was just as well, as, owing to the high wind and clouds, few men dropped on their correct objectives and the Parachute Brigade was scattered over a wide area.

Dempsey remarked that he did not propose to go into detail but this was an operation, especially the capture of the huge Merville Battery, with its four great guns, which would, he was sure, be studied for many years since it showed the importance of tough, individual training, very careful briefing, and inspired leadership. At one stage, a comparatively small group of paratroopers, whose objective was an important bridge over the River Orne, were completely lost as they had been dropped over a wide area some distance from their target and it was blowing half a gale. Suddenly, out of the sea-mist which covered the area, loomed the solid figure of their Divisional

Commander. 'Follow me!' cried Gale, and as he passed through them he was heard to shout the lines of Henry V's famous Agincourt speech:

> *And gentlemen in England now abed*
> *Shall think themselves accurs'd they were not here,* ...

The bridge was duly captured with very few casualties.

When I asked Dempsey about the subsequent fighting in the thick hedgerows of the Bocage country he emphasized how difficult this had been – hard slogging to capture very limited objectives. It was particularly difficult for armoured offensive operations, owing to the limited visibility and the splendid cover presented by the thick hedges for the enemy anti-tank weapons.

I was sad to learn that during this bitter fighting in the Bocage my old friends of the desert, both infantry and armoured, had been rather 'sticky' and had not shown the drive and initiative of the formations which had been training in the U.K. since 1940. I have always felt that this was a natural phenomenon. Those 'desert warriors' had been fighting more or less since Alamein. They had returned to the U.K., where quite rightly they were acclaimed as the veterans who had been doing all the fighting to date; but then they should have been removed to the depths of the country, where the terrain resembled what they might expect in Normandy, and put through some really tough training. This did not happen, and the Bocage could hardly have more differed from the open desert and mountainous country of North Africa to which they were used. As a result, they suffered unnecessary casualties, particularly in Tank Commanders, who were used to fighting with their turrets open and were easily picked off by the hidden German snipers in the thick hedgerows.

I have always felt that this aspect of divisional psychology was never properly studied during the last war. After a longish period of fighting, the soldiers, though capable of looking after themselves, begin to see all the difficulties and lack the *élan* of fresh troops. They begin to feel it is time they had a rest and someone else did some fighting. No doubt this is what happened in Normandy to these veteran divisions from the Middle East. It is to their eternal credit that they soon regained their old form and ended the war among the best troops we possessed. In a curious way my absence from the recent fighting proved an advantage to me, we had served together in the days of their desert victories and I had not seen them during their sticky Bocage period, so, unlike some of the other Generals, I was delighted to have them under my command.

On my way to Second Army H.Q. I came across some more of my old friends, the very experienced, high-calibre War Correspondents – Chester Wilmot, Christopher Buckley, Alan Moorehead, Richard Dimbleby, Edward Ward and Alexander Clifford. Throughout the war I made a point of always taking the press into my confidence and telling them, *beforehand*, how we proposed to fight the next battle. This enabled them to be in the right places at the right time and to report the battles accurately, which is important from the point of view of morale. Nothing annoys troops more than to read in the newspaper, and particularly in their local papers, of some brilliant action carried out by a unit which has played a very minor part in the victory for which they have been largely responsible. 'Credit where credit is due' has always been my maxim.

To start with, I got into trouble with Montgomery over these prebattle briefings, since he feared that vital information might be given away. All I can say is that not once in the whole war did one of these experienced and reliable men ever let me down. Moreover, as the war progressed it became a two-way benefit. After finishing my briefing I would say, 'It's your turn now' – and nearly always some vital information would be forthcoming. Moving round as they did, often at battalion level, with their wide experience of war, they got the 'feel' of the different formations very quickly, and would say, 'If I were you, General, I should be careful of X Brigade, or Y Division; they have been in the line too long and need a short breathing space.' Next day, I always visited the units concerned, and sure enough found that their information was correct.

'Bimbo' Dempsey having completed his briefing, I set off to join my new command – the veteran XXX Corps, which had been operational ever since Alamein. Under my predecessor, Bucknall, it had been almost continuously in action since the early days of the landing in the bridgehead.

At this stage, I think that it might be helpful if I made some remarks on how the higher formations of the Army worked in this campaign. Two facts must be stressed: first, that there did not, could not, exist any sort of manual setting out in precise terms the roles and duties of organizations such as an Army Group, an Army or even a Corps; secondly, and this follows on from the first point, that the quality of the personalities concerned and of their relationships with each other was of immense significance.

A large military formation such as the Twenty-first Army Group, for instance, is very similar to some huge civilian firm, though its dividends consist of victories in battle, and it risks not pounds, shillings and pence, but human lives. The Commander is like the active Chairman, who is responsible for making the decisions, and he is supported by a Managing Director, and by the Heads of different departments, or, in the civilian world, by the Board of Directors. We were very fortunate in the Twenty-first Army Group to have at the top two extremely intelligent and able Chiefs of Staff (Managing Directors) in the shape of Eisenhower's Lieut-Gen. Bedell Smith and Montgomery's Maj.-Gen. 'Freddie' de Guingand. Montgomery disliked conferences, so it often fell to the lot of de Guingand to represent him, and therefore to put forward the British point of view. This could have been disastrous, but Freddie was prepared to stand up to his chief if he did not agree with Montgomery's policy. He was also such a tactful, popular person that he was able to smooth over the cracks and high-level quarrels which are bound to occur in warfare, when everyone's nerves are taut.

At the top, Bedell and Freddie worked hand in hand; lower down the scale we were equally lucky. Maurice Chilton, Dempsey's Chief of Staff, and my B.G.S., first of all, Pyman, then, when he was promoted, Brigadier 'Splosh' Jones, could always iron out any difficulty. I did not come into contact so much with the Administrative and Intelligence side, but I know that both these important aspects of war were handled on similar lines.

Army Group received its strategic directions from Churchill and the Chiefs of Staff, and translated them into the overall plans. In Europe, Montgomery usually directed the major operations personally, although when he was in Normandy he was always very careful to see that Bradley was in agreement with him. Montgomery allocated the major units for the specific tasks, thus, he selected XXX Corps to lead the advance into Belgium and decided the number of divisions it should have under command. Before the Arnhem battle he gave me my orders personally at Bourg-Léopold. On both these occasions, I think that Dempsey was told what Montgomery was doing. I doubt, however, whether Dempsey had been told beforehand when Montgomery came up to see me just prior to my last battle, which was the seizure of Bremen. That Montgomery's very individualistic management of operations did not adversely affect this smooth running was due to the very close links that existed, as I have said, between the Chiefs of Staff at Army Group, Army and Corps.

Although it may seem surprising, I normally, during the actual fighting, saw very little of Eisenhower or Montgomery, who were no doubt concerned with higher strategical problems. With the help of hindsight I now think that the Higher Command faltered after XXX Corps captured Brussels. Eisenhower, Montgomery or Dempsey should have ordered me to bypass Antwerp and cut off the Germans who were escaping via the Beveland peninsula. My orders were quite clear – to bounce a crossing of the Rhine.

Dempsey visited me fairly frequently during battles, and was always a tower of strength – calm, unruffled and shrewd. He would arrive in a small Auster aircraft, which enabled him to cover quite a large part of the battlefield for which he was responsible. I also used an Auster, and my Divisional H.Q. was instructed to have a suitably large field in the neighbourhood. This had the advantage of enabling me to make quick personal contacts, but it also had the disadvantage of making it difficult to get the 'feel' of the battle in the same way as when I travelled round by car or jeep and was able to stop and speak to people, and to see the look on their faces – 'smelling the battlefield', in fact. Crerar, who commanded the First Canadian Army, operated by very different methods. He visited me almost every day during the Battle of the Reichswald, when I was under his command. Weather permitting, he used to fly daily over the fighting area, also in a light aircraft.

The Army's chief task was the allocation to Corps of the specialized troops which it controlled. Perhaps the most important of these were the heavy and medium artillery regiments that were concentrated in AGRAs (Army Groups Royal Artillery). Army also allotted the 'Funnies' of the 79th Armoured Division. Army had under its control a considerable number of other equally specialized formations such as the Royal Engineers, who would construct the Bailey bridges. If I got into difficulties and wanted more troops I would appeal to Dempsey and he would always do his best to provide them. He had also several independent brigades which did not belong permanently to any division.

A Corps is the largest formation which fights the tactical battle, so a Corps H.Q. must be a highly efficient and mobile base from which the Commander can control the actual fighting. By now I had become almost a professional at taking over Corps; three times already in North Africa I had been through this painful process since 1942 and I wondered whether on this occasion the atmosphere would be more welcoming than I had experienced before. I was lucky, as XXX Corps was probably the most experienced H.Q. in the British Isles and the whole thing worked like a well-oiled machine, under the control of two most able officers. The first was my B.G.S. (Chief of Staff) 'Pete' Pyman, and the second Brigadier in charge of Administration (Brigadier Q) George Webb, both ex-Royal Tank Corps officers. It was largely due to the influence of these two that I was made to feel very welcome from the start. We had fought alongside each other for many months in the desert and in North Africa – and there was always a great fellow feeling among those with 'sand between their toes'

I used to work out my battle plans for the Corps in consultation with my B.G.S., my Brigadier Q as well as with the Corps Commanders Royal Artillery and Royal Engineers and with a liaison officer from the R.A.F. We had a very close link between the Corps and the 83rd Group Tactical Air Force commanded by Harry Broadhurst. When I had finalized the plans, I called a conference, which was also attended by the Divisional Commanders and others concerned, in which I gave out my orders. Afterwards I worked out with my B.G.S. what alternatives we would adopt if things went wrong and we prepared alternative plans, which, however, were kept strictly to ourselves. I always took my Brigadier Q completely into my confidence over everything.

A Corps H.Q. was normally divided into two parts: Main, concerned chiefly with the actual fighting; and Rear, concerned with administration. Although separated, they were located as close to each other as possible, depending on the nature of the country and the state of the battle. When I arrived on 4 August 1944, Main H.Q. was located at Quesnay (approximately three miles north-east of Caumont) and Rear H.Q. a few miles away in close touch with the supply depots, workshops and hospitals, etc., which had been established in the beachhead. Each consisted of approximately 100 camouflaged lorries, caravans and trucks, dotted about in a wooded area 400 × 400 yards.

I was mostly concerned with Main H.Q., though I used to visit Rear H.Q. as often as possible. I lived in the caravan, with next door to it a lorry containing large-scale maps of the battle area; this was my main office. The Operations Department consisted mainly of a camouflaged marquee, complete with field telephones, and maps of different sizes; this was manned day and night. In addition to the staff officers and other ranks, both Main and Rear H.Q. were protected by troops supplied from one of the Divisions in the Corps.

We naturally lived very simply. There were four messes at Main H.Q. In mine, which consisted of a lean-to tent on the side of a mess truck, lived my two A.D.C.s (Captains or Lieutenants), the B.G.S., the G.S.O.1 (a Colonel or Lieut.-Col., the Chief Operation Staff Officer); the remainder were Brigadiers C.C.R.A. (Corps Commander Royal Artillery), C.C.R.E. (Corps Commander Royal Engineers) and the C.C.R.S. (Corps Commander Royal Signals). The whole H.Q. had to be very mobile and able to move at short notice. It was also so organized that I could go on ahead with a very small tactical H.Q. if the situation warranted.

Pyman was in command of Main H.Q. and was a tower of strength. George Webb was the exact opposite of the normal administrative staff officer, who as a rule is built for comfort rather than for speed. He had represented Britain in the Olympic Games before the war, and had a genius for administration. In addition to being in charge of Rear H.Q. he nearly always found time to visit some units in the front line at least every two days – 'just to keep in the picture', as he used to say. He was one of those remarkable people who was always up to something: one day, to my astonishment, I found that we had a farm – George had collected a number of stray cattle and poultry, wandering about loose as their owners had been forced from their farms owing to battles being fought over their land. He found a number of men who had been farmers or farm labourers before the war and put them in charge. We were thus able to supply our 'casualty clearing station' with fresh eggs, milk, meat and so on. On one occasion a very senior officer, standing by the side of the road, had witnessed a column of lorries passing and out of each came a plaintive 'moo' 'What on earth is this?' he asked. 'XXX Corps Farm, sir, moving up,' replied the staff officer at his side.

Unfortunately George Webb was killed later in the war, otherwise he would almost certainly have risen to very high rank in the Army. He was such an attractive, unusual person that his death affected me deeply – almost more than that of anyone I knew during the last war

My first problem was to get to know the rest of my staff. So I started by visiting all the different branches – particularly the Signals, as it is quite impossible to fight a modern battle without first-class communications. Montgomery had once asked me whether I would prefer to have in the Corps six divisions with not very adequate communications or five divisions with a first-class Signal layout. I opted unhesitatingly for the latter As I had expected, I found a first-class team, whose morale was high.

I always made it a rule that if I required briefing this must come from the actual officer who handled the subject and not from my Chief of Staff, as was the case in most formations (although he could be present if he wished). By this means, I got to know most of my staff personally. I also insisted that if an officer arrived from one of the forward units, it was the duty of the staff officer concerned to make him feel, however junior he might be, that he was the one man in the world whom he wanted to see.

When I took over XXX Corps on 4 August, it consisted of the 7th Armoured Division, the 43rd Wessex and 50th Northumbrian Divisions, plus the 8th Armoured Brigade. Looming in front of us was that formidable feature, Mont Pinçon, from which the enemy dominated the surrounding country. My next and most important task was to get 'the feel' of the troops in the Corps, and it soon became obvious to me that the seven weeks' hard slogging in the thick Bocage country had taken their toll and the gloss had gone from the magnificently trained army which had landed in Normandy. I have always said that in a section of ten men, as a rough guide, two lead, seven follow and one would do almost anything not to be there at all. The two leaders take most of the risks and are usually the first to become casualties. When this happens on a large scale, as had occurred in the Normandy Beachhead Battle, so much better suited to defence than to attack, the cutting edge of a division becomes blunted. This was obviously what had happened to the 43rd Wessex, one of the best-trained divisions which has ever left our shores and which was facing up, with the 8th Armoured Brigade, to Mount Pinçon. Yet the battle was going well; more and more German divisions had been thrown in against the Twenty-first Army Group front and, as a result, the Americans had been able to break out of the Cotentin peninsula.

I spent the next few days, rather like an American presidential candidate, on a whistle-stop tour of the Corps. As we edged ever closer to Mont Pinçon, at every possible opportunity I gathered together as many men as possible and showed them on a large, coloured map, which I had specially prepared for the purpose, how well the battle was going. I have always made a practice of this when out 'smelling the battlefield' because the modern soldier is much more intelligent, certainly than his grandfather, and probably than his father, who fought in the First World War. In battle he is risking his most precious possession – his life – and he will only give of his best if he has confidence in his leaders and, above all, knows what is going on. The weather was hot, the country damnable, and the Germans in the Mont Pinçon area even more bloody-minded than usual. Battle groups based on a couple of Tiger tanks were proving particularly obnoxious. I began to wonder how we would ever capture the formidable objective in front of us.

As I drove back to my H.Q. on 6 August, I was met by a jubilant Pyman, who, even before we reached him, shouted out, 'We've got it! – Mont Pinçon!' I could hardly believe my ears. Apparently Captain Denny, commanding the leading group of tanks of the 13th/18th Hussars, had found a narrow track, seemingly unguarded, leading to the top of the mountain. Showing great initiative and having received permission from his C.O., Lieut.-Col. Dunkerley, he had led two troops up the track, which was so narrow that one tank came off it and had to be abandoned. Now they were on the top, but a thick fog had come down and they could hear German voices all round them. Denny added somewhat plaintively on the R.T. that they were 'feeling rather lonely'. Pyman assured me, however, that the already battle-weary 4th Wiltshires were being led to the top by Lieut.-Col. Luce, their C.O. They reached the summit under cover of darkness and next day repulsed a somewhat half-hearted German counter-attack. So the most formidable feature in Normandy, which had been pointed out to the troops over and over again on models of the area during training, had been captured by seven or eight tanks – thanks to the initiative and courage of one young officer of the 13th/18th Hussars and his Commanding Officer. The effect on morale was tremendous. Mont Pinçon had been the cornerstone of the enemy defences in Normandy. With it now in our hands, the position was reversed. We could overlook them, not they us.

I could now sit on the heights of Mont Pinçon with my C.C.R.A., Brigadier Stewart Rawlins, directing our artillery fire by radio. If necessary we could bring all 300 of our guns to bear on an enemy position in a matter of minutes. We literally blasted the infantry forward out of the bridgehead. It was hard work for the gunners, as they had to be prepared for action day and night, but using cooks, clerks and everyone available, they formed two teams for each gun. I have always said, 'Although I am an infantryman, in my opinion the arm of the Service which did most to win the last war was the Royal Regiment of Artillery.' It was encouraging to note that our infantry were increasing the length of their advances almost daily and were capturing more distant objectives. This was due, not only to the superb artillery support, but also to the fact that many of their leaders who had been wounded were returning to their units from hospital.

Returning to the scene of battle – Montgomery had been quite right when he said, 'Jorrocks, you have arrived at the right moment.' I had once more been extremely lucky. The troops have a saying that if you want to get on in the Army you must be in the right place at the right time and your face must fit. I can think of no one to whom this applies more than to myself.

Even though Mont Pinçon had fallen, it was still not clear what the Germans proposed to do next. Their only chance of avoiding almost wholesale destruction seemed to be to withdraw with all speed to the line of the Seine, or better still the Somme. At the moment their obstinate resistance on the British and Canadian front seemed to indicate that they were now trying to pivot on that area. Beyond this, both Montgomery and Bradley were frankly puzzled as to what action they should now take. They knew that Hitler's great weakness lay in the fact that he would never given up ground. This had already resulted in the major disasters of Stalingrad and Alamein, where Rommel had been forbidden to carry out a fighting withdrawal. It seemed scarcely credible, however, that he would perpetrate a similar error for the third time. To understand, therefore, the dramatic, complex and rapidly changing situation which now developed, it is necessary first to review the rapid progress during the past week of the great American right wheel towards the east.

Chapter 3
The Falaise Pocket
EVERSLEY BELFIELD

Introduction by *Sir Brian Horrocks*

For the next fortnight, after the capture of Mont Pinçon, the emphasis of the Normandy battle shifted to the two flanks. The U.S. forces, and Patton in particular, having shaken themselves free from the Bocage, were swinging round in an easterly direction with little opposition. In this type of mobile warfare, where petrol vehicles predominated, they were much superior to the Germans, the bulk of whose formations were still horse-drawn.

On the other flank, however, the situation was very different. The Canadians, with the Poles under command, were involved in a real dogfight – the sort of battle which Corps Commanders dread. The different units were so mixed up that clear communications were impossible, which made it very difficult to produce a cohesive plan. As a result of this lack of control, casualties mounted rapidly. I watched this battle with considerable anxiety and sympathy for General Simonds, the Canadian Corps Commander. If the two prongs, U.S. and Canadian, could have joined up, the bulk of the German forces in Normandy would have been surrounded and forced to surrender, and the war would have almost certainly been over in 1944. As this – the Battle of the Falaise Gap – was unquestionably the turning point in the whole war in the west, it must be described in some detail, though XXX Corps played a modest role. Our job was a pedestrian one – to advance daily against tough opposition. But all the time during this very confused period I hoped that, if the Germans could be surrounded, XXX Corps might be called upon to play a vital part in the subsequent campaign.

* * *

Before describing the Battle of the Falaise Gap, the confused efforts leading up to it must be briefly traced. The great American offensive, code-named 'Cobra', which had begun on 25 July, had succeeded in unlocking the western edge of the Normandy bridgehead. By 1 August, Patton's newly arrived and highly mobile Third Army had started to exploit this breakout. The startling successes achieved by these fresh troops under their dynamic leader meant that the Allied plans, based on the assumption of a fairly orderly advance, had now to be continually adapted to meet the new situations arising. As the German collapse became more rapid and widespread, those responsible for the higher direction of the campaign often inevitably lost touch with the realities of the situation and made decisions which now appear in retrospect hard to justify. Perhaps the most complicating factor was the paradoxical position which developed during the first three weeks or so of August. On the one hand, Patton's breakout was so completely successful that, to all intents and purposes, no coherent front existed against his forces. On the other hand, the other Allied Armies in Normandy met some of the most tenacious resistance of the whole war, and here the front was very firmly held by the Germans.

We must now plunge into the maelstrom of events which culminated, in late August 1944, in the defeat of the Germans in Normandy. Even after Patton had broken out it was still thought that a major effort would be needed to capture the Breton ports before operations elsewhere could be started, since the Normandy beaches would be unusable once the weather had deteriorated in the autumn. However, it was soon recognized that a single Corps would be sufficient for this task, and thus Patton's forces could be deployed in an easterly rather than a southerly direction. It was now planned that the Allied forces should make a concentrated effort to drive the Germans against the Lower Seine, where the bridges had been destroyed. With the enormous Allied air superiority, the already depleted German forces would therefore be faced either with annihilation or surrender.

At this moment Hitler suddenly intervened. Studying his maps in his Headquarters in East Prussia, he saw that at the base of the Cotentin peninsula, Patton's forces had to squeeze through a corridor, between the Germans and the sea, only about twelve miles broad. Here, near Avranches, all the traffic had to converge upon and cross a single bridge. Hitler reckoned that, if a stranglehold could be applied there, the American offensive would be broken. The German Commander, von Kluge, was ordered to attack, using his battered Panzer formations. On 6 August, he launched his reluctant troops upon what was called the Mortain Counter-offensive. Aided by excellent weather and close co-ordination between ground and air units (many of whom were British), the Americans had decisively repulsed this threat by 8 August and Patton's progress was in no way affected. One important result of Hitler's intervention was the concentration of a large number of German formations into the western, or far, end of the Normandy front. This switch of their forces, together with Patton's almost unimpeded progress to the south of the Normandy battleground, presented the Allied Commanders with the opportunity of surrounding all the Germans and gaining a really decisive victory. It was one of those almost unbelievable occasions which military commanders may dream of, but which very rarely materialize.

On 6 August, Patton had reached Le Mans. He was now meeting negligible opposition and his XV Corps was ordered to carry on northwards to capture Argentan – which it did on 13 August. The new plan was that Patton's XV Corps should then advance a further fifteen miles to Falaise, which, it was expected, would be very soon reached also by the Canadians, who were less than ten miles away. This link-up by the Americans and Canadians would thus block the German escape routes to the east, thereby trapping them against a hard shoulder formed by these two Allied formations. On the afternoon of 13 August, however, Patton's XV Corps received the most definite and personal order from Bradley, their Army Group Commander, that it was not to go beyond Argentan. It was halted there and reduced in size until relieved by another Corps from the U.S. First Army on 17 August. We can now see that Bradley's decision to halt XV Corps at Argentan was one of the most momentous decisions of the whole campaign, and it was at the time much resented by Patton himself. Whatever Bradley may have said later, there can be no doubt that his main reason for issuing this most unfortunate order was his fear that Patton's unsupported XV Corps would be unable to withstand the 75,000 Germans, with their 250 tanks, who were potentially trapped west of Argentan and Falaise. Bradley was particularly anxious lest Patton's isolated troops should be overwhelmed by these remnants of nineteen German divisions, which, he erroneously believed, were already 'sluicing' back. In fact, the Germans had hardly begun an evacuation plan. During these next few days, however, they most effectively exploited this unexpected opportunity and regrouped their forces to their own fullest advantage. Moreover, like all the Allied Commanders, Bradley was then far too optimistic about the pace of the Canadian advance.

On the eastern flank of the Normandy bridgehead, the Allies had always encountered the most determined resistance. Since D-Day hardly any progress had been made on the coast, where the terrain was most unsuitable for armoured warfare, with thick woods just inland, whereas between Ouistreham and Cabourg the wide expanse of watery meadows formed by the River Dives stretched almost down to the sea. The British attempts to advance inland hereabouts also met with the most violent German opposition. It was not until after a series of very costly battles that half of Caen had been captured by 9 July. A massive armoured offensive that had tried to swing round to the east of Caen and then to push south towards Falaise, was soon halted before gaining much ground. Thus by 31 July, when the Canadian Army was formed, the Allies had only managed to penetrate about fifteen miles inland. The German leaders, fully recognizing the vital importance of holding this ground, had retained most of their armoured forces here, as any collapse on their eastern flank would have rapidly resulted in the disintegration of their whole Normandy front.

The first task of the newly-created First Canadian Army was to advance southward, from their positions just outside Caen, to link up with Patton. The responsibility for planning to break through the deep German defences astride the Caen–Falaise road was given to the 41-year-old Lieut.-Gen. Guy Simonds, Commander of II Canadian Corps. Simonds was one of the most experienced and resourceful Canadian generals, having commanded their 1st Division in Sicily and Italy, and subsequently the 5th Canadian Armoured Division in Italy. He was under no illusions about the difficulties confronting him. On 31 July he stated, 'The problem is how to get armour through the enemy gun screen to sufficient depth to disrupt the German anti-tank gun and mortar defence in country highly suited to the latter combination. It can be done: (*a*) by overwhelming air support to destroy or neutralize enemy tanks, anti-tank guns and mortars; (*b*) by infiltrating the screen in bad visibility to a sufficient depth to disrupt the anti-tank gun and mortar defence.' Code-named 'Totalize', Simonds's plan was an elaborate one. It aimed at surprising the enemy in a variety of ways. He obtained almost unlimited air backing, including British heavy bombers which were to be used for the first time at night in direct support of a ground operation. He determined to transport infantry through the main enemy defences in armoured carriers which were improvised by removing the guns from an American self-propelled gun chassis. These vehicles had armour-plated protection for their crews and were officially known as 'Kangaroos' Simonds dispensed with a prior artillery bombardment, but ordered a creeping barrage to be fired from 360 guns directly the attack began. He devised several directional systems to guide the line of the offensive through the darkness, such as Bofors, light anti-aircraft guns, firing a continuous stream of tracer shells and artificial moonlight from searchlights pointing southward at a low angle.

'Totalize' was opposed by a very mixed German force. The major formations were two fresh infantry divisions that had just arrived from the Fifteenth Army across the Seine. Although by now much reduced in strength, the 12th SS Panzer Division immediately returned from reserve to fight as fanatically as ever. Its fifty tanks, mainly Mark IVs with the long 75-mm. gun, were reinforced by about twenty of the heaviest German armour, the 56-ton Tiger tank which mounted the 88-mm. gun; both these weapons easily outranged the guns on the Canadians' Shermans and Cromwells (except for the few Shermans, called 'Fireflies', with the 17-pounder gun). Also heavily involved was a newly arrived anti-aircraft Corps which was equipped with about ninety of the powerful 88s, which were tri-purpose guns capable of being used in anti-aircraft, anti-tank or field roles. Finally the German who took over control at the crucial moment was Kurt Meyer, Commander of the 12th SS Panzer Division, a young fighting general who had had immense experience, first on the Russian front and latterly in Normandy. He it was who halted the rout of the German infantry on the night of 7–8 August and continued to direct operations for the next few days.

The first part of 'Totalize' began at 2300 hours. I noted in my diary that, although ten miles away, I could feel my tent shake as over 3000 tons of bombs from nearly 1000 aircraft were dropped on targets on the flanks of the axis of the advance. I then heard and saw 'the barrage going full blast, lighting up the sky intermittently, and on either flank of it streams of tracer shells from the Bofors guns flying leisurely through the air' By now the ground attack was in progress. In two columns there were eight lines of tracked vehicles almost nose to tail. The Caen–Falaise road was supposed to be the dividing line between the two columns, each of four lines, which were led by flail Sherman tanks with the 'Kangaroos' and Bren-gun carriers in the middle, while more tanks brought up the rear of the lines to give protection. To those taking part, the overwhelming impression was one of chaos. Through the noise and dust, vehicles whose drivers had lost their sense of direction, avoiding bomb craters and other obstacles, swerved across the paths of others who had also to take sudden evasive action. To make the scene even more alive, German anti-tank gunners hit some vehicles, which burnt alarmingly brightly. Yet despite all this apparent confusion, the columns found that, when morning came, they had driven about three miles through the German defences. With little loss, most of their objectives had been taken, including the hamlet of Tilly-la-Campagne, which had resisted three attacks since 18 July; but a few places did hold out till later, and fierce counter-attacks had to be repulsed.

Starting on the afternoon of 8 August, the second phase of 'Totalize' was dogged by misfortune and disappointments. Because some of the R.A.F. heavy bombers had been diverted by foggy conditions to other airfields, it was found that their crews could not be briefed nor their aircraft bombed up for a further attack within twelve hours. Thus, at the very last moment, heavy bombers of the Eighth U.S. Air Force were called upon. Only 500 of the 678 aircraft dispatched dropped their bombs, and many of these fell nowhere near the targets; about twenty machines actually dropped their loads on the Canadians and Poles just outside Caen. This tragedy put some of the more important units out of action. Furthermore, serious delays had already been caused by the enormous traffic jams created by the 4th Canadian and 1st Polish Armoured Divisions moving forward during the night and morning. They had to pass through masses of other transport, which was clogging the few roads and bridges in and beyond Caen, where some minefields had not yet been cleared. Another hindrance was the German shelling and mortaring from strongpoints still holding out on the flanks. Finally Kurt Meyer and his subordinates were well aware that another attack was impending and took full advantage of the morning's pause to try to repulse it.

In this second phase the Canadian and Polish armoured divisions were to continue as soon as possible onward from where the night attack had halted. The plan was that they were to advance on either side of the Caen–Falaise road to seize the hills overlooking Falaise, particularly those just to the east of the town from where the main road to Trun, now becoming the focal point in the German retreat route, could be dominated. The resumed attack immediately ran into considerable resistance and little progress was made before nightfall. On 9 August, a Canadian armoured regiment, supported by most of an infantry battalion, did manage to break out. Unfortunately the two units, the British Columbia and the Algonquin Regiments, soon lost their way (a very easy thing to do hereabouts, where the over-detailed maps were most unhelpful). Swinging much too far to the east, they soon found themselves isolated, but claimed to have captured their objective. As they sent back an incorrect map reference, they received no support, except from the pilots of a couple of rocket-firing Typhoon aircraft which returned several times to try to help. By the evening, the Germans had destroyed almost all these Canadian tanks and most of the troops were either killed or wounded and captured. To the east of the Canadians, the Poles also made only slight headway. By the morning of 11 August, Simonds called off 'Totalize', the offensive having literally ground to a halt. Thus the expected breakout had failed, but the Canadians and Poles had gained eight miles and were over half-way from Caen to Falaise.

General Maczek, Commander of the Polish Armoured Division, attributed this rebuff to a variety of causes which are worth a brief consideration. He stressed that when armoured units are funnelled through a narrow corridor they can make only a rigid, frontal style of attack, which is a most dangerous procedure. He pointed out that in this key area the German defensive system had been continuously strengthened and was much deeper than had been expected; I recorded that all round this region I found 'German dug-outs made with great care and thoroughness, many being dug into the sides of lanes and shored up with timber supports' The bombing had had little effect on these or on most of the German strongpoints; these were cleverly concealed positions in the woods, orchards, hedges and stone buildings scattered all over this terrain, which, being fairly open, provided the German tank and anti-tank gunners with good fields of fire. Maczek emphasized that the Allies were handicapped by having only the relatively light Cromwell and Sherman tanks (27 and 30 tons respectively). These had to approach to within 500 metres of the heavier German Panther and Tiger tanks (45 and 54 or 68 tons) to knock them out, whereas the 88-mm. gun in the Tiger or on the ground could dispose of the Allied tanks at two kilometres. The Panther's gun and armament were also markedly superior to those of the Cromwell and Sherman, whereas the German Mark IV was certainly their equal. Thus, although the Allied armour greatly outnumbered the German tanks, its inferiority nullified much of its theoretical advantages in mobility; the Poles lost sixty-six tanks in 'Totalize' and the Canadians many more. Although Simonds blamed the failure of 'Totalize' primarily on the inexperience of these two new armoured divisions, the 49-year-old Maczek, who had fought in Poland before escaping to Britain to form and train this armoured division, considered that they had simply been asked to do too much under the circumstances.

By 11 August, the whole of the Normandy battle began to take on a different character. By now even Hitler had had to accept that the Mortain counter-attack had failed. The Commander in the field, von Kluge, was becoming increasingly anxious for the safety of all the German troops west of the Seine and was trying to prevent their being trapped in what, on the map, was ominously coming to resemble a pocket. The best exit from this embryo pocket was the 15-mile gap then existing between Falaise and Argentan. Through this the Germans had now to channel all their troops and equipment before moving in a north-easterly direction towards Rouen, since part of Patton's Third Army was already approaching Paris. Predictably, the Germans were therefore still holding on grimly to the north of Falaise.

Simonds had now decided that both sides of the main Caen–Falaise road were almost impassable, especially Quesnay Wood which the Germans had turned into a fortress and which had withstood two costly Canadian attacks. He thus planned to break through just to the east of Falaise, less than ten miles distant from his forward units. He then intended to sever the roads running east and south out of the town. Code-named 'Tractable', this ambitious plan would, if successful, cut across the main German lines of retreat, thereby trapping most of their troops.

In broad daylight on 14 August, Simonds attacked with two infantry brigades, in armoured carriers, escorted by two armoured brigades, followed by a further two infantry brigades, their flanks being concealed by a thick blanket of artillery smoke. They were supported by a high proportion of the massed medium artillery of the Twenty-first Army Group. The R.A.F. sent over the full weight of Bomber Command. I wrote in my diary, 'The weather was perfect as the first wave of heavy bombers plastered Quesnay Wood which had been holding us up for so long. Everybody felt very elated and excited and we were all congratulating ourselves on their accuracy.' The first wave of bombers had indeed done an excellent job, but the second wave arrived, and in my diary I continued,

> ... suddenly to the east of where we were sitting on the open ground watching this attack, there was a vast billow of black smoke and the earth rocked as more and more Lancasters dropped their bombs there. Then some began to come over us at about 3000 feet, their bomb doors open and the bombs plainly visible. We dashed for some nearby German slit trenches, fearing the worst, but all the bombs seemed to fall the other [the east] side of the road.

After this there was a lull, but then I saw a third wave of bombers approaching; my diary records:

> I leapt into a jeep with one of the mechanics and made for one of the Austers (which were parked nearby). As he started it up he offered to go up with me, but I refused, as his extra weight would have reduced the climbing performance. I climbed at full throttle and with great difficulty (I had forgotten how it worked) fired off a red Verey cartridge at about 2000 feet and another at 4000 feet.

At about 6000 feet I was just below a large formation and twisted and turned to attract their attention.

I am certain that none of this third wave bombed our own forces, as I was in the midst of the stream of planes and noted, when one formation passed just above me, that I could plainly see the large bombs in the open bay. I was very fearful of bombs falling on me as I was over the area that they had been bombing earlier.

Subsequently a Court of Inquiry found that the Pathfinder crews of the second wave had not checked their timed run from the coast with sufficient accuracy. Almost certainly they mistook a wood which was four miles, about a minute's flying time, nearer the coast for their target of Quesnay Wood. This tragedy was also partly the result of complete lack of communications between the Services. When first bombed, the troops correctly lit yellow flares, the standard Army recognition indicators for friendly formations. In Bomber Command, however, yellow flares were their target indicators; nobody had warned the aircrews of this possible confusion. The red Verey lights I fired seemed to have helped, despite Air Marshal Harris's comment in the Official Inquiry that 'they were likely to give a misleading indication of target indicators' One of those taking part in this raid said later that they were warned to fly forward of the Auster, as it was an easily recognizable aircraft that did not operate over enemy lines. It was additionally most unfortunate that none of the Army's wireless sets seemed able to work on the frequencies used by R.A.F. Bomber Command. Watching this great bombing attack was the Commander-in-Chief of the R.A.F. Tactical Air Forces, Air Marshal Sir Arthur Coningham, and even he was helpless as he sat bouncing up and down inside the Corps Commander's armoured car with the bombs falling all round him. R.A.F. Bomber Command never made a similar error during this campaign.

This mishap caused the loss of 150 Canadian and Polish lives and 250 wounded. (Only a week earlier heavy bombers of the U.S. Air Force had mistakenly bombed the Canadians and Poles, killing 65 and wounding 250.) The offensive had got off to a bad start.

Unfortunately, the Germans knew when and where the attacks were coming. On the previous day, an officer, although forbidden to do so, had taken a copy of the battle orders for his unit, had lost his way in his armoured car, driven into the German lines and been killed; the Germans had thus had time to adjust their dispositions. Nevertheless, despite these setbacks the Canadians, covered by dense clouds of dust and smoke, soon gained their first objective, the River Laison. The Germans quickly recovered and counter-attacked, and the battle thereafter degenerated into a series of confusing minor actions which the Army, Corps and Divisional Commanders found themselves powerless to control. Reports were often unreliable and usually so belated as to be useless. Many of the troops were locked in such close combat that even those in the forefront of the fighting were uncertain who was doing what and to whom. The Canadians in fact had recreated something not unlike the first days of the Battle of the Somme in 1916. The efforts of the pilots of the Spitfires and Typhoons to help the troops on the ground were sometimes bedevilled by this lack of precise information. It was also peculiarly exasperating that at the critical stage of the forthcoming battle some of the most confused fighting should have taken place at the junction of four map sheets. This was an especially serious problem in the very close and rugged countryside at the exits from the Pocket near Chambois, where map reading proved very difficult at speeds of 200–300 m.p.h. The airmen's task was complicated by misleading and erroneous reports of the precise positions of Allied troops who often either were uncertain of their own whereabouts or found themselves sandwiched between German formations. A considerable number of Allied soldiers and vehicles were unavoidably shot up by their own airmen.

By 15 August, the Germans were being rolled back along the whole front except around Argentan, where, on 13 August, it will be remembered, Bradley had ordered Patton to halt. Falaise, which had been the linchpin of the German Armies, was now as good as lost. On the British Second Army front, formations were over the River Orne and were striking south. First U.S. Army had curled right round the western and southern faces of the great German salient that stretched from Tinchebray to south of Argentan. Here, at last, the Americans had linked up with Patton's stationary 2nd French Armoured Division which, at the nearest point, was only eleven miles away from the British on the north side of the Pocket. Farther to the south, Patton's columns had romped into Dreux and Chartres. Far away on the Mediterranean coast, Devers's Army Group had landed with remarkable ease and was rapidly pushing inland.

At Hitler's headquarters there had been consternation throughout the day. Von Kluge had gone forward early to get the feel of the battle, and all efforts to get in contact with him had been abortive. Hitler suspected him of defecting to the Allies. In fact a low-flying Allied aircraft had smashed von

Kluge's radio. When he eventually did get back, he rang to say that the time was long past when any counter-attack could restore or stabilize the situation, even for a day or two. Many of the German vehicles had run out of petrol; for survival, it was imperative that withdrawal should begin immediately between Argentan and Falaise. None the less, permission from Hitler to pull out did not arrive until late in the afternoon of 16 August, by which time the Allied forces on the west had pushed on several miles farther.

Meanwhile, like the previous offensives, 'Tractable' had soon run out of steam. Powerful counter-attacks north-east of Falaise therefore achieved their limited purpose and kept open the German escape route. On 15 August, Simonds received fresh orders to plug the gap in the shrinking Pocket which was now clearly seen to be lying between Trun and Chambois. The American troops also were instructed to resume their advance north-eastwards from Argentan to Chambois. Owing to infuriating delays in transferring responsibility from Third to First Army, it took three-and-a-half critical days before they began, on 18 August, their move to link up with the Canadians in order to exploit this new situation. The Canadians had to change the direction of their thrust from a southerly axis directed at Falaise to a south-easterly one aimed both at Trun, about twelve miles from Falaise, and at Chambois another four miles farther on. For this final effort Simonds decided to employ again his two armoured divisions and one of the Canadian infantry divisions, but it took two days to disengage and regroup them. Their new task was to prove most demanding. General S. Maczek sadly commented in his book *Avec mes blindes*, 'A great air of optimism prevailed amongst the higher staffs. According to them, it was a matter now of rapidly blocking the last escape routes; then it only remained for us to collect the German prisoners and take possession of their equipment.'

From 17 to 21 August the concluding stages of the Falaise Gap battle took place in the vicinity of Trun and Chambois. The extremely bitter fighting at very close quarters often resulted in the whereabouts of many units being unknown for considerable periods of time. It was unfortunate that, at this critical juncture, some of the relatively inexperienced Allied formations should have had to contend with the most sophisticated battle techniques developed during the war. Not only were various German groups trying to extricate themselves, but veteran SS Panzer units, already outside this pocket, were also breaking back to keep a gap open through the Allied troops in order to enable their best-trained soldiers, such as the SS men and tank crews, to escape. This retrieval operation had been ordered by Field-Marshal Model, the new Commander of Army Group 'B' who had replaced von Kluge (on being summoned back to Germany, von Kluge had committed suicide on 19 August). Model's manoeuvre, new to the western Allies, had been successfully developed by the Germans during their long retreat on the Russian front. If well co-ordinated, it forced their opponent's formations to face two ways: in this case, westward to stem the tide of those trying to escape, and eastward to ward off the attack of those breaking back to save those who were trapped.

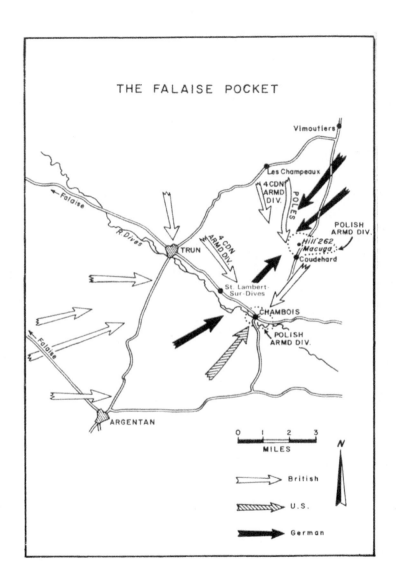

By the evening of 17 August some Canadians were near Trun, most of which they had captured by the following day, but from 18 to 20 August they made little further progress. The chief reason was that the extreme violence of the enemy attacks fragmented units, and concerted action could not be organized by the Canadian staff. The main fighting was between Trun and Chambois, for the control of the roads leading towards Vimoutiers. The Pocket itself had now shrunk to a strip barely seven miles long and six miles wide. The fighting reached its climax on 20 August. Terrible casualties were inflicted on the retreating Germans, especially by the Allied artillery. By the evening of 19 August, over 3000 guns had been moved to within range of all the German forces, and the intensity of the bombardment was reminiscent of Verdun and Passchendaele in the First World War. In this mêlée, however, one of the most serious problems encountered by those directing the artillery fire was to distinguish friend from foe, so intermingled were the two sides; close air support was by now virtually impossible. Along the Trun–Vimoutiers road, the Canadians were still unable to prevent sizeable groups of Germans from smashing through, especially when the fanatical SS units were involved. By 21 August the worst was over, but even then a Canadian officer wrote, 'A host of white flags appeared and hundreds of the enemy crowded in to surrender. Many others were unable to give up, for every move towards our lines brought bursts of fire from certain SS troops patrolling the low ground behind them in an armoured half-track.'

During this climax of the struggle to plug the Gap and while the Canadians were almost engulfed, the Poles were also trying to stem the tide of the German thrusts. Originally they had been told to advance on Trun, but by 17 August the situation had altered and their new orders were to cut through the German positions north-east of Falaise and then to swing south to Chambois, a distance of about fifteen miles. On 19 August, two Polish regiments managed to carve their way through to Chambois, where they joined up with formations from an American infantry division. (At no time during this period were reliable communications between the Canadians and the Americans established in this area.) These two formations found the village with its important crossroads in a terrible condition. An American later reported, 'When I entered Chambois the blood was flowing in streams in the gutters. The buildings blazed and the stench of death and burning flesh was almost unbearable. There was an incredible pile of German dead. I had never seen such a mass of harness in my life, nor had I seen so many horses, wounded horses.' With the German infantry still largely dependent on horse transport, the mangled remains of these, and of innumerable cows, provided the most gruesome and foul-smelling evidence of the efficacy of the endless artillery and air attacks to which the retreating Germans and the animals were being subjected.

Perhaps the most dramatic episode in the battle of the Falaise Gap was the struggle waged by the remainder of the Polish Armoured Division. On the night of 17–18 August, one of its tank regiments had set out for Chambois, led by a French civilian who knew this wooded and hilly terrain. Unfortunately he mistook the name of the village the Poles were seeking, and he took them, not to the more distant Chambois, but to the nearer village of Champeaux. There was, however, one major compensation for this mistake and the resultant delay. During the night march, the Poles had passed through the lines of newly-arrived formations of II SS Panzer Corps which were being assembled just outside the Pocket for their break-back operation. The prisoners they took gave them the first information of this new threat to the closure of the Gap.

On 18 August, the main Polish force made little headway towards Chambois. On the 19th, new Intelligence reports led to General Maczek being then ordered to cut through the German positions and seize a strategic hilltop, known either as Point 262 from its height, or as 'Maczuga', the Polish name for a mace, which its shape resembled. This place was about three miles north of Chambois and dominated the main road to Vimoutiers. Here about 2000 Poles with seventy-two tanks and some anti-tank guns were isolated in a steadily diminishing perimeter during the critical period of the Falaise Pocket battle. For forty-eight hours they were cut off from any direct support, partly because their exact whereabouts were not known, and partly because no force was immediately available to break through the enveloping Germans.

The situation in which the Poles on Maczuga found themselves had developed so rapidly that it was unforeseen by the commanders on both sides. The Germans had anticipated that the break-back by the armoured groups of II SS Panzer Corps would be sufficiently powerful to hold open a passage long enough, for thirty-six hours at least, to enable the élite German troops to escape. Furthermore, Model had assumed that the Allies could not quickly establish a strong force astride the escape roads to Vimoutiers, in the region of Trun and Chambois. For their part, the Allied commanders had confidently expected that the Canadians would very soon link up with the Americans and the other Poles in Chambois, thus closing the Gap and allowing the British divisions already approaching from the south, together with the rest of the

Canadian, Polish and American troops, to mop up the scattered remnants of the German Seventh Army. The Allied Intelligence had seriously underestimated the ability of the German leaders to form effective battlegroups out of the more fanatical of their men who were determined to escape or die in the attempt. Nor had sufficient account been taken of the tremendous pressure generated by tens of thousands of German troops surging back across the River Dives to reach the comparative safety of their comrades waiting for them only a few miles away. As a result of this miscalculation, the Germans managed to keep open a corridor across the River Dives near St Lambert, a hamlet about half-way between Trun and Chambois. They did so despite the heroic efforts of 200 men and a few tanks under Major D. V. Currie, awarded the V.C. for his efforts, who had got into St Lambert and stayed there, causing heavy casualties to the fleeing Germans. More Germans filtered through other routes across the Dives, and yet others circumvented the defenders in Chambois. But nearly all those who escaped this net had then to try to work their way round the Poles on Maczuga, who were also holding back II SS Panzer Corps's armoured groups attacking them from the opposite direction.

One of the Poles marooned on Maczuga compared their situation to that of a person in the middle of an antheap on the march — except that the ants here were heavily armoured! At one of the most critical moments, sixteen Tiger tanks approached the position and were taken on by twelve Shermans, half of which were soon knocked out. Attached to the Poles was Captain Sevigny, the forward observation officer of a Canadian 5·5-inch medium artillery regiment, who ordered his regiment's sixteen guns to bring down fire almost on his own trench. Dozens of 100-lb shells arrived exactly on the target and the attack was crushed. Captain Sevigny, who had earlier registered several likely targets, had a panoramic view of the battlefield and, like many other artillery observers during this period, he directed heavy concentrations of shells which did terrible damage to the Germans, who were mostly in the open. Many of the artillery officers were cut off from their regiments and had the unusual experience of facing their own guns when directing their fire!

The most critical day for the Poles was 20 August; Captain Sevigny recalled in a pamphlet *Boisjois Côte 262*:

> ... But I could not believe my eyes, the Boches marched against us singing, *Deutschland, Deutschland über alles*. We let them come to within fifty yards, then we mowed down their ranks ... but other waves followed ... the fifth arrived! Not having any more ammunition, the Poles charged the enemy with the bayonet. ... On this day we had endured eight such assaults ... what fanaticism! One of the wounded, near me, had the appearance of a child. I read in his pay book the date of his birth, April 1931! He was thirteen. How horrible.

That night the wounded Polish officer in charge of this sector called together the fifteen men still capable of fighting and told them that he did not believe that the Canadians could come to their aid, and that they were down to the last five shells for each of their guns and to the last fifty rounds per man for the rifles. One of these attacks, however, produced a welcome reinforcement in the shape of fifteen German prisoners who turned out to be Poles; they speedily changed uniforms and sides to fight with their compatriots! When the Canadian Grenadier Guards fought their way through, helped by a final Polish counter-attack, they found that 'the picture at Point 262 was the grimmest the regiment had so far come up against ... unburied dead and parts of them were strewn about by the score ... they had several hundred wounded who had not been evacuated, about 700 prisoners of war lay loosely guarded in a field' One of the prisoners was a German corps commander. The numbers of the Poles were terribly depleted; no food or ammunition or medical supplies had reached them, as none of their soft-skinned vehicles had been able to get through the surrounding Germans. To a greater extent than any other group these Poles had thwarted the massive German efforts to break out of the Pocket. They had also endured the brunt of the attacks from both directions.

In the Falaise Gap battle the Polish casualties were about 1450, of whom nearly 450 were either killed or missing, amounting to about 20 per cent of their combat formations. The Poles claimed more than 5000 prisoners, while from 19 to 23 August II Canadian Corps alone had collected 13,680 prisoners. No statistics exist for the numbers who escaped during the Falaise battles: the highest, i.e. the German, estimate was 50,000, the lowest about 20,000. Before bad weather on 20 August ended their attacks, the airmen had achieved one of their most impressive victories of the war. It was impossible to count the total losses they had inflicted on the retreating Germans, but in the area around the Falaise Gap alone over 3040 items were listed, excluding horses and carts. The count did not extend beyond Vimoutiers, although the aircraft were operating up to the Seine during this period. Altogether about 40,000 Germans were captured in the Pocket, and during 10–22 August over 25,000 were killed.

In conclusion, taking the battle for Normandy as a whole, the Allies had, by the end of August, destroyed Army Group 'B' (the Seventh and Fifteenth Armies) as a coherent fighting force. It had lost about 400,000 men, of whom 200,000 were now prisoners of war, 135,000 of these having been taken between 25 July and 31 August. The Allies' losses in Normandy totalled nearly 210,000, of whom nearly 37,000 had been killed.

Sir Brian Horrocks comments: Nevertheless, despite the slaughter in the Falaise Pocket, claimed everywhere, and rightly, as an outstanding victory, one-third of the Seventh German Army, many of them without equipment, had managed to escape before the encircling prongs had closed round them. This should not have happened; many reasons have been put forward, but to my mind few Germans would have escaped if Bradley had not halted Patton's northerly advance. Montgomery, the master of the tactical battle, realized this only too well; to be quite honest, it was because of their lack of battle experience that he had little confidence in the U.S. Commanders.

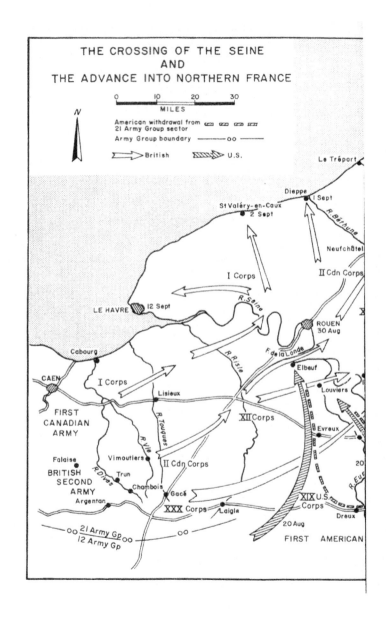

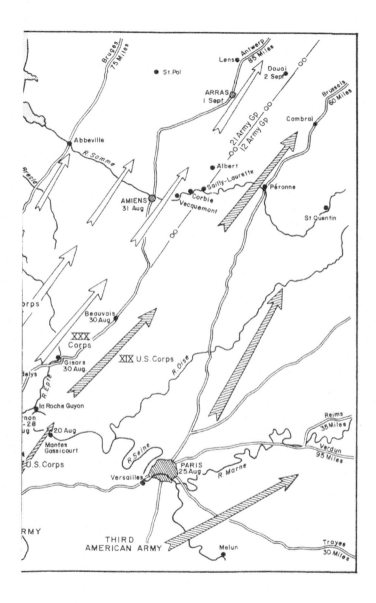

Chapter 4
Crossing the Seine

I. The Crossing at Vernon
SIR BRIAN HORROCKS

During the period of the Battle of the Falaise Pocket, XXX Corps H.Q. became very mobile. In order to keep in close touch with the rapidly changing situation between 4 and 21 August it moved six times; though we did not know it at the time, this was very good practice for the many and much longer moves that were to come. On 14 August, 11th Armoured Division came under XXX Corps, and so began a long and happy relationship between the two of us.

Some 4,300 prisoners were captured by the Corps between 30 July and 4 August. By 19 August it was becoming evident that another forty-eight hours would see the end of the struggle within the Falaise Gap. The arrival of Patton's XV Corps at Mantes-Gassicourt and the capture of a bridge over the Seine there on 20 August had opened up to Montgomery, Bradley and Dempsey a further chance to destroy what still remained of the German Army west of the Seine. If the XV Corps had now thrust rapidly down the west bank of the river to the coast it could have cut the escape routes and pushed the Germans, estimated to consist of 75,000 men (mainly from their Fifteenth Army) plus 250 tanks, towards the mouth of the Seine, which would have offered ideal targets for the Allied Air Force. This plan, although on the face of it very attractive, had one grave disadvantage: U.S. XV Corps would be operating straight across the British front, thus causing very awkward supply problems for the logistic staff. Bradley generously offered to provide trucks to move British troops through his own rear areas, but Dempsey only thanked him for his kind thought. Actually, this would have avoided much confusion, because there were liable to be incidents at the crossroads, etc., when the U.S. troops on traffic control were suddenly confronted with strange vehicles which they had never before seen moving east, while their own six-wheelers were driving north – moreover, vehicles belonging to the German forces were also trying to escape in an easterly direction and some had infiltrated into the Allied columns, particularly in the dark.

Although uncertain as to Eisenhower's future plan once he had crossed the Seine, Montgomery on 20 August issued his orders. These were to complete the destruction of the enemy forces in north-west France, and then to advance northwards with a view to the eventual destruction of all enemy forces in north-east France. This demanded that the Twenty-first Army Group, once all the Germans in the Pocket had been eliminated, should advance to the Seine with all speed. The Second Army were to cross between Mantes and Louviers, where the Americans had secured a bridgehead, and the First Canadian Army in the neighbourhood of Rouen. Once across the Seine, the Second Army would drive north to the Somme between Amiens and the sea. From Rouen the Canadian Army was to wheel left and quickly secure the whole of the Le Havre peninsula and the important rail system connecting with the port. Meanwhile, Bradley's Twelfth Army Group was to assemble to the west and south-west of Paris, ready to take it on orders from the Supreme Commander. Thereafter it was to advance to the general line, Orleans–Amiens, so disposed as to be ready to operate north-eastward towards Aachen and Brussels, with or without a portion directed due east to the Saar.

In his later years Montgomery was wont to assert that he did not mind what anybody said about him. This was not entirely true. At this time he deeply resented American suspicion that his handling of the Normandy battle showed evidence of caution and timidity, and that he would never be equal to the demands of exploitation and pursuit. The apparent failure of Eisenhower and others to understand that, after five years of war, British interest demanded victory in 1944, that the war was bearing heavily on the mass of the people of Britain, and that their manpower was running out, hurt him deeply. Already he had been forced to break up the 59th Division to fill the depleted ranks of the infantry in the rest of his Army. In his heart of hearts he knew that the moment had come, to use his own words, 'to throw his bonnet over the windmill and soar from the known to the unknown'

His directive of 26 August, the last he was to issue as Commander of the Allied Land Forces, is redolent of this conviction. So far as the Twenty-first Army Group was concerned he announced his intention 'to destroy all enemy forces in the Pas de Calais and Flanders and to capture Antwerp and the Belgian airfields' Its eventual mission would then be to advance eastwards on the Ruhr. Above all other considerations, Montgomery now emphasized the need for action and movement.

The abrupt change in the tempo of operations confronted Dempsey with a peculiarly complex problem. Speed was the all-important consideration. He could not, however, readily deploy his Army until the Canadians on his left had veered northward and the Americans on his right had wheeled across his front to make way for him. By grounding his VIII Corps in the Vire area he added this transport to the general pool, increasing the mobility of the rest of the Army. He directed XXX Corps to make the right-hand crossing over the Seine at Vernon. XII Corps would cross later at Louviers, once the Canadian advance to Elbeuf had cleared their right flank. XXX Corps was now advancing rapidly, virtually unchecked. Their main difficulties came from mines, booby traps and blown bridges, rather than from active resistance offered by the fleeing Germans. A prize capture at this time was Lieut.-Gen. Kurt Radinski and his staff. It was lucky for them that they were captured, for the French Forces of the Interior (F.F.I.) thereabouts were now emerging from their hiding places and shooting German stragglers on sight.

Battery Sergeant-Major J. Anthony's experience riding a motor cycle at this time vividly highlights the general confusion. He had been compelled to fall out of the column of 50th Division owing to a puncture. Having repaired it, he met a party of F.F.I. including some girls, who eventually directed him to Laigle. When he got there he found himself in the middle of a battle between Americans and Germans. As he could see no sign of British troops, he decided to drive back the way he had come. On his way he saw to his astonishment in the distance a German tank coming towards him, and wisely decided to pass it at speed. When he eventually got back to his battery he found that he had traversed sixty-eight miles of occupied territory. He is also said to have brought back 'much useful information' Traffic control generally presented many unanticipated problems. One indignant military policeman went so far as to quit his post to protest at the nearest Brigade Headquarters.

'Look here,' he demanded heatedly. 'How can I control the ruddy traffic when a Tiger tank keeps coming up and shooting at me?' His particular problem was quickly dealt with and the tank knocked out.

By 25 August the Americans had seized four bridgeheads over the Upper Seine between Melum and Troyes, as well as a fifth at Mantes-Gassicourt, thirty miles west of Paris. On the previous day, U.S. V Corps had forced its way into the suburbs of the city, brushing aside sporadic and at times serious opposition. Fortunately, von Choltitz, the Commander of the Paris Garrison, ignored Hitler's orders 'to make another Stalingrad of Paris', and surrendered, with all the bridges intact, to the American First Army. The story of de Gaulle's dramatic entry is well known. Eisenhower, with his normal consideration for the feeling of others, and his good manners, invited Montgomery to join him in making a formal call upon de Gaulle on the morrow. Montgomery, who had found de Gaulle an embarrassment ever since his landing in June, politely declined Eisenhower's invitation on the ground that he had other important engagements. At the same time, he issued orders forbidding visits by British troops to the city, thus avoiding the placing of temptation in their way at a time when memories of 1940 were still painful.

Although Bradley's Army Group was now well poised for another advance on a front of over a hundred miles, the fighting on the bridges on the Canadian front was by no means at an end. In Model the Germans had a Commander who had already shown himself in Russia to be at his best in a desperate situation. In the north, he had collected most of the troops of the Fifteenth Army who had held the coast defences between the mouth of the Seine and the Dives, as well as the survivors of the Seventh and Fifth Panzer Armies. He was now conducting an orderly withdrawal on to the eighteen ferries operating over the Seine beyond Rouen. In the process, he capitalized on the German Army's remarkable capacity for resilience by skilfully exploiting the closely wooded country on the west bank of the Lower Seine. Earlier, the American XV and XIX Corps, who had struck northwards across the British front, had soon found themselves faced by obstinate and well-handled rearguards. The Canadians too, including I British Corps, still had to continue to fight their way forwards instead of flowing free as Patton's Divisions had been doing in the south. Needing time to get the battered survivors of his Army Group across the river, Model feared a thrust along the eastbank from Mantes towards Vernon and les Andelys, and he ordered his troops to defend the crossings at these two places.

Bridging equipment for the crossing of the Seine had begun to arrive early in August – columns of Royal Engineers specially trained in England were now available. One of these, consisting of 366 task vehicles, carrying storm boats, close-support rafts, Bailey and bridging pontoons, plus folding boat equipment, had been allotted to XXX Corps. The 43rd Wessex Division was an obvious choice for the actual crossing. Its Commander, Major-General G. I. Thomas, though a very difficult man, was an immensely able Divisional Commander, and nobody in the British Army had given more detailed thought to the problem of crossing rivers in the face of opposition. For two-and-a-half years before D-Day he had exercised his troops in this most exasperating and complex type of operation, including the crossing of the Medway, the Rother, and the aptly-named Reading Sewer, preferably in the tidal reaches and by night, in heavy rain and mid-winter. With the forcing of a crossing at

Vernon, in the teeth of enemy fire, of one of the great rivers of Europe, over 650 feet wide, with a strong current and muddy bottom, his hour was about to come.

On the evening of 22 August, I summoned him to my H.Q. to receive orders for the crossing of the Seine. After reviewing the progress of the Allied Armies, I gave him as my intention, 'To force the crossing of the Seine at Vernon on or about the 25 August – to cover the construction of a Class 9, and a Class 40 bridge – to form a bridgehead of sufficient depth to allow the passage through of the remainder of the Corps' (i.e. two armoured divisions, one armoured brigade and one infantry division). I then proceeded to deal with further details.

Suddenly I began to feel very ill. The skeleton was emerging from my cupboard – I was in for one of my bouts of pain, accompanied by sickness and high temperature, which usually lasted for anything up to a week. I managed to complete the orders without Thomas suspecting anything. I then retired to my caravan and lay down, feeling very unwell.

Within a few minutes the door opened and in came my A.D.C. to say that Montgomery was coming to my H.Q. first thing next morning. This was the worst possible news; if he saw me in my present state I was almost certain to be sent home, unfit for active service. So I told him to send a message to ask the Commander-in-Chief to postpone his visit, as I would be very busy and away from my H.Q. during the next few days.

A couple of hours later the caravan door opened again and, to my horror, in came Montgomery. 'Ah, Jorrocks!' he said, 'I thought there was something odd happening, so I came to see for myself.' He then went on, 'I know why you sent that message, but you needn't worry – if we can get you fit out here there is no question of your being invalided back to the U.K., but I am not taking any chances. Your caravan will now be moved to my Tactical H.Q. and you are not to move from it back to your Corps until I give you permission.' Montgomery rightly stressed that there was nothing I could possibly do for the next few days anyhow. 'Thomas has got his orders, and will get on with the battle much better without the Corps Commander fussing round him.'

So my caravan was established next to Montgomery's, and during the next two days every medical specialist in the Army came to see me. Each day Montgomery paid me a visit, and these talks proved more than usually interesting, as this was the time when the big argument about the future conduct of the war was going on between himself and Eisenhower. This was, in fact, the period when the Broad *v.* Narrow Front was argued out between Eisenhower and Montgomery, so that the latter was not in a position to issue any orders for operations on the Seine other than the establishment by the 43rd Division of as deep a bridgehead as possible.

Montgomery argued like this: 'The Germans are now completely disorganized, as a result of their defeat in Normandy. If we can prevent their recovery, there is a good chance of the war being won in the autumn of 1944. We should therefore stage a powerful thrust, preferably up the coastal plain, which must keep on and on without a halt, so that the Germans never get time to draw breath. We shall then be able to bounce a crossing of the Rhine before they get their defences organized. We can then encircle the Ruhr from the north and cut it off from Germany, and the war will be over.'

Eisenhower considered this narrow thrust to be too risky and eventually decided to advance on a broad front up to the Rhine. This was a safer course but it had certain drawbacks. First, the war could not possibly be won before 1945, which meant prolonging it by at least six months. Secondly, as a result of this Broad Front policy almost all the available formations would be in the line all the time, and there would be very few reserves available to meet any unforeseen eventuality, such as the German counter-offensive in the Ardennes, for instance. Which plan was right? I have thought about this a great deal, and at the time it seemed to me that each Commander was right in his own sphere. Montgomery, as the Ground Forces Commander, was right from the point of view of the actual fighting. His plan might well have succeeded, but it could only have done so if unceasing pressure was brought to bear on the Germans the whole time. This meant that every lorry and supply aircraft in the theatre would have to be made available to bring up petrol, food, ammunition, and all the many requirements of modern war, so that the mobile thrust would never have to halt for lack of supplies. The only way to get all that transport would be to halt a large proportion of the U.S. Divisions in France and remove their vehicles in order to maintain this thrust, which would be, after all, a predominantly British affair. Had anything gone wrong with Montgomery's plan – and there was of course a distinct element of risk – the political repercussions would have been great. So Eisenhower, as the Supreme Commander, seemed to me at the time to be correct in turning it down at his level. Many people may disagree with me but that was my opinion. Anyhow, Montgomery was ordered to stage as powerful a thrust as possible up the coastal plain, using his own resources, and the spearhead of this was to be XXX Corps.

With the benefit of hindsight I now realize that, provided some of the aircraft tied up in the U.K. as part of the vast

Airborne Army (which was not used until Arnhem) had been made available to supply Montgomery's thrust, we could almost certainly have seized the bridgehead over the Rhine and the unfortunate Battle of Arnhem need never have taken place. Anyhow, I had had a ringside seat at one of the most vital personal duels which took place during the entire war. I was released from my pleasant bondage at Montgomery's Tactical H.Q. on 26 August, and returned to prepare for as exciting a role as any Commander could wish.

Let me now turn briefly to the 43rd Division and the difficult task I had set them. There is no doubt that General Thomas had every right to be extremely proud of his Division. Until I arrived in Vernon on 27 August and saw the situation for myself I had not realized what an almost impossibly difficult operation this had been.

The whole town, and two broken bridges over the Seine, were completely dominated by thickly wooded hills on the far bank, so every movement on the bank of the river, some 250 yards wide, and in Vernon itself was visible to the enemy. Thomas told me that they had been opposed by tough, experienced German forces. Undeterred by numerous setbacks, the 43rd continued their assault crossing, in which the 5th Wiltshire, 4th Somerset and 1st Worcestershire Regiments were particularly prominent. By dawn the bridgehead was firmly established on the far bank. Meanwhile, in spite of hostile artillery fire and low flying attacks by German fighter aircraft, the Divisional Royal Engineers had completed a light bridge 650 feet long over the river, while tanks and anti-tank guns were being rafted across – a slow process.

Work on the Class 40 bridge, which would take tanks, had also been going forward steadily, and by 5.15 p.m. on the 27th had been completed.

On the 28th, the 43rd Division had advanced against little resistance and had occupied a bridgehead four-and-a-half miles deep. The battle had cost 550 casualties, but the way was now open for our advance up the coastal plain. On the afternoon of the 28th the bridges passed to the control of XXX Corps and the 8th Armoured Brigade started to rumble over.

II. The Canadian Advance to Elbeuf
EVERSLEY BELFIELD

About fifteen miles downstream, near les Andelys, XII Corps crossed the Seine without too much difficulty. By 29 August, they had constructed a light and a heavy bridge and were ready to begin their advance on XXX Corps's left flank. When II Canadian Corps reached Elbeuf and took over from the Americans who had been halted there, they encountered far stiffer opposition than anywhere else on the Seine crossings. Once again it was Model who was skilfully directing the delaying operations. He exploited the rugged wooded terrain in the large loop of land opposite Elbeuf and Rouen. Here he had been operating at least eighteen ferries for some time and had brought back from the Pas de Calais a fresh regiment to help protect these crossing places. From 26 to 29 August the Canadians could make little headway. Bad weather also hampered close air support, which at this stage was not very efficient. Furthermore, the Canadians were now suffering from their weeks of continuous fighting in Normandy, and in this respect they were much worse off than the British. Experience in Africa had led the Staff to expect that in a division 48 per cent of the casualties would be amongst the infantry, and provision for reinforcements had been made accordingly. By 17 August, the Canadian figure had reached the terrible total of 76 per cent, and there were simply not sufficient men to replace these losses. In particular, the nine battalions of their 2nd Infantry Division were 1910 men short of their establishment fighting strength of about 5600. Moreover, many of their newly-arrived reinforcements had to be sent into action at very short notice and had had little training. In the fighting for the Seine crossings this Division suffered a further 577 casualties. (It is not generally known that in the Second World War the Canadian military losses per head of their male population were the heaviest of the western Allies.) Anyhow, on 30 August, Model withdrew and the Canadians entered Rouen. Here the Seine is tidal and wider than where the British Corps had their bridges. Certainly there was terrific congestion at Rouen, where I British Corps also had to cross the river. Early in September, my diary recorded, as follows:

> After several false attempts we got to the marshalling yard where the only usable bridge lay; here was confusion, lines twisted, engine houses destroyed, locomotives rusting. Beside the bridge was an assorted collection of German transport that overflowed on to the structure itself, blocking it even more. A long-dead horse added its stench to the confusion. Amidst this scene of wreckage, blue-overalled railway workers picked their way in unco-ordinated helplessness, a stream of civilians were crossing and re-crossing the river, dodging in and out of the waiting vehicles. The delay was due to a Belgian ammunition lorry that had slipped half over the side in the night and partly blocked the

passage. The bridge itself was a solid steel affair that had collapsed in one place, caving in either under the bombs that had fallen on it or as a result of a German attempt at demolition. It had been roughly repaired with timber and made usable for lighter types of transport, though it creaked unpleasantly and needed careful driving to cross safely. An irate Engineer Brigadier turned up after we had waited an hour and things began to move again. Alongside the quay on the other side of the Seine was a huge line of lorries and chalked on their side was the notice that they were bringing food to Rouen.

This food was a mere drop in the ocean compared with Paris for which, at the end of August, 2500 tons was asked for daily, 1500 tons being sent by road and 500 coming temporarily by air at the expense of the armies. The Rouen scene may have been an extreme example, but there were many bottlenecks en route not only at rivers, but also on hastily made by-passes carved round towns or villages damaged in the fighting. The journeys to the forward areas were rarely straightforward and placed very heavy strains on both the drivers and their vehicles. When a little later I was flying above the main routes north of the Seine I remember seeing many traffic jams caused sometimes by broken down lorries, sometimes by accidents and for other reasons.

On 1 September, Eisenhower officially took over the control of the land battle from Montgomery. Known as S.H.A.E.F. (Supreme H.Q. Allied Expeditionary Force), Eisenhower's H.Q. was in Normandy, and under it came: Twenty-first Army Group, commanded by Montgomery, and consisting of First Canadian and Second British Armies; Twelfth Army Group, commanded by Bradley, and consisting of First and Third U.S.

Armies; Sixth Army Group, commanded by Devers, operating from the South of France.

Of more immediate relevance to XXX Corps during the forthcoming advance was the Order of Battle, which read, from left to right, as follows. First Canadian Army – to move up the coastal plain to Bruges, with orders to capture the Channel Ports of Le Havre and Dieppe; on their right was Second British Army with, left, XII Corps and, right, XXX Corps; then came First U.S. Army, with their XIX Corps, under General Collins, on the British immediate right; finally, on the right flank was Patton's Third U.S. Army, directed on Verdun.

Chapter 5
The Advance to Brussels and Antwerp
SIR BRIAN HORROCKS

To resume my narrative: fortunately the medical specialists reported to Montgomery that my sharp attack of fever was nothing serious and would last for only a week at the most.

When I was released by Montgomery on 26 August and returned to my Corps, the 43rd Division had already established a firm bridgehead over the Seine at Vernon. In front of me now lay the most exciting role that any commander could envisage. My orders were to break out and seize the crossings over the River Somme in the neighbourhood of Amiens, some seventy miles distant. On no account was I to get involved in a set-piece battle. My Corps was to consist of the Guards Armoured Division, the 11th Armoured Division, and the 8th Armoured Brigade, while, bringing up the rear and cleaning up any opposition which the Armoured Division had bypassed, was my old friend, the 50th Division. We were advancing on a fifty-mile front behind a screen composed of two superb Armoured Car Regiments, the Household Cavalry on the right and the Inns of Court on the left. As I had under command upwards of 600 tanks, it would have been impossible to direct an operation of this sort from a Corps H.Q.

As a result of my experience when in command of the 9th Armoured Division during exercises in Britain, I realized that the only way to command a formation consisting mainly of tracked vehicles was to be in one myself. In this particular case it was obvious that my Corps H.Q., with its many soft-skinned vehicles, could not possibly advance until 50th Division, helped by the French Resistance, had mopped up the small centres of opposition which the Armoured Division had bypassed. So, unless I could move freely among the leading formations, I would soon be completely out of the picture and quite unable to 'smell the battlefield' In a fluid operation like this it is important for the Corps Commander to be able to visit and talk to Commanders personally. My visit to Roberts's H.Q. is just one example of this. As will be seen, it was essential that we capture the bridges over the Somme before the Germans destroyed them. This was only possible if the 11th Armoured Division, which had been advancing all day, continued during the night. Before ordering this to be done, it was important that I should meet 'Pip' Roberts, the Divisional Commander, personally, and discuss the situation with him, so as to make sure that his Division was capable of carrying out this extremely hazardous operation. So my Command Post was a tank, from which the gun had been removed to make room for a small table on which we could work. My staff consisted of one young G.S.O.2 Operations, a Signal Officer and my A.D.C., Harold Young. The whole operation was controlled by wireless and it was the primary role of the G.S.O.2 to keep my B.G.S. at Corps H.Q. informed of everything which was happening up in front. I never saw the rest of my H.Q. for over a week. In addition, I had an escort of three tanks. This may sound unduly cautious, but the Armoured Divisions and Brigades were advancing along the road and disregarded what was happening on their flank. In order to visit them I had to move across country which, in many cases, was still in German hands. We were very lucky, however, because all we encountered were defences hastily thrown together by the German administrative troops.

Montgomery had made it clear to me that there must be no relaxation of pressure by day, nor, if necessary, by night. 'The Germans are very good soldiers,' he said, 'and will recover quickly if allowed to do so. All risks are justified – I intend to get a bridgehead over the Rhine before they have time to recover.'

During this advance, on my right would be the U.S. XIX Corps, and as I had never fought in close contact with the American troops before I went over to meet my next-door neighbour, General Collins. As with all the U.S. Battle Commanders whom I met, he proved to be a very friendly man.

When it came to mobile warfare, the U.S. forces could outstrip the Germans every time, and very often the British as well. I once found myself on the 'Red Ball' route which was one of the main American supply arteries and the contrast between the British and U.S. supply columns was astonishing. The British moved at a steady speed – each vehicle at regulation distance from the one in front – very orderly, very correct, very sedate, and, I am afraid, very, very slow, compared with the U.S. columns. Convoy after convoy of their far more powerful six-wheel lorries, endowed with far greater acceleration and much better hill-climbing capability than was possible with our smaller four-wheel Fords and Bedfords, swept past me, usually driven by cheerful-looking Negroes with a cigar in their mouths. They seemed to be made of rubber; as often as not, one leg dangled out of the window of the driving cab, while the other presumably operated the accelerator pedal. No such nonsense as vehicle spacing for them; they just raced flat out for their destination and, in spite of not having the vaguest idea as to where they were going, they usually, thanks to the indefatigable military police on powerful motor bikes, got themselves to their correct destination in the end. I began to wonder whether our tactical training, and in addition our supply system, were not too rigid and a bit out of date. There were, of course, good and bad U.S. Divisions, just as there are in every army, but the good ones were very good indeed and far quicker into battle than was usually the case with us.

Although all this happened over thirty years ago, the next few days proved the most exciting and exhilarating period of my life. On 29 August we burst out of the positions held by the 43rd Division, with, from right to left, the 8th Armoured Brigade and the 11th Armoured Division leading. The Guards Armoured Division was coming up fast on my right flank, but they had farther to go before joining the Corps, as they were operating with another formation some distance away before being transferred to me. Moreover, crossing the Seine always took time, as the bridges had to be negotiated with care by armoured vehicles. I have always maintained that the British Yeomanry Regiments are second to none, and of these the best, in my opinion, were the 8th Armoured Brigade, which consisted of the Sherwood Rangers (Nottinghamshire Yeomanry), the Staffordshire Yeomanry, plus one regular Cavalry Regiment – 4th/7th Dragoon Guards. We were together for most of the war, from the battle of Alam Halfa in August 1942 to Bremerhaven in Germany, where the war ended. There was a close family atmosphere about the Yeomanry. Most of the officers and troopers in each squadron had grown up together and came from the same town or group of villages. This, of course, made for a unique spirit of comradeship between officers and men.

I don't suppose any Commander has ever had a better-led and better-trained Corps under his command than my 'Corps de Chasse' (the 43rd Wessex Division, which had fought almost continuously since D-Day, deserved a well-earned rest and were left behind in reserve, though their transport was used from time to time to supplement the vehicles supplying XXX Corps).

One of the interesting things about this advance was that the two Armoured Divisions operated quite differently. The 11th Armoured was the more flexible of the two. 'Pip' Roberts, one of the most experienced Tank Commanders in the Army, would switch his troops rapidly, attacking with tanks only, tanks and infantry, or infantry supported by tanks, according to the situation. The Guards, on the other hand, always worked in regimental groups, Coldstream tanks and Coldstream infantry, Grenadier infantry and Grenadier tanks, etc. This system was not calculated to get the full value from the mobility of an Armoured Division, but it ensured the closest possible co-operation between the two arms, as the infantry and tank crews all came from the same regiment and had more or less grown up together. Nevertheless, I preferred the standard Armoured Divisional practice of the 11th Armoured Division. Fortunately, however, by now I had gained sufficient battle experience not to interfere with the way a Divisional Commander handled his command.

During the first day's advance on 29 August we covered some twenty-one miles, which in my opinion was not good enough; the Germans might recover quickly, and it was vital that we should capture the bridges over the Somme before Gen. Dietrich had time to organize a strong defensive position on the river. Although the weather was terrible and the troops had been advancing and fighting all day, I had to harden my heart and, arriving at Roberts's H.Q. at 4.15 p.m. on the 30th, I ordered him to continue the advance throughout the night, as Amiens had to be captured by the next morning. This was particularly hard on the tank drivers who had been on the go for some thirty-six hours and were already exhausted. But Roberts never hesitated and gave the necessary orders at once.

Curiously enough, I was recently visiting one of the main workshops of Bovis Engineering (I am a non-executive director of this company) when an elderly fitter to whom I was talking suddenly said, 'Do you remember the night of 30–31 August 1944, sir? I was a tank driver in the 11th Armoured Division and we had been on the move all day, we were very tired and were settling down in a comfortable little bivouac area for a good supper, for which we had collected some of the ingredients during the day. Suddenly we were told that, on the Corps Commander's orders, we were to continue our advance during the night. The names we called you that night, sir, won't bear repeating! I have never forgotten that terrible night.' I replied that I remembered it well and I hoped he also remembered that at first light next morning he had been rumbling in his tank through the streets of Amiens, with the bridges intact, and cheered by a delighted populace.

It had been a fantastic night's advance, with drivers falling asleep at every halt. Visibility was nil, owing to the rain, and at times there were actually German vehicles in our column. But on and on they went. Only a first-class, well-trained Division, with a very high morale, could have carried out that night's advance.

When I arrived at Roberts's H.Q. early on the 31st, he had succeeded, with the help of the French Resistance, in seizing intact all the bridges over the Somme and his lorried Infantry

Brigade was then debussing in the centre of the town. He also showed me with much pride a sinister-looking figure who was apparently General Eberbach, to whom Dietrich had been in process of handing over the defences of the Somme. To add insult to injury, he had been captured in his pyjamas, which was a little undignified for the erstwhile Commander of the Fifth German Panzer Army.

On the right flank the 8th Armoured Brigade captured Gisors, where the Germans blew up an ammunition train just before they entered the town. In the outskirts of Beauvais they knocked out an anti-tank gun and, in the middle of the town, guided by the Maquis, a huge Tiger tank. Streets which up to a few minutes before had been utterly deserted were suddenly thronged by crowds, delirious with joy, waving flags, showering the tanks with apples and flowers, and hurling out luckless German soldiers who had sought shelter in their houses, shooting them and trampling them underfoot. It was a fantastic spectacle, with a kiss at one end of the street often followed by snipers' bullets at the other. Much of the German transport was horse-drawn and, as one British Cavalry man wrote, 'It went against the graih to set about it with a gun but it was drawing Germans and German supplies, and there was nothing for it but to harden the heart and let fly.' By 30 August, the Guards Armoured Division was complete across the Seine, and I was able to pull back the 8th Armoured Brigade into reserve. Meanwhile, exciting things continued to happen on this flank. There are still many people with cause to remember that wild stormy night of 30–31 August. Although the 11th Armoured Division was firmly established in Amiens on 31 August, I was determined to make every effort to see that the whole of XXX Corps was north of the Somme by the end of that month. This was more difficult for the Guards Armoured Division than for the 11th Armoured because, during the past twenty-four hours, they had covered a hundred-odd miles in order to catch up, driving much of the time along narrow winding roads. Fortunately for them, their Armoured Car Regiment – the 2nd Household Cavalry Regiment had been probing in front of the 8th Armoured Brigade.

I must break off here for a moment and just pay my own tribute to the Household Cavalry.

If you are walking down Whitehall in London towards Parliament Square, you will see two mounted sentries, in full ceremonial dress consisting of breastplates and all, on duty outside the Horse Guards Parade, H.Q. of London District. You may think that this colourful uniform belongs to the past and not to warfare in the twentieth century. Make no mistake about it – those mounted sentries belong to the best Armoured Car Regiment in the British Army, the Household Cavalry. Normally, armoured cars bear a role out of all proportion to their size, as they are the eyes and ears of the Corps Commander. Advancing usually on a wide front, they constantly report back by wireless to their Liaison Officer at Tactical Corps H.Q., and to be successful three things are required:

Firstly, the man in charge of the leading scout car (usually a Corporal of Horse in this particular regiment – the equivalent of a Sergeant in the infantry) should be very alert and intelligent.

Secondly, an Armoured Car Squadron must be prepared to fight for their information; in other words, exert pressure, so that the enemy is forced to disclose his location.

Thirdly, and probably the most important of all, their wireless communications must never break down.

The 2nd Household Cavalry Regiment were superb in all three respects.

They had been very thoroughly trained by their C.O., Lieut.-Col. Sir Henry Abel Smith. In fact, he made life so hard for them in the U.K. – out on exercises day after day and night after night – that any other regiment would have been almost driven to mutiny; but now, during this rapid, somewhat chaotic advance into Belgium and Holland, their training paid a very high dividend indeed.

This, their first operation with XXX Corps, was typical. Just after midnight, on 30 August, their C.O. reported to Tactical H.Q. XXX Corps, where he received the following orders: '2nd Household Cavalry Regiment will capture three bridges over the River Somme at Sailly-Laurette, Corbie, and Vecquemont by 0800 hours today [it was then past midnight and therefore 31 August]. The bridges will be known as "Faith", "Hope" and "Charity" Move at once, as the 5th Brigade of the Guards Armoured Division has been ordered to advance at 0200 hours.'

In the words of Leit. Orde's brilliant History of the 2nd Household Cavalry Regiment, in which he served.

> A night march through enemy territory is at the best of times a tense affair. The drivers peer out of their visors, intent on avoiding falling asleep or landing in the ditch. The car commanders also stare ahead, trying to penetrate the gloom for signs of the enemy and check-ups on the right route. The operators live in a strange world of their own at the bottom of the turret, tormented by crackles and demoniac wireless noises while map boards and chinagraph pencils drop on to their heads. Gunners grip the trigger mechanism as much for support as anything else, for they are almost blind at night. Over everyone

the desire for sleep descends in recurrent and overpowering waves.

As in the case of the 11th Armoured Division, this advance became a squadron affair. Each squadron was advancing by a separate route on a comparatively wide front. Suddenly, hostile fire would open from a wood, an isolated farm, or from some hastily constructed trenches covering, perhaps, a crossroads. The leading troops would deploy and return this fire. Sometimes the Germans would surrender. If not, the remaining troops, benefiting from the local knowledge of the Maquis, would outflank the opposition, using by-roads, tracks, etc.; while one of the troops would then turn back and engage the enemy post from the rear, the remainder of the squadron would continue the advance. Once the enemy post was cut off, the occupants usually surrendered, and the Household Cavalry troops would then hand them over to the tender mercies of the Maquis and continue the advance, rejoining the rest of the squadron. It was a night of utter confusion but the Squadron Leaders realized that the one vital thing was speed of advance. On anyone reading the history of this night, the outstanding impression is the fearless initiative displayed by all ranks throughout – on and on they went, and the operation of each individual squadron deserves a complete chapter to itself.

They captured 'Faith', 'Hope' and 'Charity' with literally not more than one or two hours to spare, for they found that each bridge was 'wired up' to large bombs ready to be blown. The detachments of Royal Engineers attached to each squadron showed their usual courage in dismantling bombs which were strange to them.

This regiment had advanced over sixty miles in forty-eight hours, fighting many individual battles on the way, and – what is almost as important – succeeding in holding these three bridges against German counter-attacks for several hours of daylight before being relieved by the Grenadier Guards, the leading tank regiment of the Guards Armoured Division. So by 1 September we had pierced the first defensive position on which the enemy hoped to hold us up. During the night a map was captured in an enemy staff car which showed that the Germans had intended to withdraw to and consolidate the line of the Somme as the right-hand sector of a new defensive position extending to Switzerland. This was the third time I had employed armoured troops at night and, strange as it may seem, each operation had been completely successful.

The race for the Rhine was now on, and the next few days were the most exhilarating of my military career. The German Fifteenth Army, holding the coastal area, and still awaiting our major invasion in the Pas de Calais, suddenly found their lines of communication threatened by a powerful armoured thrust. With the Guards Armoured Division on the right and the 11th on the left, we swept through the inadequate *ad hoc* defences which were all the Germans could manage in the time, like a combine harvester scything through a field of corn. The armoured car screens formed by the 2nd Household Cavalry Regiment on the right and Inns of Court, under their thrustful C.O., Bertie Bingley, on the left, would report enemy defensive positions, hidden Panthers and so on; if the opposition was likely to be serious, our leading tanks which had been advancing down the road would deploy across country to attack the enemy from the flank or rear, supported by their artillery which could drop into action at a moment's notice. If the opposition proved tougher, the Motor Battalion and/or the lorried Infantry Brigades would de-bus and attack from the front – this, however, was rarely necessary. All this sounds easy, but success depended on high-class training and, above all, perfect wireless communication. The French inhabitants of the various villages which were liberated went mad with joy. They poured out of their houses with champagne and flowers for 'les Anglais' I don't believe we have ever before or since been so popular with the French, and this, of course, had an inspiring effect on the morale of the troops, which mounted almost visibly. They certainly deserved this after the months of hard slogging in the French Bocage.

The chief danger came from the German garrison in Lille, which made threatening noises against our left. The 8th Armoured Brigade and the 50th Division proved perfectly adequate to protect this flank, and the Armoured Divisions, obeying their orders to avoid becoming involved in set-piece battles, swept forward.

The main artery along which the Corps advanced was indicated by signposts bearing a black club on a white background; by now the 'Club Route', as it was called, jutted out well in advance of the rest of Montgomery's forces. By the end of the war it had become one of the most famous military highways in British history, stretching from the Normandy beaches across France, Belgium, the Netherlands and Germany to Bremerhaven on the North Sea. The speed of our advance was such that if a vehicle broke down it was left behind, under the protection of the local Resistance group, whose help throughout this advance was invaluable. Besides taking over our German prisoners, if for some reason or another our advance was held up, they always knew alternative routes and acted as guides. It was the French Resistance which had prevented the enemy destroying the bridges over the Somme at Amiens. Their only fault was the very natural one of overestimating the number of Germans, or 'Poches de Boches', as one of their leaders described them.

On 1 September both Armoured Divisions and the 8th Armoured Brigade which had rejoined them, were all off at the crack of dawn. They were now on the open rolling plains, over which the decisive battle of 18 August 1918 had been fought – ideal country for armoured operations. The leading troops of the 1st Welsh Guards soon reached the high ground immediately north of Arras, about noon, with the rest of the Division hot on their heels. They had been the last battalion to leave Arras in 1940; it was peculiarly appropriate that they should be its liberators four years later. For General Adair, too, Commander of the Guards Armoured Division, it must have been a moving moment, for it was here that he had won the Military Cross in the First World War.

The 11th Armoured Division had reached the outskirts of Lens, rounding up German stragglers and overrunning VI or flying bomb launching sites *en route*. These unpleasant, pilotless weapons had been causing great misery and destruction to south-east England and the London area, so everyone felt that they were directly helping those at home. By the early afternoon, therefore, the whole Corps was on its objective, the watershed between the Somme Valley and the Flanders Plain, dominated by the huge Canadian Memorial on Vimy Ridge, for which so much blood had been shed in the First World War. It was now in a position to strike at will anywhere across the Belgium frontier – only a few miles away.

Progress on 2 September was slow in contrast to what had gone before, as Second Army H.Q. ordered a standfast, so that an operation by airborne forces from the U.K. might be launched to seize the bridge at Tournai – in fact, this was already occupied, having been captured intact on this day by XIX U.S. Corps. So, late that night the airborne operation was fortunately cancelled and plans were made for the resumption of our advance into Belgium at first light. It was curious that during the whole of the advance we were constantly being 'threatened' by this sort of operation. It soon became obvious that the vast, highly-trained airborne army in the U.K. was bursting to go. Plan after plan was devised for their use, only to be discarded at the last moment as their objective had invariably been captured by our ground forces before they could get there. I almost began to apologize for the speed of our advance.

Naturally, I have certain outstanding memories of our breakneck dash to Brussels and Antwerp. On 2 September I paid my daily visit to the H.Q. of the Guards Armoured Division, then established at Douai. My regiment, the 1st Battalion Middlesex, having formed part of the Guards Brigade at Aldershot prior to the war, I had become accustomed to their peculiarities, notably their tradition of extreme understatement and concealment of emotion. I knew, for example, that it was possible to carry on quite a lengthy conversation with Warrant Officers or N.C.O.s of the Grenadiers without their making any other contribution than 'Sir!' But by long practice they had acquired a remarkable facility of indicating approval, agreement or strong resentment simply by the tone of voice in which they uttered this single word.

On my arrival at their H.Q. I was greeted with the usual friendliness. After a short pause I said, 'Your objective tomorrow will be' – another pause – 'Brussels!' There was a gasp of astonishment and delight and for once their emotions burst through their reserve. Not only did they appreciate the honour of being asked to liberate Brussels, one of the finest prizes of the war; they were responding to a challenge, for the Belgian capital was still some seventy miles away. Next day, with the Welsh Guards on the right and the Grenadier Guards on the left, there was a keen competition to get there first. For a time it was level pegging, but the Grenadiers were held up at Pont à Marcq by a group of stubborn SS Germans, who seemed determined not to surrender. The losses sustained here by 'The King's Company' and No. 2 Squadron of tanks cast a shadow over the day's triumphs. Meanwhile, the Welsh and the Household Cavalry Regiment armoured cars were roaring along their route, encountering only negligible opposition. A Belgian friend of mine living in Brussels described their entry:

> Throughout the war we had become accustomed to the noise of German tanks moving through our streets, so when I heard the familiar rumble outside I just glanced casually out of the window. Then, suddenly, my attention became riveted! There was something different about these tanks and armoured cars. The Allies were advancing, we knew, but they were many miles away; but then a young Tank Commander looked up at me and waved. The impossible had happened – they were British! It was unbelievable that the Occupation was finally over. I seized a bottle of champagne which I had been keeping for just such an occasion, and dashed out into the streets. Everywhere doors were being flung open by cheering crowds. '*Les Anglais* at last – !' It was the most wonderful evening of my life. Odd shots were still to be heard in the distance but nobody took the slightest notice.

My best moment of the whole advance was when I crossed the frontier into Belgium. I have always maintained that I was about the last man out of Belgium during the retreat to Dunkirk; it had been a miserable business, as only a few days earlier we had driven up to the River Dyle, through cheering, waving crowds and now, with our tails between our legs, we were leaving these unfortunate people to their fate. As I passed through the ashen-faced crowd, I kept on saying, 'We'll be back', and now I was fortunate enough to be in command of the relieving forces. As I crossed the frontier, a young man ran up to my tank – presumably he had seen my red cap badge. He was weeping with joy as he reached up to shake me by the hand. 'I knew you would come back!' he said. Such moments are rare – not just in war, but in life generally. Subsequently, when talking to some of the older officers, notably from the Guards, and the 50th Division, I was told that for them also the return to Belgium had been an emotional experience.

As a Belgian Brigade was attached to my Corps, I was determined that they should share in the triumphant return to their capital, so I waited until next day, when, escorted by the Belgians, I entered Brussels. It was almost impossible to move through the cheering crowds. I kept on pointing to my escort and shouting, 'Belge!' They were commanded by a General Piron, who subsequently rebuilt the Belgian Army and became a well-known figure in the military circles of Europe.

What with champagne, flowers, crowds, and girls perched on the top of wireless trucks, it was difficult to get on with the war. Whilst the Guards had every right to enjoy their well-earned welcome, I still had to control the operations of the 11th Armoured Division, the 50th Division, plus the 8th Armoured Brigade. The only hope of any peace appeared to be in the grounds of the Royal Palace of Laeken, which had high railings round it. The Palace was occupied by Queen Elisabeth, the Belgian Queen Mother, who consented to us using it. The night after my Corps H.Q. arrived, we invited her and her lady-in-waiting, La Baronne Carton de Wiart, a relation of our famous General Carton de Wiart, V.C., to dinner. It was a pretty rough and ready meal, consisting of rations, and eaten off some six-foot tables in our small mess tent, but the Queen told me afterwards that she had never enjoyed a dinner so much. During the next few days she constantly wandered round the H.Q. and became a great favourite with all ranks.

As our Corps sign was a wild boar, she presented us with a baby boar from the Ardennes, who was named 'Chewing Gum' because his nose, when pressed against one's arm or leg, felt just like this essential ingredient of the American way of life. He accompanied us right to the end of the war and became quite a famous figure. As, after the war, the authorities would not allow his entry into Britain owing to quarantine regulations, he ended his days as a very important historic person in the Antwerp Zoo.

However, the great thing was that, isolated in this park, and far from the madding crowd, we could get on with the war. Although we did not realize it, this was the high point of the 1944 offensive. From now on, things began to go wrong. It's always easy to be wise after the event, but I have since felt that at this point those responsible for the higher direction of the war in the west faltered.

First of all, we were ordered to halt, since we were outstripping our administrative resources, which we were still receiving by lorry from the beachhead some 300 miles away. We were told that supplies, particularly of petrol, were running short. This was a tragedy because, as we now know, the only troops available to prevent us reaching the Rhine were one German Division, the 719th, composed of elderly gentlemen, most of whom had stomach ailments, and who had hitherto been guarding the coast of the Netherlands and had not seen a single shot fired in anger, plus one Battalion of Dutch SS and a few Luftwaffe detachments. I cannot believe that Eisenhower's Intelligence did not realize that this was all the opposition there was in front of us. We could have brushed them aside without difficulty and might easily have bounced a crossing over the Rhine. It was infuriating because we still had 100 litres of petrol per vehicle, plus a further day's supply within reach. Moreover, we had captured Brussels Airport and, had we run into trouble, supplies could have been flown in without difficulty. We also heard on the grapevine that at the end of August, Patton's Third Army on the right flank had also been halted for a similar reason.

Although the order for us to halt came from my immediate boss, General Dempsey, Commander of the Second Army, I am certain that it did not have the blessing of Field-Marshal Montgomery. I think it was the direct result of the Broad Front policy insisted on by Eisenhower, mainly for political reasons. Montgomery had stressed to me over and over again, 'Never let up the pressure, Jorrocks, or the Germans will recover. They are very good soldiers. Keep on at them day and night!'

Some historians have suggested that the troops were exhausted. This is completely untrue. There had been very little hard fighting, and liberating villages is 'heady stuff' – we were all suffering from 'liberation euphoria' In fact, I had rarely seen morale higher. The Royal Army Service Corps drivers may well have been tired, but the fighting troops were raring to go. So much for the first mistake.

For the second mistake I must take at least part of the blame. When the 11th Armoured Division had been ordered to capture Antwerp, 'Pip' Roberts had asked me for a definite objective; an armoured division was not the ideal formation with which to capture a large town – even with the help of the Belgian Resistance. I replied, 'Go straight for the docks and prevent the Germans destroying the port installations.' My reason for this was that I still retained painful memories of the delays imposed on the Eighth Army during their advance along the North African coast; the Germans always destroyed the port facilities and thus slowed down the unloading of our supplies. Marvellous to relate, Roberts captured the docks in full working order, including those on the north bank of the Scheldt. This was an almost unbelievable stroke of luck, for the sluice gates and the dockside equipment, all electrically operated, could easily have been put out of action. Here the Belgian 'Armée Blanche' appeared in force. With their assistance, 159th Infantry Brigade assaulted the many concrete emplacements surrounding the German H.Q. in the park. By 8 p.m., after a tough battle, it was in their hands, and along with it General von Stolderg, the Commander of the Antwerp Garrison. In all, they took 6000 prisoners, and, for want of other secure accommodation, lodged them temporarily in the Zoo. Inevitably, Hitler's Government protested through United Nations H.Q. in Geneva that his soldiers were being subjected to gross indignities. In fact, had it not been for the protection given them, their chances of survival would have been slim indeed.

Further back, the 50th Division, protecting the exposed left flank of the Corps, had had a tough day but had cleared the country south of Lille, and XII Corps had reached a point twenty-five miles short of Ghent. On the morrow, the 83rd Group R.A.F., with its H.Q. near Brussels, was to have five wings on the airfields round the outskirts of the city. Though we did not know it, 4 September, the day Antwerp fell, was the apogee of 'Overlord', and at the same time it was, as will be seen, the day we lost the Battle of Arnhem.

It never entered my head that the Scheldt would be heavily mined, so that Antwerp could not therefore be used as our forward base for some time, or, worse still, that the Germans would succeed in ferrying across the estuary from Breskens to Flushing and also from Terneuzen – until it was captured by the Polish Armoured Division – the remaining troops of the German Fifteenth Army, which had been holding the coast. General von Zangen, the Army Commander, reckoned that he had saved the remnants of eight German divisions, a total of 82,000 men and 530 guns. If I had ordered Roberts to bypass Antwerp and advance for only fifteen miles north-west, in order to cut off the Beveland isthmus, the whole of this force, which played such a prominent part in the subsequent fighting, might have been destroyed or forced to surrender. Napoleon, no doubt, would have realized this, but I am afraid Horrocks didn't. My only excuse is that a Corps is the highest formation which fights the tactical battle, and is not concerned with strategical matters, which lie in the province of the higher formations – Army, Army Group, etc. My eyes were fixed on the Rhine, and I knew that the Canadians, plus XII British Corps, were coming up on my left flank.

As this was the turning point in the whole campaign it deserves further consideration. First of all, in a peculiar way, I suddenly became isolated, without any contact on my flanks, and with a complete blackout as to what forces opposed us. I had no worries as regards my left flank because the 50th Division and the 8th Armoured Brigade had blocked any German sally from Lille. Moreover, XII Corps was advancing on my left. There is always rivalry between Corps, and considerable amusement had been caused when we were told how our Brigadier in charge of Administration happened to be at the entrance to his H.Q. when an armoured car poked its nose round a corner and opened up with a blast of machine-gun fire. The Brigadier leaped into the road, waving our 'Club Route' sign. When the armoured car got level he shouted angrily to the Commander, 'What do you think you are doing? You are now passing Rear H.Q. XXX Corps.' XII Corps, during its advance on our left flank, had been forced to fight hard by the front-line German troops holding the Pas de Calais, while we had only been opposed by their administrative formations, so it was naturally echeloned to our rear, but it was nevertheless getting closer to the Meuse every day. Of the Canadians and Poles I had no information at all, and I would have been horrified to learn that 82,000 first-line troops and over 500 guns were being ferried across the estuary and would soon be threatening our left flank. Looking back it is difficult to understand why this move, which was being observed from the air, was never reported to my H.Q.

During the whole of the Second World War, our Intelligence was of a very high order indeed: in fact, it was unheard of for a fresh German formation to appear on my front without 24–48 hours' warning. I learnt afterwards that, at a very high level, our experts had broken the German secret code, so that our top Commanders were always well informed of German intentions all over the world.

Yet no information about the forces likely to be opposed to XXX Corps was ever disclosed. In fact, as will be read in a later chapter, Montgomery, for the first and last time in his long and brilliant career as a tactical Commander, completely underestimated the opposition which we were likely to encounter during our advance to Arnhem when he started his orders by saying that the disorganized German Army was straggling back to the Fatherland or words to that effect.

I was astonished to hear this, because we knew that the Germans had made a remarkable recovery, and during our advance to the Meuse–Escaut Canal we had been fighting hard against Gen. Student's paratroops, under the command of the redoubtable Van der Heydte, plus SS Panzer formations. I had been heavily involved in a desperately hard fight carried out by the Guards Armoured Division and later on by the 50th Division. Fortunately, these were two of the best divisions in the British Army, but even they had had a struggle to overcome this tough resistance.

Why did I receive no information about the German formations which were being rushed daily to our front? For me this has always been the sixty-four thousand dollar question. Looking back, I believe that the fly in the ointment was General Brereton's powerful Allied Airborne Army in the U.K. By now it was bursting at the seams, having had no fewer than sixteen operations cancelled at the last moment, owing to the rapidity of our advance. It is probable that the Arnhem operation had already been decided upon at the beginning of September, and the powers that be were not risking another cancellation at the last moment. Back in Washington, General Marshall, the Chief of Staff of the U.S. Army, was urging Eisenhower to use this immensely powerful force in one great operation to finish the war in 1944. So Patton's two flanking thrusts on the right and my XXX Corps on the left were halted.

This was a great pity; if those transport aircraft, which had been sitting in the U.K. doing nothing, could have been used to supply us both, the war really would have been over in 1944. The fortnight's delay before the complicated Arnhem operation could be launched proved fatal, for the enemy was growing stronger every day.

Chapter 6
The Battle for the Arnhem Start Line
SIR BRIAN HORROCKS

Although ordered to halt in Brussels and Antwerp, I chanced my arm to a limited degree and ordered the Guards Armoured Division to occupy Louvain, as I wanted to ensure that we held the bridges over the River Dyle, where, incidentally, we had first encountered the Germans at the beginning of the war. We were not permitted to resume our advance until 7 September – four vital days had been wasted. When we were allowed to advance again the situation had worsened drastically. We were no longer sweeping up the coastal plain on a 50-mile front. Every day fresh German formations appeared on our front, and we found ourselves concentrated on a 5-mile front, fighting hard again.

It can now be seen that the German military machine possessed some valuable assets which were then not easily identifiable. In every country that has been engaged in a long war there are half-forgotten formations which have come to exist almost in their own right, and these were to be found even in Nazi Germany, as late as the autumn of 1944. The most important of them were the Parachutists, out of favour after Crete, but who could still muster about 3000 first-class troops, mainly engaged in training recruits and scattered throughout the Netherlands and Western Germany. There were also considerable numbers of well-trained men in Luftwaffe and naval units, as well as the battle-hardened Panzer troops who had escaped from Normandy. Finally, there were the men on leave from the Russian front, the convalescents and the recruits. Not ideal material with which to hold up an invading force, but useful as a stopgap, while reinforcements, and in particular the Fifteenth Army, were being collected together into conventional formations. Equally valuable were excellent leaders such as Student, who had been disgraced and kept out of high command, or Lieut.-Gen. Chill. Both these men responded with energy and determination to the challenge; Chill, whose division had been almost wiped out, showed remarkable initiative in going forward with the remnants of his troops to the Albert Canal, where he had prepared defensive positions and had gathered up thousands of stragglers before Student's men had arrived to strengthen the line.

That they were working on internal lines of communication was a further advantage to the Germans as the Allies approached their borders. They could move large numbers of men along a relatively undamaged railway network.

On 7 September, the Guards Armoured Division set out from Louvain to capture two bridges over the Albert Canal. Despite the enthusiastic crowds of civilians, their advance was rapid – one bridge was found to be blown but the other at Beringen had been only partly destroyed. A very brave Belgian, waving a white handkerchief, raced across this damaged bridge to tell the Welsh Guards that the Germans were leaving the small town of Beeringen, and thus, by the afternoon, they were able to establish a bridgehead in pouring rain, watched by a large crowd on both banks, and helped by a few German prisoners. The Royal Engineers soon started to build a Bailey bridge. Meanwhile the local bargees, not to be outdone, marshalled their barges and anchored them a couple of hundred yards to the north, to provide an alternative means of crossing. The bridge was rapidly completed, and the Welsh Guards' tanks promptly crossed over. But only just in time – as German reinforcements were now arriving in strength and bringing down vicious shell and mortar fire on to the approaches to the bridge. As their orders were to push on without delay, the Welsh Guards ignored the fire and pressed on towards Helchteren and Hechtel, the key road centres of the mining district between the Escaut and Albert Canals. After a stiff fight against the enemy defending Helchteren, the Welsh Guards clashed for the first time since leaving Normandy with a force of paratroopers. Although supported by anti-tank and self-propelled guns, these were no match for the British armour and at least 500 were killed and 300 taken prisoner. This hard fighting, however, delayed the advance on Hechtel, which was not reached until nightfall, and then was also found to be strongly held by paratroopers. It was therefore decided to postpone the attack upon it until the next morning.

For the Irish Guards also it proved to be the first of several days packed with dramatic incidents. When the Welsh Guards went forward, the Germans had stayed in the town of Beeringen, growing stronger from hour to hour; within the town the Irish Guards casualties began to mount, as the enemy shelling increased. The fire was obviously being directed by observers from two high slag heaps 300 yards to the north of the Canal, which completely dominated the town. Major R. Eames, commander of the 439th Battery of the West Somerset Yeomanry, Royal Artillery, was accompanying Lieut.-Col. Joe Vandeleur, commanding the Irish Guards. Just before Eames had his leg blown off he had found an upstairs room in a convent which overlooked both the vital roads that ran between the slag heaps and the Canal, and also the important road running north towards the large town of Bourg-Léopold. From this room Vandeleur directed the day's battle, his viewpoint being the convent window.

Almost as soon as he had installed himself there five Panther tanks arrived and took up a position just below. Fortunately, they could not elevate their guns sufficiently to hit him and his party in the room above their heads. In addition to the 439th Battery, he had a call on a medium regiment firing at maximum range, but, having lost his Battery Commander, he had to direct the fire of these guns himself. Selecting as his primary target the tanks just below him, he thus risked their hitting the convent itself, but with most gratifying results; two tanks immediately burst into flames and the remainder scuttled off.

Vandeleur next launched an infantry company, under Major M. V. Dudley, and a weak squadron of tanks under Major D. R. G. Fitzgerald, against the slag heaps and mine offices, supporting them with the fire of both batteries and the machine-guns of the Northumberland Fusiliers. Half-way to their objective they were held up by the enemy, skilfully hidden on the reverse slope. After negotiating some boggy ground the tanks found a way round and overran the Germans in their slit trenches. By last light the slag heaps and the mine offices were captured. Among the prisoners was the German artillery officer who, sitting in a bucket suspended on the overhead cable between the peaks of the slag heaps, had been directing the fire of the enemy guns. Although he remarked on the Irish Guards' extravagance in wasting a vast amount of ammunition, they stood him a glass of champagne before dispatching him to the rear. Altogether, it had taken eight hours to get the last German out of Beeringen. A suicide squad consisting of an officer and about forty German paratroopers later made their way along the Canal bank, with orders to destroy the bridge. They got to within half a mile of it before clashing with a transport column *en route* to the neighbouring 50th Divisional front. The Germans succeeded in destroying thirty lorries before they were beaten off in hand-to-hand fighting, leaving thirty prisoners behind them.

It was obvious that the days of easy victories were over. What had been almost a military vacuum forty-eight hours previously was now rapidly filling up with paratroopers from all over Germany. Although many of them were young and inexperienced, they were all dedicated Nazis and fought better than many of the regular forces. Beaten to Beeringen by only a short head, these new formations were now endeavouring to form a ring round this tenuous bridgehead.

The operations now developing were extremely complex. The British east flank was wide open and the 50th Division was meeting stiff resistance short of the Albert Canal. For three days the Guards Armoured Division was in a very vulnerable position, isolated and dispersed. Germans were reported in every wood, and were offering obstinate resistance, particularly the paratroopers in Bourg-Léopold and Hechtel, where they now had strong forces including tanks and self-propelled guns. In particular the crossroads at Hechtel had become a veritable No-Man's-Land. The German Commander obviously meant to deny us the use of the main road leading into Holland. The 11th Armoured Division therefore was brought forward from Antwerp to guard the XXX Corps's exposed right flank. To keep up the momentum, I ordered the Guards Armoured Division to push on and capture a bridge over the Escaut Canal, about ten miles from Hechtel. Adair had to leave the

Coldstream and Welsh Groups to destroy the enemy in Bourg-Léopold and Hechtel, and decided to move the Grenadiers and Irish Guards across country. The chances of capturing a bridge by surprise outweighed, in his view, the danger to his lines of communication. As this was a most remarkable feat of arms I propose to describe it in some detail.

Since the main route to Hechtel was now blocked, a troop of Household Cavalry under Lieut. Cresswell set out on 10 September to find a way round. Moving out to the west, he discovered a rough track through the sandy country which rejoined the main road about two miles north of Hechtel. Using this bypass, the Grenadier Guards Group of tanks and infantry fought its way northwards until it reached a level crossing. This was about a mile short of the De Groot Bridge over the Escaut Canal which is on the direct road to Eindhoven and Arnhem. In the meantime, Cresswell had found a fine new road not shown on the military maps, which also led to the Escaut Canal, and, driving a lorry along it without being spotted, he got to within three kilometres of the De Groot Bridge. From this point he saw that the road ran parallel with the Canal and that a large factory hid the bridge from view. Realizing that if he took his armoured cars farther forward he was bound to be discovered, he borrowed two bicycles from some civilians and, accompanied by Cpl of Horse, Cutler, set off to the factory. On arrival they climbed to the top of the building, from which they got a perfect view of the bridge and its defences. These consisted of four 88-mm. guns and numerous infantry in sandbagged trenches. Returning to his troop, he reported by wireless what he had seen to Lieut.-Col. Joe Vandeleur of the Irish Guards Group, who was about eight miles away. He stressed the fact that the bridge was intact and visible from the factory. Vandeleur promptly headed his column down the road which Cresswell had discovered, as far as the factory, keeping out of sight of the De Groot Bridge. On reaching the factory he hid this column behind him and ran upstairs, from where he noted that a curve in the road below him denied the Germans' 88-mm. guns a clear view of the troops attacking from the direction of the factory until they were within 100 yards of the bridge. The rest of the story is vividly told in his own words:

> The problem is now – will the Germans blow the bridge before we can get to it? We therefore decided to put it to the test. The plan was a very simple one. David Peel's squadron was to send one troop of tanks, commanded by Duncan Lampard, to the corner of the curve. This was to be accompanied by a platoon of the 3rd Battalion, commanded by John Stanley-Clarke, which was to be the assault force, with Michael Dudley's company and the remainder of David Peel's squadron engaging the enemy point-blank with fire for twenty minutes. If at the end of these twenty minutes the bridge had not been blown, John Stanley-Clarke and Duncan Lampard were to charge, followed immediately by Hutton of the Royal Engineers and six Guardsmen to remove the explosive charges. We had no artillery support, and were fifteen miles north of Brigade H.Q., so there was no wireless touch. The signal for the assault was to be a green Verey light. It all came off perfectly. I then formed a minimum bridgehead of two companies and a squadron of tanks on the north bank, and prepared the positions for all-round defence. It was obvious that the Germans would try to recapture the bridge, and in all probability from the rear. A large number of German troops had been cut off from their line of retreat, and they were not going to take this lying down. Early next morning we were attacked by enemy infantry, supported by armour and self-propelled guns, from our left flank. I was shaving in a top-floor room, when I

suddenly saw my van burst into flames. This van was fitted with broadcasting apparatus and a gramophone for entertaining the troops. The road was littered with gramophone records and my kit. A German tank came straight down the road towards us, and knocked out the anti-tank gun protecting Battalion H.Q., Sgt Cahill and his detachment being killed. David Peel, who had commanded the assault squadron, was killed a few minutes later. My Adjutant, Edward Rawlence, was killed stalking a German tank. My Regimental Sgt.-Major, R.S.M. Grant, was badly burnt. We had quite a job beating off this German counter-attack. We remained in this bridgehead for a week and were severely counter-attacked in a wood north of the Canal, but the position held firm. 1st Grenadier Guards and 15th/19th Hussars came up to support us in the bridgehead after two days. The main casualties in the battle were in holding the bridgehead. We had got off very lightly in the assault.

I was so impressed with Vandeleur's brilliant and inspiring leadership that I gave orders for the De Groot Bridge to be called 'Joe's Bridge', and it would be from this bridgehead that, within a week, the 'Market Garden' (Arnhem) battle would be launched. 'Joe's Bridge' it *was* called, and as such it will always be remembered in the annals of the British Army, in which Vandeleurs have served since the War of American Independence – in twenty-four campaigns and in twenty-six different regiments.

The Germans continued to reinforce Hechtel, even when the place was almost surrounded, and here the Coldstream and Welsh Guards had a gruelling time; when, after being supported by a particularly heavy concentration of guns and mortars, they finally overcame the opposition, they counted over 150 German dead, 200 wounded, and took 500 prisoners, all from the First Parachute Army. This force apparently consisted in equal proportions of men who had seen service in Russia and recruits from the Hermann Göring Training Battalion, a combination of hardened soldiers and hard-bitten young Nazis.

The only available Brigade of the 50th Division had, on 7 September, come up from Antwerp with orders to secure another bridgehead over the Albert Canal – the place chosen was south of Ghell, fifteen miles west of Beeringen, where the original road bridge had been destroyed. The leading Battalion – the 6th Green Howards – approached the Canal, at the end of a long day's march in the rain, as the light was fading. There was no time for detailed reconnaissance and they had been able to bring only two assault boats and twelve reconnaissance boats with them. At half-past one in the morning, two companies launched one boat each, and silently started to cross the Canal. To their astonishment, the boats reached the far bank undetected. The tedious process of ferrying over the Battalion, a section at a time, with only two boats, now began and was completed about an hour before dawn. So far the enemy had remained quiet. When daylight came, however, in the language of the period, 'all hell was let loose' The large German garrison responsible for defending the Canal had been overrun in the dark, not only on the far bank but also in a hamlet on the near bank. One company of the 6th Green Howards which had been isolated was now reinforced from the 7th Green Howards. Although the boats were by this time leaking badly, the 7th, under heavy fire, also crossed into the bridgehead, which held firm for the rest of the day, and that night the 5th East Yorkshires expanded the bridgehead on the west flank. The other Brigade of the 50th Division, consisting of the 6th, 8th and 9th Durham Light Infantry Battalions, was brought up to expand the bridgehead still further and to cover the construction of a folding boat bridge; a four-day battle now erupted, first against the Luftwaffe Regiment and then against the 2nd Parachute position, which the Durham Light Infantry had last met and defeated at Primasole Bridge in Sicily in one of the bloodiest battles of the Second World War.

The fighting in the Ghell Bridgehead, with both sides throwing in tanks, proved to be almost equally grim. It went on until 12 September, when the Parachutists' last attack was beaten off. The bridgehead had been completed, smashed and built again under heavy fire before the Germans fell back behind the Escaut Canal, leaving large numbers of dead. It had been the bitterest battle the Durham Light Infantry had fought in the whole campaign, and that is saying a very great deal.

The glamour of the pursuit to Brussels and Antwerp and the wide publicity which has been accorded to the Arnhem operation have tended to obscure the significance of the fighting between the Albert and Meuse Canals, whereas on 3–4 September the German Command system had been in obvious disarray, there was now increasing evidence that Army Group 'B' was being handled by Model with great drive and skill, in response to a clear and firm directive from von Rundstedt. Sound tactical sense too was apparent in the orders issued for the defence of the crossings over the two canals and the key road centres on the main route to Arnhem. The troops that were being rapidly fed into the gap had already shown themselves to be effective. German morale too was rapidly reviving owing to the fact that the Allies were now directly threatening the very borders of their Fatherland.

Chapter 7
The Arnhem Spearhead
SIR BRIAN HORROCKS

I. Montgomery's Instructions and My Orders to XXX Corps

On 12 September I was summoned by Montgomery to meet him on a forward airfield near Bourg-Léopold; I am almost certain that Dempsey was present as well. Montgomery did not give us detailed orders but described his outline plan for the whole operation, which he said was the largest between air and ground forces which had ever taken place.

He started by saying that the German Army was still disorganized after their defeat in Normandy, and were streaming back to the Fatherland as fast as they could go. At long last he had got permission to use part of General Brereton's First Allied Airborne Army. An Airborne Corps, under the command of General Browning, would consist of 1st British Division, with the Polish Parachute Brigade under command, and the 82nd and 101st U.S. Divisions. This Corps would seize the bridges at Grave, Nijmegen and Arnhem. They would thus form a bridgehead through to the north side of the Neder Rijn. They would also lay down an aerial carpet from Eindhoven to Nijmegen. Browning would plan this operation and issue his orders at his H.Q. in the U.K., and I was to dispatch a liaison officer to be present.

Dempsey and I, in our respective H.Q.s in Belgium and Holland, were to plan the breakout from the Meuse–Escaut Canal, and the subsequent advance of XXX Corps through the airborne carpet to the Arnhem Bridgehead, from where we were to advance right up to the Zuider Zee. VIII Corps on the right and XII Corps on the left were to advance, clearing up my flanks. He insisted several times that speed was essential. So the orders which I issued at Bourg-Léopold to the officers of XXX Corps on 16 September had been worked out with the approval of the Army Commander, General Dempsey, who allocated to my Corps the additional troops which would be required for this operation.

In the course of the war, I had received many orders and instructions from Montgomery, but this was the first time that he, the master of the tactical battle, completely underestimated the enemy strength. I had no idea whatever that the 9th and 10th Panzer Divisions were refitting just north-east of Arnhem, nor had Dempsey so far as I know, yet both Montgomery and Browning knew that they were there, as they had been identified by air photographs. I can only imagine that both were determined not to scrap once again the operation of the Airborne Army. Moreover, General Marshall, in the U.S., was urging Eisenhower to use this powerful force in one magnificent gesture to finish the war in 1944, and Montgomery eagerly grasped the chance of an advance at last on a narrow front, which had originally been turned down by Eisenhower. A lot had to be done in five days and there was much to-ing and fro-ing by air between the U.K. and ourselves, as D-Day was 17 September 1944.

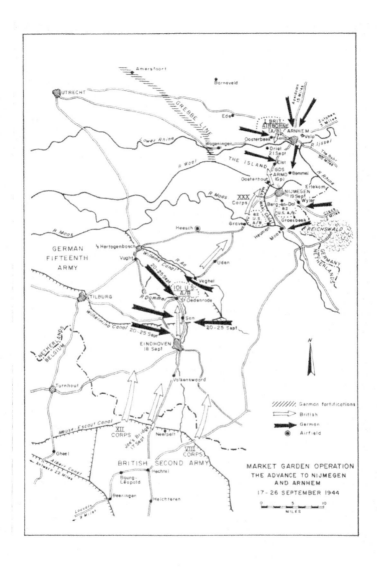

Preliminary Reconnaissance and Issue of Orders at Bourg-Léopold

During the next few days in September the remaining Corps of the Second Army came up and joined us on the Canal. VIII Corps were on our right and XII Corps on our left; the 11th Armoured Division now came under command of VIII Corps.

My first problem was to find out the nature of the enemy defences opposed to our bridgehead, which we had widened to a width and depth of approximately 3–5 miles. The German forces in front of us were paratroopers, and more were appearing every day. I wanted to find out just how deep were their defences, and whether the bridge over the River Dommel, leading to the first little Dutch town of Valkenswaard, was still intact and strong enough to take tanks. This was obviously a job for the Household Cavalry, who, I expected, would find a way round as usual, but this proved impossible as the country in front of us was thick, wooded, and mined. The highly dangerous and difficult job of obtaining the vital information for the next move forward was handed over to the troop commanded by Lieut. Buchanan-Jardine, who realized very soon that the only thing to do was to bluff his way through. He therefore left behind his two armoured cars which were certain to be destroyed, and decided to drive his two scout cars flat out straight down the one main central road, right through the enemy positions. This he did, encountering numerous enemy defences on the way; but the two little Daimlers roared on, nothing daunted, and their speed carried them through. By 2 p.m. they were well inside the Netherlands and stopped at a small café, from where the bridge could be seen. They were now clear of the German defences and reported this important fact by wireless. They also saw a German Mark IV crossing the bridge, so we now knew that it was strong enough to take tanks.

No sooner had they arrived than a band of overjoyed Dutch surrounded them, shouting and slapping them on their backs, making noise enough to attract the attention of any German within miles. Buchanan-Jardine warned them that this was not the Liberation – that would come later. It was only a reconnaissance. He obtained from them much valuable information, all of which was wirelessed back. Now came the problem of his return. There was only one thing for it – the two little cars once more set out through the German lines, flat out again, with everything firing at them. Nose to tail they raced back and got through successfully to our lines. Everything on the outside of the cars was punctured and broken by small arms fire – including even the precious cooking utensils. Sad to relate, they learned later on from a Dutchman that after their departure the Germans had gone to the café and shot three civilians in cold blood.

I have always felt that this was about the most gallant reconnaissance ever carried out. I am glad to say that Lieut. Buchanan-Jardine was subsequently awarded the Military Cross and the Order of the Bronze Lion of the Netherlands for being the first soldier to set foot in that country since the German Occupation.

As D-Day for Arnhem was on the 17th this did not allow much time for all the complicated details of this complex advance to be tied up neatly. Part of the planning had to be done in the U.K. and part at my H.Q. Fortunately, I had a most experienced staff, many of whom had been together since Alamein. By the 16th everything was ready, including the arrival of the seaborne tail of the Airborne Division; a certain number of road vehicles were always handed over to the formation which was most likely to be the first to join up with airborne troops, and this, of course, added to the congestion on the one major road available.

Conference at Bourg-Léopold on 16 September

The little Belgian town of Bourg-Léopold briefly earned its niche in history, for it was here, in the scruffy little cinema opposite the station, that I had arranged to give out my orders to the subordinate commanders of XXX Corps for the Arnhem operation. The inhabitants must have wondered what on earth was happening as they found the British Military Police almost occupying their town early in the morning, and from about 0900 hours onward a motley stream of officers in cars and jeeps of every description beginning to pour in. When their identity cards had been checked by the police, the officers were ushered into the cinema where a vast, hand-drawn map had been fixed on the stage.

I had learnt from attending many of Montgomery's conferences the value of simplicity: clear, concise orders, if possible, were pointed out on a map which all could see. When describing my audience, I have used the word 'motley' because no one was wearing standard uniform with steel helmets. I myself was dressed in a high-necked woolly with a battle-dress top and a camouflaged airborne smock, while nearly all the officers from the various armoured units wore berets of every colour. I have deliberately mentioned this because in the American Army the strictest rules as regards dress prevailed. If George Patton could have seen my audience that day, he would have gone through the roof. It is an interesting fact that two of

Britain's best battle commanders, Wellington and Montgomery, never cared how their troops were dressed, providing the clothing was serviceable and comfortable; but woe betide anyone whose weapons were not spotlessly clean!

The atmosphere of the conference was casual and cheerful. I always did my best to keep it like this. I had attended many U.S. briefings and the atmosphere there was always much more formal. After all, a Corps fights the tactical battle, so the Corps Commander must be out all day 'smelling the battlefield' I therefore knew most of the audience at Bourg-Léopold personally. Some of us had fought together side by side ever since Alamein, apart from the time when I was in hospital, so they were far more my old friends than subordinate commanders.

All the officers in the British Army are trained to give out their orders in a certain sequence. This helps to prevent anything being forgotten. On the pages overleaf I give very briefly the outline of my orders that day at 1030 hours in the cinema at Bourg-Léopold.

ORDERS FOR ARNHEM

Information

Enemy

German Commander Model very experienced, has fought a lot on Russian front. Troops opposing us mostly airborne formations under General Student – and in particular opposite Joe's Bridge, 6th Parachute Regiment, commanded by Van der Heydte. Additional troops arriving from Germany every day, mostly consisting of young paratroopers, highly indoctrinated, therefore very brave, while their N.C.O.s are the best and most experienced in the German Army.

Own troops

This is the biggest combined airborne and ground forces operation which has ever been attempted. Code-name: 'Market Garden' 'Market' – for the airborne troops; 'Garden' – for the operation of the ground forces.

'Market'

First Airborne Corps commanded by Lieut.-Gen. Sir Frederick Browning (known to everyone as 'Boy' Browning) consisting of 1st British Airborne Division, which includes the Polish Parachute Brigade.

Role: To capture Arnhem Bridge and establish a bridgehead to the north of the Neder Rijn.

82nd U.S. Airborne Division, commanded by Gen. Jim Gavin.

Role: To capture Grave Bridge, the railway and road bridges over the River Waal at Nijmegen and to seize and hold the high ground south-east of the town.

101 U.S. Airborne Division, commanded by Gen. Maxwell Taylor.

Role: To capture and hold the road from Eindhoven to Grave.

Intention

'Garden'

XXX Corps, consisting of:

>Guards Armoured Division
>50th Infantry Division
>43rd Infantry Division
>8th Armoured Brigade
>A Dutch Brigade

will break out of the existing bridgehead on 17 September and pass through the airborne carpet which has been laid down in front of us, in order to seize the area Nunspeet–Arnhem and exploit north to the Zuider Zee.

Flank formation

VIII and XII British Corps will be advancing on our right and left respectively, but as most of the available resources have been allotted to XXX Corps they will not be able to advance so rapidly and we shall be out on our own, possibly for quite a long period.

Administration

(a) The Corps will advance, and be supplied, along one road – the only major road available. Some 20,000 vehicles will be involved, so traffic control posts will advance behind the leading troops and will be established at intervals along the road, linked by wireless to a central traffic control station. In order to avoid congestion no unit must put more than five vehicles on the road without a timing from Traffic Control H.Q.

(b) All units will take as much food, petrol and ammunition as they can carry, since XXX Corps will be isolated for some time and supply may be difficult.

(c) *Break-out:* Tough opposition must be expected and the country is very difficult – wooded and marshy – only possibility is to blast our way down the road. Guards Armoured Division will lead break-out and I have arranged for their leading Regiment, the Irish Guards Group (Infantry and Tanks), to be preceded by a barrage fired by 350 guns which are now in position and camouflaged.

The Typhoons of the 83rd Group R.A.F. will give close support to the leading formations and their control vehicle will be with H.Q. Irish Guards.

50th Northumbrian Division will be responsible for the flanks, as counter-attacks will certainly be launched against us.

Remaining formations will be in reserve ready to move up as and when required.

(d) Speed absolutely vital, as we must reach the lightly equipped 1st British Airborne Division *if possible in forty-eight hours.* [I emphasized this several times over.]

(e) *Zero Hour*: I will give Zero Hour as soon as I know for certain that the Airborne Divisions are on their way. Timings must depend, therefore, on weather. There will be a 30-minute concentration from our artillery on known enemy gun positions before the Irish Guards tanks start to advance.

(f) *Difficult country* between here and Nijmegen, low-lying, intersected by canals and large rivers; bridges will almost certainly have been prepared for demolition. We have collected in one area 9000 Sappers and vast supplies of bridging material. Air photos of each bridge have been taken, and each handed over to a separate Royal Engineers unit which has made its own plan to repair or replace its bridge. As soon as a report is received of any demolition the road will be cleared of all traffic and the Royal Engineers unit earmarked for this particular bridge will be rushed up along what I hope will be a completely open road.

My Command Post will be established on the roof of a factory [pointed out on map]. I then intend to follow the Guards with a small tactical H.Q. to join up as soon as possible with Browning's H.Q. which will be in the Nijmegen area.

END OF ORDERS

Note 1. As I have already said, I had no idea at all that the remnants of the 9th and 10th SS Panzer Divisions had been moved back to an area north-east of Arnhem to refit. We could have defeated them quite easily, but they were too heavily armed for the lightly equipped Airborne Troops.

Note 2: It may seem rather late in the day to issue orders, as D-Day was on the 17th – the next day – but the formations in XXX Corps were experienced troops and most of the preliminary arrangements had been made, such as dumping ammunition, surveying the guns into position, and the complicated plans which had to be made for the Royal Engineers. I had found from experience that it was dangerous to issue orders too early, as someone might be captured and give the whole show away.

There were surprisingly few questions at the end of the orders, though I must say the audience looked very thoughtful as they left the cinema – particularly the Irish Guards.

II. Break-Out

On Sunday, 17 September, at approximately 11 a.m. I climbed on to the flat roof of the same factory from which Joe Vandeleur had made his plan for the capture of Joe's Bridge.

From there I had a clear view of the ground over which the initial assault of the battle would take place. My small Command Post had already been established there: it consisted of a G.S.O. 2 – a young Staff Officer from the Operations Branch, my A.D.C., a Signal Officer, and a couple of operators who manned the wireless link and the telephone back to my Operations Room in Corps H.Q. located a few miles to the rear and hidden in the woods. This was my normal Command Post team, and we had fought many battles together.

It was a lovely sunny Sunday morning, completely peaceful, except for the occasional chatter of a machine-gun in the distance. It was rather a terrible thought that on my word of command 'All hell' would break loose. I was uneasy that this vast operation was starting on a Sunday, not, I am afraid, on account of any religious scruples, but because no attack which I had launched on a Sunday had ever been completely successful.

All the same, I was confident of success; this may sound odd after what I have written in the previous chapter, but I was still suffering from the 'liberation euphoria' – cheering crowds, welcoming us whenever we entered even the smallest village. I had also become used to the sight of depressed, bedraggled, unarmed German soldiers straggling back towards the Fatherland, and usually only too glad to be made prisoners of war as they were reasonably safe with us, which was not always the case if they fell into the hands of the Maquis, who had many old scores to pay off. Moreover, during the last few days' hard fighting which had taken place between Brussels and the line of the Canal, our troops had proved more than a match for the young paratroopers, even though they were commanded by very experienced men of the Student/Van der Heydte class. After all, the Guards, the tough little Geordies from Durham and Northumberland, the staunch countrymen of the 43rd Division from the west of England, and last – but by no means least – the Yeomanry, had shown over and over again that they were more than a match for the Germans, whose morale in 1944 was considerably lower than during the advance to Dunkirk, or in Rommel's splendid Desert Afrika Korps.

I knew that it would be a very tough battle; especially so, owing to the nature of the country, with its numerous water obstacles and the single main road available for thousands of vehicles; but failure never even entered my head.

While these thoughts were passing through my mind I was told over the wireless that the weather was O.K. and the Airborne Armada was on its way. Even now I was determined not to give Zero Hour until I actually saw them overhead, as weather conditions could change quickly.

I felt a very lonely figure, leaning over the parapet of that factory roof. This was always a difficult time for me, knowing that thousands of men were about to risk their lives in a plan for which I was responsible. I kept on going over the details in my mind. Had I overlooked anything?

The troops I knew would also be 'taut' – but, being British, they would of course be cracking the same old corny jokes as usual. In one attack I had seen the occupants of an armoured carrier crossing the start line all wearing black top hats, which, no doubt, they had found in their billets, as the Germans in those days always wore them for funerals. Their sense of humour struck me at the time as somewhat macabre, but typically British.

What worried me most was the long period which had elapsed since we had had the enemy on the run, during our advance to Brussels. Ten days had passed since then, giving the Germans time in which to recover, and I had already seen signs that the German military machine was beginning to function once again with its usual efficiency.

Suddenly, seemingly out of the blue, hundreds of aircraft were overhead, many transport planes, some towing gliders, with fighter cover swarming everywhere as the Armada flew steadily northwards.

I ordered Zero Hour for 1435 hours. At 1400 hours exactly, there was a roar overhead as our 350 guns, hidden in the woods behind, opened up. I could see the Irish Guards, with their infantry riding on the tanks, moving up to the start line. I had taken the trouble to find out who would be commanding the leading troop, so, at 2.35 p.m. exactly, I could imagine Lieut. Keith Heathcote of 3rd Squadron, 2nd Battalion Irish Guards picking up his 'mike' and ordering 'Driver advance!' – the battle for Arnhem had started.

The Irish Guards pressed forward behind a screening barrage from our guns, which had hitherto been concentrated on known enemy positions, particularly their artillery, while further ahead wave upon wave of Typhoons from the 83rd Group kept the German defences under continuous rocket attack.

To start with, everything seemed to be going our way. But suddenly nine of the Irish Guards' tanks were knocked out almost all at once and a furious battle began in the woods in front of me. In the midst of the tumult and uproar the Micks showed just what great fighters they were, jumping from the tops of the tanks and hurling themselves at the German anti-tank guns. Under this furious assault the enemy suddenly broke, and by evening the Guards had reached the little town of Valkenswaard. As anticipated the Germans soon counter-attacked, but we were well prepared and the 50th Division repulsed them without much difficulty.

The Irish Guards halted for the night on the orders of Brigadier Gwatkin, the Commander of the 5th Guards Brigade, and it has been suggested that this showed a lack of urgency on the part of XXX Corps. This criticism is totally unfounded. First of all, Gwatkin was a most experienced Commander and a great 'thruster', but he had received a message to the effect that the Germans had succeeded in blowing the bridge over the Canal at Son. The Guards still had a long way to go. They had been fighting hard and tanks require maintenance. In my opinion it was the act of an experienced Commander to halt, rest his troops, etc., while the bridge was being repaired.

All in all, the day had been a successful one. By now the first waves of airborne troops had been dropped behind the enemy line; and we had seriously damaged the German defences at a very reasonable cost to ourselves.

III. The Other Side of the Hill

Meanwhile, what had been happening on the German side? After the war many people believed that the Allied plans for Arnhem had been revealed to the Germans by a Dutch traitor. In fact, according to reliable sources, our initial attack took them completely by surprise, and General Model, the German C.-in-C., himself narrowly escaped capture by the 1st British Airborne Division, who virtually came down on top of him on the 17th.

Apparently the Supreme Commander and his senior staff were lunching at a hotel in Oosterbeek, a small town just west of Arnhem, when Allied aircraft appeared overhead. The Germans, who mistook them for bombers, were astonished when the sky suddenly filled with parachutes. They had to beat a hasty retreat, for the dropping zone was a mere two miles away.

In fact Model's closeness to the Allied landing enabled him to organize resistance immediately. Leaving Oosterbeek he raced to Zutphen, twenty-eight miles north-east of Arnhem, where he alerted General Willi Bittrich, the commander of II SS Panzer Corps. The 9th and 10th Panzer Divisions had only just arrived in the area to refit after the fighting in Normandy; their presence, as yet unsuspected by my own Intelligence, was to prove decisive in the days that followed, for our paratroopers were simply not equipped to deal with this kind of opposition. Not only did the Panzer Divisions have an overwhelming superiority in firepower, despite their recent losses; to make matters worse, they had been trained in Normandy specifically to combat airborne troops.

This was our first bit of bad luck; the II Panzer Corps might have been sent anywhere else to refit, but it had gone to Zutphen, and instead of being faced by second-rate lines-of-communication troops, our 1st Airborne Division came up against some first-class front-line soldiers. In addition, there was an SS Panzer Training Regiment, billeted in farmhouses in the woods just east of Oosterbeek. On his way to Zutphen Model paused at this H.Q., alerted the Regiment, and ordered the C.O. to deploy into positions from which they could hold the 1st British Airborne's easterly advance. He also placed them under Bittrich's command and these were the first enemy troops Urquhart's paratroopers encountered.

Model and Bittrich were experienced soldiers, and they appreciated the situation very accurately. Their main task, as they saw it, was to prevent the spearhead of the Second British Army, represented by my Corps, from crossing the Lower Rhine (Neder Rijn) and joining up with the 1st Airborne Division. If they could do this, they reckoned that they could collect sufficient troops to seal off the lightly-equipped Airborne Division and deal with it subsequently at their leisure. In General Bittrich's own words:

> In spite of the obscure situation at Arnhem and the likelihood of continued and increasingly strong air landings in the area north of the Rhine, I advisedly chose to direct the main effort against the enemy forces in the Nijmegen area. So the 9th SS Panzer Division was ordered to prevent the British from seizing the Arnhem bridge, and then to push the Airborne Division out of the town to the west while additional forces were collected to seal them off from the north and west. The 10th SS Panzer Division

was dispatched to the south to prevent the British Second Army from occupying the all-important bridges over the River Waal at Nijmegen.

Model also alerted every available German formation within reach and ordered them to move against our lines of communication stretching over some sixty miles from the Belgian frontier to Nijmegen.

One further piece of good luck came the German way. General K. Student, who, it will be remembered, was commanding the German Parachute Army on our immediate front, and which we were fighting so bitterly, writes in his book as follows:

> Two hours after the air armada first appeared in the skies over Holland, the Allied Operation Order for 'Market Garden' was on my desk. It had been captured from a glider forced down near Vught – which was my command post.

The capture of this vital document was a great boon to the Germans, who thus had a complete picture of what we intended to do.

Meanwhile, great excitement prevailed at the Führer's H.Q. in East Prussia. As report after report came in of our airborne landings in Holland, Hitler became very worried at this rapier thrust into the under-belly of the German Reich. 'Holland has top priority over all reserves!' he ordered. Every available reserve formation in Germany, and even as far afield as Denmark, was alerted and ordered to move down to defeat the British/U.S. penetration. In addition, a steady stream of good soldiers was exerting pressure against our left flank. They belonged to the Fifteenth German Army, which had been holding the coast and was now escaping through Beveland into the Netherlands mainland. It was the arrival of these formations which finally turned the tide against us.

So much for the German side of the picture. Now let me get back again to our own battle. We have seen that on the 17th the Guards had broken through and reached Valkenswaard just inside Holland.

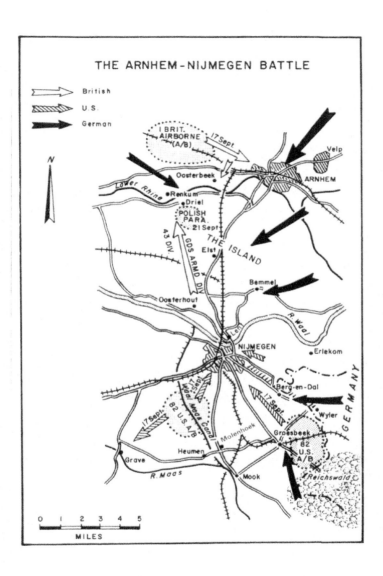

IV. The Battle of Arnhem and the Advance to Nijmegen

Next morning, 18 September, they advanced, with the Grenadier Group leading. They had some sharp brushes with the enemy forces, but from Eindhoven onwards they found the road to the north held by the 101st U.S. Airborne Division as far as Grave and then by the 82nd U.S. Airborne Division.

I followed up the Guards in my car, with my small Command Post. As we drove northwards through the seemingly peaceful countryside we were greeted at the crossroads and bridges by cheerful-looking groups of the U.S. Paratroops. Their Commanding General, Maxwell Taylor, told me that the initial landing had been completely successful, the best the Division had ever carried out, as an entire regiment had come down in full view of their Commander. In fact, between 1300 and 1330 hours, 6769 men had jumped, with casualties of less than 2 per cent. The gliders had not been quite so successful; only 53 out of 70 came in without accident.

I don't believe any division other than one of these two Airborne Divisions could have kept the 25 kilometres of this one road open, with increasing German pressure coming in from both sides. In spite of all their efforts, however, the Germans succeeded in cutting the road three times, and the 50th Division was put under their command to help them.

So much has been written about this battle that I propose to concentrate only on the outstanding events, from my own personal point of view as the Commander of XXX Corps.

The 82nd U.S. Airborne Division had been, if possible, even more successful than the 101st. Thanks to a crash landing, almost on their objective, they had captured intact the road bridge over the River Meuse, at Grave. Had the Germans succeeded in destroying this enormous bridge, our advance might well have been delayed by several days. The 82nd had also seized another important bridge over the Maas-Waal Canal at Heuman, and were holding the high ground above Berg-en-Dal, which dominated the road on the east. They had also penetrated to 400 yards from the main road bridge in Nijmegen itself – a truly magnificent performance.

Arnhem is the only battle which I propose to describe in some detail, since it was the most difficult and unpleasant in which I have ever been involved. The key to the whole of this operation was the Dutch town of Nijmegen. When I arrived, after a completely peaceful drive along our one road, the whole place seemed to have erupted into chaos. In the southern suburbs the Dutch civilians, quite oblivious to the tumult raging elsewhere in their town, were busy in the streets, shaving the hair from women who had cohabited with the German garrison during the Occupation.

This attractive Dutch town is dominated by two vast bridges over the River Waal, the road bridge on the east and the railway bridge on the west. It was astonishing how quickly the Grenadiers co-operated with a battalion of the 505 Regiment of the 82nd Division. There was now a desperate urgency about this battle, as no word had come through from the 1st British Airborne Division, some ten miles away on the far side of yet another obstacle, the Neder Rijn. Moreover, the German resistance was formidable. We were opposed not by elderly gentlemen, or inferior lines-of-communication troops, but by tough Nazi-indoctrinated SS troops, who were perfectly prepared to die, if necessary, for Hitler. Every square had been fortified and they set fire to every fifth house in a defensive perimeter round both bridges.

The Germans had every right to consider that Nijmegen was impregnable, but fortunately we had at our disposal two of the finest divisions of all the Allied Armies in Europe, the 82nd Airborne and the Guards Armoured, who co-operated closely in the bitter fighting which now ensued. The Grenadier Guards and a battalion of the U.S. 505 Parachute Regiment had plunged into this blazing inferno to try to capture the bridges, which, to our astonishment, had not been blown. The Grenadiers attacked from the south-east in an attempt to capture Huner Park, which dominated the road bridge and was occupied by some 500 tough German SS troops in strong defensive positions. In addition, the central square, from which all the roads radiated, had been turned into a veritable fortress with a network of trenches and barbed wire. The U.S. Paratroopers, showing their usual initiative, were working along the tops of the houses, so as to be able to fire down on to the German troops in their trenches at ground level. If they were held up on a roof they blew holes through the walls of the top floors and so continued to dominate the Germans below. Later a Grenadier Guards officer described it as being a 'jolly sight to see those paratroopers hopping from roof to roof'.

On arrival in the southern outskirts of Nijmegen on the 19th I met General ('Boy') Browning, who, with his H.Q., had landed by glider. We established our respective H.Q.s side by side in an empty school house in a southern suburb. Most of the staff work, particularly on the administrative side, had to be done by XXX Corps H.Q., as it was far more experienced and much larger than the Airborne H.Q. which had flown in by glider.

'Boy' Browning and I were old friends, and from now onwards we took all the major decisions together without any semblance of friction. Owing to the fact that he was always immaculately dressed, some people were inclined to underestimate him. In my opinion he was a first-rate Commander, always prepared to take the difficult decisions unhesitatingly. While he of course issued all the orders to the airborne troops, I did the same with XXX Corps. But in spite of great gallantry the progress towards the bridge was desperately slow.

During the afternoon of the 19th, after visiting the forward area to smell the battlefield, Browning and I met in our H.Q. to discuss the situation. Suddenly the door opened and in came a tall, good-looking American General, who, like Maxwell Taylor, the Commander of the 101st Airborne Division, was as unlike the popular cartoon conception of the loud-voiced, boastful, cigar-chewing American as it would be possible to imagine. They were both quiet, sensitive-looking men with an almost British passion for understatement. Yet both of these two Commanders, under their deceptively gentle exteriors, were very tough characters indeed. They had to be, because their Divisions, which were recruited from the whole of the U.S.A., were composed of individual killers who were, in fact, the toughest troops I have ever come across in my life, and not easy to command – yet in both Divisions these men worshipped their Divisional Commanders.

When Jim Gavin entered the room I did not realize – nor did he mention it – that he had damaged his back very badly on the 17th when he had landed by parachute on the Berg-en-Dal ridge, having dropped from just under 400 feet, while at the same time being engaged by hostile fire from the nearby wood. From then on he was almost always in constant pain and at one time it was feared that he had broken his back. As there were not sufficient aircraft for the whole Division to fly in on one day, three flights were required; but unfortunately, owing to bad weather, his air landing brigade had been unable to take off from the U.K. He had been ordered to land on the Berg-en-Dal ridge, an open space some eight miles long, with thick woods on its western side, dominating the main Eindhoven–Nijmegen road and leading down on the east side to an open valley dotted with farms, stretching up to the Reichswald in the south and to Cleve in the north. The German frontier ran down this valley, Wyler being the first German town on the eastern slopes of the spur. This spur was vital because it was here that the air landing regiments, and all subsequent flights, would also touch down. It seemed incredible that part of one division in scattered platoons could have managed to retain the vital Berg-en-Dal ridge, against constant attacks from the east. While the 508 Regiment was on the ridge, the 505 had advanced into Nijmegen and one battalion was co-operating with the Grenadiers in the capture of the road bridge, while the remainder had been directed on to the railway bridge. The only reserves appeared to be the 504 Regiment plus the Irish and Coldstream Guards groups of the Guards Armoured Division.

We pointed out to Jim Gavin that the attacks on the road and railway bridges in the town were making very slow progress and that it was absolutely vital that both should, if possible, be captured intact – though we could see that they were heavily defended and had been prepared for demolition.

We could not make out why these two bridges had not already been blown. We did not, of course, then realize that, whereas Gen. Bittrich was determined to blow them, he had been forbidden by the C.-in-C. to do so. Model was so confident of success that he wanted these bridges available for a subsequent massive counter-attack to destroy the Second British Army. We suggested to Gavin that there was only one solution – to cross the River Waal by assault boats just west of the town, while maintaining the pressure on the road bridge, and thus to capture first the railway bridge and secondly the road bridge from the rear. It is to Jim Gavin's eternal credit that he agreed at once to this apparently suicidal river crossing in the flimsy British assault boats which the U.S. troops had never even seen, let alone handled, in the swiftly running river.

We hoped to be able to carry out the crossing that night under cover of darkness, but this proved quite impossible owing to the difficulty of getting the lorries containing the boats up the one long narrow road which constituted our lines of communication and which, in spite of all our efforts, was from time to time completely blocked by burnt-out vehicles. The delay in getting these precious boats forward was infuriating, and it was the only time that I saw Gavin really angry. Having flown in, he did not understand the chaotic situation at ground level in the rear, and as Zero Hour for the crossing had to be constantly postponed, he turned towards me and said, 'For God's sake try! It is the least you can do.'

At first light on 20 September the Irish Guards tanks and 502 U.S. Parachute Regiment cleared the western suburb of the town and by mid-day they arrived at the river bank. There was now about to take place what I have always considered to be the most gallant attack ever carried out during the whole of the last war, but the delay in the arrival of these wretched boats meant that Zero Hour had even still to be constantly postponed and this was very hard on the leading waves of paratroopers, many of whom must have thought that the crossing of this wide river, in face of determined enemy opposition, was sheer murder – all the more so because, as the wind increased in strength, the smoke screen put down by the Guards and the Artillery diminished in intensity. Then, at 1200 hours, the long-awaited boats arrived.

Just as this vital attack was about to be launched, Jim Gavin received a wireless message from his Chief of Staff begging him to return at once, as heavy German attacks were developing from the east, and if the Berg-en-Dal feature was lost it would mean complete disaster for the operations in Nijmegen. So, much against his will – as he realized the vital importance of the attack across the Waal – he set off for his H.Q. What eased his mind somewhat was the fact that he had complete confidence in Col. Tucker, the Commander of the 504 Regiment, which was involved in the crossing.

Now let me turn to Jim Gavin's own account which he recently sent to me of what happened during the next few hectic hours:

> The day that we made the river crossing, however, the Germans made a major, well-planned attack, coming from two directions. The first came out of the Reichswald down the road towards Molenhoek and overran a battalion of the 505, which stayed in the town and fought from the cellars. It was this attack that caused the Chief of Staff to urge frantically that I get back to Divisional H.Q. and make some decision before we lost the whole area. I set off at once. When I got to the railroad overpass it looked as though everything was just about lost, since we could see no troopers, except one who was in a rather frightened state in a foxhole near the railway overpass. I sent for the Coldstream Guards Battalion, and asked them to double time. They were about three miles away. I had the jeep driver do that. I then had a Sergeant who was with me and a Lieutenant lie on the railroad

embankment and shoot any Germans who were trying to get out of the town. We captured our first prisoner there; he was a young, apple-cheeked, fine-looking paratrooper. From him we learned that this attack was part of another attack that was to come up through Berg-en-Dal and that they were to meet north of Groesbeek. In any event, Col. Ekman got the situation quickly in hand, after the battalion was overrun, and he launched his counter-attack, which retook Molenhoek and drove the Germans back, so by the time the Coldstream Guards got there – and they arrived in great form – the situation had quietened down.

It must be rare indeed for a Divisional Commander, suffering from a badly injured back, a Sergeant and a Lieutenant to halt the advance of a German regiment. Altogether, Gavin and his two fellow paratroopers halted three dangerous German advances by what he describes as 'engaging them quickly to give the impression that we had a lot of fire power' Jim Gavin continues:

With our Heuman bridge safe, I hurried up to Berg-en-Dal as fast as I could. We had been fighting along that ridge spasmodically ever since we landed. We did not realize it at the time, but the small town of Wyler was in Germany. We had originally planned a road block there when we were in London and every time we took it the Germans reacted with increased strength, so we had been fighting back and forth across the ridge ever since we landed. When I got to Berg-en-Dal I ran into Colonel Mendez who, you may remember, was a fine soldier, and he knew what he was doing. He was managing to contain the Germans with a platoon or two wherever they seemed to be making headway. He had enormous gaps in his front, but the Germans did not seem interested in probing to find out where they were.

The only thing that troubled us was the Panzers, since we had no effective anti-tank weapons until we captured the 1st German Panzerfausts [anti-tank weapons]. It seemed to me that if we could hold the Germans until dark we would have them, knowing that they usually liked to stop fighting at dark and bring up food. We counted on it. They obliged nicely and we planned our counter-attack to go off well before daylight the following morning.

The attack went off and, since we had momentum and were driving the Germans well ahead of us, I wanted to continue on to the flatland. A day or two later you came out to visit us. We finally rested our left flank on the Rhine River. From there our front line ran through the small German town of Erlekom and on to Wyler. Seemingly then we had to hold at least that much real estate to protect our operations around Nijmegen and the bridge crossing sites.

The utter confusion of those early days in the battle for Nijmegen is exemplified by Gavin's next comment:

To add to the complications, you may recall a German train came through our area some time after midnight, the first night there. I got the 505th on the phone up at Groesbeek and they admitted they hadn't put up a barrier adequate to block the rails, and a German train did go right through us, blowing its whistle on its way. With that, the 505th prepared themselves in the event another train attempted to come through. An hour later a locomotive and several cars came up the tracks. The 505th fired into the locomotive and it came to a grinding halt. German troops bolted out of the cars and were all over the wooded area between Groesbeek and Nijmegen the next morning. They weren't really harassing us; they were just trying to get out of there and back to Germany.

To those of us who worried about the Division as a whole, and what it was doing, that was one of the most exciting and close-call days that we had during the entire war. Making the river crossing under such marginal conditions was difficult enough but, as you can imagine, I could not see myself sitting there with a regiment of infantry while Urquhart was being cut to pieces eleven miles away, so we simply had to get across the river and get the other end of the bridge. Then, to have a major counter-offensive launched at that very moment, when we were very short of infantry and had enormous gaps in our front, made for a very busy few hours. I have often thought about the operation. The Germans were so methodical and so predictable that we were able to cope with them. With a little more skill and better reconnaissance, they probably could have made their way well into the woods between Groesbeek and Nijmegen, creating all kinds of havoc, but I believe we had the feeling, after the link-up, that as long as we had the Guards Armoured with us there was nothing they could throw against us that we couldn't cope with.

I always thought that the Guards were the best soldiers that I saw on either side in the war – not only because of their soldierly qualities, but because of their nonchalance and style; they seemed to enjoy what they were doing, and I shall always remember some of the teas they gave after things quietened down. It was a remarkable Division.

The arrival of a Divisional Commander in person in the front line saved the day. No wonder those tough paratroopers worshipped Jim Gavin. When he arrived in the Netherlands, Dempsey had offered him a caravan in which to sleep, but in spite of the continuing ache in his back he refused – 'as the boys would not like it'! I have always understood that the veterans of the 82nd Division regard the Berg-en-Dal Battle as their finest hour.

Meanwhile, under Tucker's command, the attack across the Waal had been completely successful. The Waal is 400 yards wide, with a strong current (it is really the main stream of the Rhine). The Germans were holding the far bank in strength, yet at 3 p.m. the leading U.S. paratroopers entered the river in British assault boats with which they were totally unfamiliar. Supported though they were by fire from the tanks of the Irish Guards, and approximately 100 guns, they nevertheless suffered heavily and only half the leading wave, some in boats, some swimming, succeeded in reaching the far bank. Yet this mere handful of men charged up the steep embankment and secured a small bridgehead a couple of hundred yards deep. Gradually more and more troops were ferried across until by evening they had penetrated a mile inland to the village of Lent, where the railway crosses the main road. They had thus cut off both bridges from the rear, a truly amazing achievement, but they had suffered very heavy casualties in the process.

The assault on the road bridge continued and, attacking from a different direction, the British/U.S. forces advanced literally yard by yard and house by house. By the late afternoon they captured the two key tactical features dominating the bridge, and of the many battle honours which the Grenadier Guards can claim none can have been more richly deserved than Nijmegen. At 7 p.m. Sergeant Robinson, in command of a troop of tanks, advanced rapidly to the bridge with guns blazing. Including the embankment on both sides, he had to travel 1200 yards completely in the open, when he was an easy target to enemy anti-tank guns firing from the far side and also to Germans firing bazookas from positions in the girders above the bridge. It looked to be a suicidal attempt and two tanks were hit, but somehow the troop got across and skidded broadside through the road block, knocking out two German anti-tank guns. The troop was followed by the remainder of the squadron, commanded by Lord Carrington, and only came to a halt when the Guardsmen met the remnants of the 505 U.S. Regiment, who had crossed the river lower down. Perhaps the bravest of all these very brave men was Lieut. Jones, a young Sapper officer, who ran on foot behind the leading tanks, cutting the wires and removing the demolition charges. I could hardly bear to watch Sergeant Robinson's apparently suicidal advance, as I expected the bridge to be blown sky-high at any moment. By the evening of the 21st almost a miracle had been achieved: both bridges had been captured intact.

V. Fighting on the Island

Gavin told me afterwards that he and the men of his Division felt bitterly disappointed that we had not sent a task force straight for Arnhem Bridge, after the capture, intact, of the two Nijmegen bridges. In fact, at the time, he felt that the British had let them down badly.

This sort of criticism is a constant phenomenon of battle. The forward troops always think that those in the rear are leading a life of ease and should be doing more, but even Jim Gavin, the Divisional Commander, could have had no idea of the utter confusion which reigned in Nijmegen at that time, with sporadic battles going on all over the place, and particularly on our one road to the rear, where chaos reigned. Moreover, the country in front between Nijmegen and Arnhem, which we called the Island, was almost impassable for tanks; all the narrow roads ran along the tops of embankments, with wide ditches on either side, and any vehicle on an embankment was a sitting duck for the German anti-tank gunners hidden in the orchards with which the Island abounded: one knocked-out vehicle could block a road for hours. It was infantry country, and realizing this I had ordered up the 43rd Wessex Division to move through Nijmegen and launch a divisional attack towards Arnhem. I did not realize at this time that they also were badly blocked on that one 'blasted' road which was constantly under fire and so often cut. In many cases the front line of the 101st Division was the ditch on the side of the road. The administrative situation at this time was deteriorating rapidly, and artillery ammunition, like almost everything else, was beginning to be in short supply. At this very moment a German formation had just penetrated St Oedenrode and stopped all traffic on the road for several hours. As regards the troops immediately available, the Irish Guards Infantry were reduced to five platoons.

I now began to feel as though I was in a boxing ring, fighting a tough opponent with one arm tied behind my back. I was, in fact, trying to fight three battles at the same time. The first was to keep open my tenuous supply line, which stretched back along one road for over fifty miles to Eindhoven and beyond; much of which was being frequently cut by an increasing number of German forces operating on both sides of this single road link. The second battle was to prevent the Germans closing in on Nijmegen itself, especially from the wooded country to the east of the town. Finally, I was desperately trying to force a way through to the north bank of the Neder Rijn to join up with the embattled parachute troops.

I still had had no word from the British Airborne Division, but I realized that their plight must be getting desperate. Though we did not realize it at that time, it was already too late to capture Arnhem Bridge. Just three hours previously, Frost's gallant force, which had been holding the north end of Arnhem Bridge for three precious days against continuous attacks by superior formations from the 9th SS Panzer Division, had at last been overrun.

The story of the magnificent fight put up by the 1st British Airborne Division has been told over and over again, so I do not propose to go into any detail here, except to say that the outstanding hero of the whole battle was unquestionably Lieut.- Col. Frost, commanding the 2nd British Parachute Battalion. The Reconnaissance Unit of the 9th SS Panzer Division had seized Arnhem Bridge just 30 minutes before the arrival of Frost's force. He could not force his way over, but by holding grimly to the north end, in spite of repeated attacks, he prevented any movement across the bridge. The 10th SS was therefore forced to cross by ferry farther to the east, and this delayed their arrival at Nijmegen until we had captured the town and its two vital bridges intact.

The next day the Guards Armoured Division failed to advance more than two miles against increasingly heavy opposition; unfortunately, ground to air liaison was not working well, and little support could be obtained from the 83rd Group R.A.F. Now that German reinforcements could cross Arnhem Bridge, they began to appear in ever-increasing numbers.

Still, there was no need to despair. Two-thirds of the Polish Parachute Brigade (for this operation, under the command of the 1st British Airborne Division) had dropped on the 20th, just south of the Neder Rijn at Driel, and I hoped, when the 43rd arrived, that, with a fresh infantry division available, I would be able to join up with them and force a crossing over the river.

Brigadier Essame, Commander of 214 Brigade, the leading formation of the 43rd Division, arrived well in front of the Brigade, at the Headquarters of Brigadier Gwatkin, who put him in the picture and pointed out the difficulties of fighting on the Island. He then reported to my Tactical H.Q. and described to me the chaos which existed on our one road to the rear, and the difficulty which the Division was experiencing in its forward move through Eindhoven and Grave. We had done our best to keep the road open by installing the strict traffic control which I have already mentioned, but the German pressure from both sides was increasing all the time and even if the enemy had not physically cut the road (which they did several times) stretches of it were under fire, and blockages were constantly being caused by burnt-out British vehicles. All this was bad enough, but the chaos in Nijmegen had to be seen to be believed: part of 214 Brigade had been directed wrongly over the road bridge instead of the railway bridge, and Essame had in the dark experienced considerable difficulties in finding this unit and concentrating his three battalions.

Fortunately, Essame was an experienced and tough Commander, and I do not believe that anyone else would have succeeded in collecting the scattered elements of his 214 Brigade so rapidly on the night of the 21st and launching his first attack early the next morning.

I spent the morning with him, and nobody could have done more than he. Unfortunately, artillery ammunition was running short and the 7th Somerset Light Infantry, his leading battalion, at once ran into strong natural defensive positions, round the village of Oosterhout, held by approximately a battalion of

Germans, supported by tanks, some self-propelled guns and mortars.

As the Guards had earlier found to their cost, it was quite impossible for the 43rd Division to deploy armoured vehicles in an attack across this difficult country intersected with high banks and dikes, in which the enemy enjoyed all the advantages of cover and the attacker none. So the Somersets advanced with practically no support at all, either from tanks or guns. The first attack failed and the leading Company Commander, Major Sidney Young, was killed. The C.O., Lieut.-Col. Borradaile, one of the best C.O.s in the Division, now launched another attack round the right flank, which seemed to offer the best opportunity of success; but this also was held up. The Brigadier then decided on a third attack, which, in spite of the embargo, he determined to launch with the whole of the Divisional Artillery in support.

This third effort, which started at 3.20 p.m., was completely successful, and by 5 p.m. a gap had been opened in the German position, through which Essame slipped a mobile column which he had been holding in readiness. This consisted of one squadron of the 4th/7th Dragoon Guards (tanks), 5th Duke of Cornwall's Light Infantry, one platoon of machine-guns of the 8th Middlesex, and some DUKWs filled with ammunition and much needed stores for the beleaguered British paratroops.

George Taylor, the thrusting C.O. of the 5th Duke of Cornwall's Light Infantry, divided his forces into two; in front, an armoured column with two companies of infantry riding on the outside of the tanks, and behind, the remaining two companies of his battalion in charge of the soft-skinned transport vehicles. They set off from Oosterhout just before last light, and the head of the armoured column covered the ten miles to Driel in thirty minutes; here it joined up with the Poles, but the Germans managed to infiltrate five Tiger tanks and some infantry into a gap which had opened between the two columns.

C.S.M. Philp, travelling in a carrier at the tail of the armoured column, rammed the leading enemy tank and killed the German Commander as he peered out of his turret, before he himself and his driver bailed out into the ditch beside the road. Learning that his force had been split into two, Taylor sent back two platoons under Major Parker, with extra P.I.A.T.s (infantry anti-tank weapons) and some '75' anti-tank mines, to clear up the mess. In a remarkably successful little operation, this small force, working in the dark, succeeded in stalking and destroying all the Tigers. Private Brown, a young soldier, spotted an enemy tank with a track damaged by some of the mines, so he left the cover of the ditch where he was lying and, knowing full well the risk he ran, walked to within a few yards before firing his P.I.A.T. The tank was completely destroyed, but he himself was blinded by the blast and he lost the sight of one eye. As he was carried away he was heard to say, 'I don't care – I knocked the ———— out!' After an eventful night's drive along narrow by-roads the whole force joined up with the Poles.

It has been suggested by people who should have known better that 43 Division were slow and 'sticky'; I have therefore described this operation in considerable detail, in order to remove the slur on the reputation of this first-class West Country Division.

On the morning of the 22nd the Household Cavalry, taking advantage of the morning fog, managed to slip some armoured cars through the German lines. They succeeded in joining up with the Poles at Driel, so from now onwards we knew at least what was happening in that area, i.e. on the river bank.

The morning of the 22nd was a black day for me. I had witnessed the failure of the initial attack of 214 Brigade, and no advance had been made anywhere on XXX Corps front. I arrived at my Headquarters to be told by my B.G.S. that contact had now been made at last with the 1st Airborne – curiously enough, on the wireless frequency used by our 64th Medium Regiment. This meant that we could at least help with artillery support but, according to the message, things were apparently going very badly for them. They had been forced to withdraw from the Arnhem area and were now occupying a small perimeter round Oosterbeek, where they were being attacked furiously from all sides. Ammunition was short, and unless we could get help to them within twenty-four hours they would probably be overrun: such was the gist of the message. In fact, their situation could hardly have been worse. While I was pondering over this information, my B.G.S. returned to say that once more a German armoured formation had succeeded in cutting our road to the rear.

There was only one thing for it – I ordered the 32nd Guards Brigade to turn back and open the road by attacking from the north. Though this eventually succeeded, the road was closed to all traffic for twenty-five very important hours. Looking back, I realize that the next few days were among the worst in my life. Nothing seemed to succeed. I had to be very firm with myself; I was beginning to find it difficult to sleep, as my mind was always filled with the picture of those gallant airborne troops, fighting for their lives on the far bank of the Neder Rijn and, as I knew only too well, a Commander who fails to sleep will soon be no good. Montgomery had often said to me,

'However bad the situation may be, *the Commander must always radiate confidence.*' I did my best, but this was becoming increasingly difficult day by day.

On the 24th I climbed to the top of Driel Church, where I could get a view of the Neder Rijn. There seemed to me to be a distinct danger that the airborne troops might be cut off altogether from the river. The trouble was that the Germans were holding the high ground on both sides of the airborne perimeter and could sweep the river with fire from machine-guns firing on fixed lines, and the losses in our assault boats had been very heavy indeed. In fact, the only possibility was to cross at night under as much artillery fire as we could afford.

I issued orders to General Thomas, commanding the 43rd Division, and to Major-General Sosabovsky, Commander of the Polish Parachute Brigade:

Firstly: In order to relieve pressure on the bridgehead, Thomas was to carry out an assault crossing that night, with at least one battalion of his own, to be followed by the Poles, with as many stores as possible – particularly ammunition. This, of course, depended, I realized, on how many assault boats he could muster. I promised him the support of the Corps Artillery, though ammunition was getting dangerously short.

Secondly: Thomas was to carry out a reconnaissance farther to the west, because if things went well that night I hoped to side-slip the 43rd Division, cross the Neder Rijn farther to the west and carry out a left hook against the German forces attacking the western perimeter of the airborne troops.

Having issued these orders I then drove back twenty-five miles towards Eindhoven to meet Dempsey at St Oedenrode. This was very necessary because I had not seen either him or Montgomery for some days and we had reached the crisis point of the battle. Dempsey agreed that unless 43rd Division's left hook could be staged very quickly and with a considerable chance of success, the only thing to be done was to withdraw the remainder of our airborne troops to the south bank of the Rhine.

When I turned round to return to my H.Q., now located in a farmhouse on the Island north of Nijmegen, I found that the road to the rear had been cut by the enemy once again. The hazards of travelling along this stretch of road were typified by the experiences of four Auster aircraft whose pilots were flying senior officers on urgent duties. Major A. Lyell, one of the pilots in this squadron, wrote in *Unarmed into Battle*:

> In September, 1944, after the road from Eindhoven to Nijmegen had been cut between St Oedenrode and Uden, Captain McCorry and a passenger were flying with an urgent message that the supplies had been dropped at Arnhem into German hands, when his aircraft was shot down near Uden and both were killed. At about the same time Captain Stunt with the B.R.A. Second Army (Brigadier Parham) and Captain Salter with the Chief of Staff Second Army (Brigadier Chilton) were flying north and were also heavily engaged by 20-mm. and small arms fire between Uden and Veghel. Stunt and the B.R.A. managed to get through intact, but Salter's aircraft was so severely damaged that he had to crash land a few hundred yards from the wreck of the other aircraft; fortunately, neither he nor his passenger was hurt. The Chief of Staff sat in a ditch and burned his secret documents with a cigarette lighter, before he and Salter, guided by a Dutch farmer, made their way safely back to our lines.
>
> A fourth Auster, carrying Air Vice-Marshal Darvall, who commanded the transport aircraft supplying the Arnhem drop, was also forced to land after being fired on here, all this occurring within the space of half an hour over one short length of road.

The Air Vice-Marshal was flying to Nijmegen personally to investigate complaints by his aircrews that they were being engaged by our own A.A. guns. When he met Brigadier Parham later that day at Nijmegen, where they were both stranded till the corridor was reopened, he was most apologetic, not having realized, as he said, that the British Army had advanced fifty miles on a frontage the width of one road.

I was more fortunate than these three officers, and with the help of the carrier platoon from the Durham Light Infantry I was able, by going across country, to get round the German positions astride the road. At 1000 hours on the 25th, I arrived back at my H.Q. to find a gloomy situation awaiting me. The 4th Dorsets had crossed the Rhine during the night. They had shown the greatest gallantry in their attempts to reach the embattled 1st Airborne, but owing to the murderous enemy fire down both banks and all along the swift running river itself many of their boats had been sunk. Very much reduced in numbers, the battalion had only been able to reach the far bank in small, scattered parties, and all contact with them had now been lost. Artillery ammunition was really becoming dangerously short, one regiment was down to five rounds per gun. Reserves of everything that we wanted – ammunition, assault boats, etc. – were unfortunately on the far side of the 'cut', and, although we did not know it at the time, on this occasion the road was not opened again for four days; so Browning and I decided that the only thing to do was to withdraw the 1st Airborne Division to the south bank that night.

So, on the night of 25–26 September, supported by almost all the artillery ammunition which was left, 2163 airborne troops, 160 Poles and 75 Dorsets came back across the Rhine, some in boats, some swimming; the rain was pouring down and it seemed as though even the gods were weeping at this grievous end to a gallant enterprise. And so the Battle of Arnhem was over.

The main criticism has always been that XXX Corps was very slow. If this is so, it was my fault, because all the troops were imbued with a sense of desperate urgency. I blame myself very much for one oversight. I cannot now imagine why I did not insist on having a high-ranking Dutch officer at my H.Q. The Dutch Army must have carried out numerous exercises over this same ground. I believe that he would have advised me not to attempt the direct approach from Nijmegen to Arnhem, but to order the 43rd Infantry Division to cross the Waal (which we could have easily bridged) farther to the west of Nijmegen, and carry out a left hook against the German forces on the western edge of the airborne perimeter. The Dutch had a brave and very intelligent resistance movement, which supplied us with first-class information. Somehow, I don't feel we made the best use of it.

But even if we had crossed the Neder Rijn and joined up with the Airborne Division we could only have formed a limited bridgehead north of the river. I am certain that an advance to the Zuider Zee would have been out of the question because of the vulnerability of our lines of communication. Anyhow, with the failure of the Battle of Arnhem, all hopes of finishing the war in 1944 were over. The saddest part of it all was that the brave Dutch, who had suffered more than any other occupied country, were thus forced to endure one last terrible winter under German domination.

I cannot end this account of the battle without once again paying a tribute to the splendid courage and intelligence displayed by the Dutch Resistance. Of all the resistance movements we had encountered, the Dutch were easily the best, because their information was always accurate. The Germans never discovered their telephone system along the Waal, which they used to control the waterborne traffic on the Rhine, and as a result we were able to get valuable information very quickly. On one occasion, a member of the Dutch Resistance had come up on the air and reported by wireless that he was in the window of a house at Renkum and could see German troops in considerable numbers crossing the Neder Rijn from north to south. He added that, although he was not a trained artillery observer, he could describe fairly accurately the fall of our artillery concentrations, and this he did with surprising accuracy, causing the Germans considerable casualties. In addition, of course, the Dutch men and women showed great bravery when they hid our wounded and those British soldiers who had managed to escape from the Germans. Thanks entirely to the Dutch, a large number of them eventually got back to our lines.

Perhaps I can best conclude by saying that any great military operation is considerably affected by unpredictable elements. Whereas almost everything had fallen in our favour and gone according to plan during the Normandy landings, Arnhem was just the reverse; nothing seemed to go right.

Chapter 8
The Coastal Flank and the Opening of Antwerp
EVERSLEY BELFIELD

The Arnhem ('Market Garden') battle was the last major attempt by the Allies to reach the Ruhr in 1944. It is understandable that Montgomery, convinced that such an invasion of the heart of Germany could end the war that year, should have resolved to subordinate all other considerations to achieving this goal. It was, however, ironic that, in his single-minded pursuit of this elusive victory, he should have been largely instrumental in producing just the kind of strategic situation that he was most insistent should always be guarded against, namely getting the Allied forces 'out of balance' Probably the most important single reason for the ultimate failure at Arnhem was the logistical lack of balance which was now seriously affecting the whole campaign. Looking back, it can also now be seen that the massive supply problems which had developed can primarily be attributed to the decisions taken (or, more accurately, shelved) on the conduct of operations on the western flank of the Twenty-first Army Group. Here, during September, it was clearly demonstrated that, in the final analysis, this whole campaign had to be regarded as an intricate exercise in team work. Lack of proper concern for the progress in one sector could, and did, throw the course of the war out of gear for months. Although Montgomery must take most of the blame for this misjudgement of priorities, Eisenhower cannot be entirely exonerated; as will be seen, he lacked the firmness and sense of urgency to enforce the carrying out of his directives by Montgomery.

As mentioned earlier, the 11th Armoured Division had captured the docks of Antwerp intact on 4 September and no further orders were given to XXX Corps to advance in this area. Although the 11th Armoured Division did, on their own initiative, try to secure a bridge across the Albert Canal just north of the city, they had not succeeded in doing so before they were ordered to move on 6 September. At this time the Allied Higher Command do not seem to have fully appreciated that this great prize was useless so long as the Germans held both banks of the Scheldt Estuary. On the other hand, the Germans had always recognized the vital strategic value of retaining this 50-mile stretch of low-lying land. Furthermore, they were well aware of the need to delay the whole Allied progress up the coast to the mouth of the Scheldt. During September 1944, the German High Command was determined to impose the maximum possible delay on the Allies and this for two main reasons: first, to gain time for the new war-winning weapons which were soon supposed to be coming into service, and secondly, simply to keep the enemy off their soil. Montgomery, who had a very free hand in pursuing his policy here, virtually turned his back on his western flank, concentrating only on thrusting eastward.

This chapter will have a twofold purpose. First, it will describe the many problems that beset the First Canadian Army in bringing to fruition XXX Corps's *coup de main*, the seizure of the great port of Antwerp and its installations undamaged. Secondly, in doing so, it will draw attention to one of the grimmest and longest battles of this campaign. During

September, the Canadian Army (over half of whose troops were British or Polish) was treated as a kind of odd-job organization, and thus given a very low claim to supplies. Nevertheless, the 4th Division and the Polish Armoured Division both moved very rapidly forward, mopping up pockets of resistance and taking several thousand prisoners *en route*. By the middle of the month, they had taken Bruges and Ghent. Beyond, they met very powerful German resistance based on the system of large canals which connect these inland ports to the coast and the Scheldt Estuary. With its networks of dikes, this southern end of the Estuary was most unsuitable for armour to operate in, nor were adequate numbers of assault boats available. Thus these two Divisions were virtually grounded for the rest of the month. By 23 September the Germans had completed their evacuation. Over 82,000 men and more than 530 guns as well as considerable quantities of equipment had been transported across the Lower Scheldt mainly from Flushing to Walcheren and from Terneuzen to South Beveland. As on the Lower Seine during August, the Allied air attacks had done little to hinder these German ferries.

Along the coast in this early forward drive occurred two moving events: on 1 September, 2nd Canadian Division captured Dieppe, where, during the Raid just over two years before, this Division had lost more than 3000 men. This was indeed more than a symbolic return; Dieppe was taken almost intact and by the end of September it became the largest useable Channel port, handling nearly 7000 tons a day. On 2 September, 51st Highland Division entered St-Valéry-en-Caux, where most of the original Division had been taken prisoner in June 1940.

On 9 September, the Canadian Army's priorities within the Twenty-first Army Group were specified. The first was the capture of Boulogne; the second that of Dunkirk; the third was to eject the Germans out of the region round Ghent; the last, 'to examine and carry out the reduction of the islands guarding the entrance to Antwerp' The rest of September was therefore principally devoted to besieging and capturing the Channel ports. Unaccountably not specifying Dieppe and Ostend, both of which fell without a siege, Hitler had ordered all the other Channel ports to be classed as fortresses and held at all costs.

The first siege to be tackled was that of Le Havre, the largest port in northern France, which had been earmarked for American use. The attack on Le Havre was made by 49th West Riding and 51st Highland Divisions, which then formed I British Corps and stayed with the Canadian Army for the rest of 1944. The approaches to Le Havre were well protected, on the western side by flooding and elsewhere by mines, anti-tank ditches and huge concrete gun emplacements primarily designed for sea defences. The garrison of over 11,000 (underestimated at about 8700) was also strongly provided with artillery. In this siege massive bomber support was received, 4000 tons being dropped beforehand and a further 5500 tons during the attack itself which lasted from 10 to 12 September. The 15-inch guns of H.M.S. *Erebus* and *Warspite* were also brought to bear on the biggest gun emplacements, H.M.S. *Erebus* being hit twice by German batteries during her bombardment. In addition to the divisional artillery, two heavy and six medium regiments (5·5-inch guns firing 100-lb shells) took part in the softening-up process. Under the weight of this physical and psychological pressure the German resistance was less tenacious than had been expected, and this extremely well planned operation was over in forty-eight hours, with less than 400 casualties. The German demolition of the docks had, however, been so thorough that it was over four weeks before the port could be used.

Much farther north on the elongated 200-mile Canadian Army front, 2nd Division was pushing along the rear of the Channel defences. The defenders of Dunkirk, under the redoubtable Admiral Frisius, were most resolute and by means of extensive flooding almost cut themselves off from the hinterland. It was soon apparent that it would need a major effort to capture Dunkirk, and it was decided to abandon any attempt to do so; the garrison was contained and did not surrender until 9 May 1945. On the other hand, Ostend was taken on 9 September without a fight and became a most valuable, if small, port, being the nearest to the Twenty-first Army Group battle front until the opening of Antwerp.

The next port on the list was Boulogne, and here the Royal Artillery devised an original way of supporting the Canadians before and during the siege. An Auster spotting plane was flown out above the Channel to direct the fire of the Dover 14-inch and 15-inch batteries (four guns in all) against the fortified gun emplacements around Cap Gris Nez. At least one direct hit was scored on these large German guns and they were silenced throughout the siege of Boulogne. The pilot had his revenge on an anti-aircraft battery which fired at him by using his huge weapons on their site. Before the gun barrels were so worn out that the shells would no longer carry across the Channel, over 200 rounds had been fired and thus these guns had ended their life just before there was no further use for them.

On 17 September, the first day of the Arnhem battle, the siege of Boulogne began. With I Corps grounded from lack of transport, the only available formation was 3rd Canadian Division, less one brigade, but it was reinforced by some armour and medium regiments of artillery. Although smaller than Le Havre, Boulogne had been well prepared and was a tough nut to crack, with its deep underground fortifications, as well as the usual surrounding forts, minefields and anti-tank defences; in addition it was protected by many gun batteries, most of which emerged unscathed from the only heavy bombing raid, which took place on the opening day. After a much less thorough softening-up process and with about half the number of troops, it took the Canadians six days to capture Boulogne and they suffered 634 casualties, proportionately far higher than those incurred at Le Havre. Over 9500 prisoners were taken, some of whom had finally to be forced out of the very deep concrete bunkers by pumping flame down the ventilation shafts.

By 25 September, the forces of 3rd Canadian Division had moved up to Calais, where much the same procedure was followed as at Boulogne except that more heavy bombing raids took place. Although these did not destroy the solid structures of the forts they had a very demoralizing effect on their defenders. At Calais there was no high ground protecting the town, but the Germans had flooded much of the country, leaving only narrow strips of dry ground along which the attackers had to approach the outlying forts and the citadel itself. Unlike Boulogne, no civilians had been evacuated beforehand; 20,000 of them had so complicated the shrinking German defences that, on 28 September, a 48-hour truce was arranged to get them out. When the fighting was resumed, the garrison had lost heart and their resistance soon ended on 1 October. The Canadian casualties were under 300, and the 7500 prisoners brought the total taken during the clearing of the coastal belt to 30,000. In their northward progress, the troops of First Canadian Army had also overrun very many of the VI, or flying bomb, sites, so ridding southern England of this menace to life and property. But neither the capture of Boulogne, not opened until 12 October, nor of Calais, out of action until November, was of any immediate help in alleviating the supply crisis. On 1 October, therefore, the only two harbours working north of the Seine were Dieppe and the smaller harbour of Ostend, whose combined capacity was about 10,000 tons daily, compared with Antwerp's potential 40,000 tons. It would have been wiser to have masked Boulogne and Calais, whose garrisons like that of Dunkirk were no threat to the Allies. In the meantime, by 21 September, Canadian and Polish Armed Divisions had managed to push forward, to occupy about twenty miles of the southern shores of the Scheldt Estuary, from near Antwerp to the port of Terneuzen.

The confused state of affairs at this period was brought home to me when on 20 September I was told to fly a liaison officer from the II Canadian Corps to try to find the exact whereabouts of the Poles. The Corps H.Q. was then near Ardres, just outside Calais, about seventy-five miles away from where the Poles were thought to be. A light aircraft was the best, and at times almost the only, means of speedy communication. I wrote in my diary:

> I first landed, against orders from the ground, on a short piece of double-track road with a broken bridge at one end and two damaged Austers beside it. This was near Ecloo, where the 4th Canadian Armoured Division was known to be. I was directed

on from there to the small town of Lokeren, half-way between Ghent and St Nicolas. I found a strip there and landed, but the liaison officer never managed to catch up with the Polish divisional commander, nor his chief artillery officer, as both were away with the forward troops and we had to go back without finding them.

Before returning, I had to go on to refuel at the big airfield just outside Antwerp. I remember being surprised on being warned to be very careful not to fly much to the north of the aerodrome as the Germans were still only just the other side of it, on the nearby Albert Canal.

It has now generally been agreed that the most serious strategic blunder in this whole campaign was the delay in opening up Antwerp. Three major causes contributed to this unfortunate state of affairs. The most important of them was the prevailing conviction, from the most senior officers downwards, that victory was only just round the corner. Hence the policy of pushing on into Germany at all costs seemed the obvious, as well as the swiftest, way to end the war in 1944. Secondly, the acute shortage of supplies complicated the issue by posing most awkward questions about priorities, particularly whether or not it was justifiable to try to halt advancing forces in order to divert their very limited resources for a future operation which, as has been mentioned, many leading commanders considered as probably being unnecessary. The third reason for delaying the clearance of the approaches to Antwerp lay in Eisenhower's lack of firm leadership and Montgomery's unwillingness to face facts. The circumstances which caused this state of affairs are worth examining in some depth.

On 3 September, an accurate warning of the impending situation was given when Admiral Ramsay, the Naval Commander-in-Chief, sent a telegram to both S.H.A.E.F. and the Twenty-first Army Group stressing that 'both Antwerp and Rotterdam are highly vulnerable to mining and blocking. If the enemy succeed in their operations the time it will take to open these ports cannot be estimated.' Neither of these two Headquarters heeded this professional advice. In his lengthy report of 9 September, Eisenhower gave priority to the capturing of the deep-water ports of Brest (taken on 18 September after the Germans had completely wrecked it) and Le Havre; but the need to occupy both the banks of the Lower Scheldt as soon as possible was virtually ignored. On 13 September, Eisenhower mildly rebuked Montgomery, remarking, 'I also understand that you are pressing hard to open the Scheldt Estuary.' On 16 September, from the somewhat unexpected quarter of the Combined Chiefs of Staff Meeting in Quebec, Eisenhower received the following message emphasizing 'the necessity for opening up the north-west ports of Antwerp and Rotterdam [*sic*] in particular, before the bad weather sets in' On 22 September, at a top-level S.H.A.E.F. conference, Eisenhower required that the Twenty-first Army Group should 'open the port of Antwerp as a matter of urgency', but equal importance was given to its developing 'operations culminating in a strong attack on the Ruhr from the north' Eisenhower must have been aware which of the two courses of action Montgomery preferred and that the Twenty-first Army Group had insufficient resources to accomplish both simultaneously. On 4 October (a month after XXX Corps had taken Antwerp) Field-Marshal Sir Alan Brooke, the Chief of the Imperial General Staff, intervened. He flew over to

S.H.A.E.F. H.Q., Versailles, where Eisenhower had convened a meeting of the naval and air commanders-in-chief, army group commanders and other very senior officers. Here it was bluntly stated that 'the fact stood out clearly that access to Antwerp must be captured with the least possible delay' The formidable Alan Brooke was obviously exasperated. He wrote in his diary, 'I feel that Monty's strategy for once is at fault. Instead of carrying out the advance on Arnhem, he ought to have made certain of Antwerp in the first place. He [Eisenhower] nobly took all the blame on himself, as he had approved Monty's suggestion to operate on Arnhem.'

It is interesting to trace Montgomery's reactions. During the most critical period, 3–14 September, he issued no formal directives to his Armies, but only somewhat vague individual letters and orders. This apparent paralysis may have been a part of a policy designed to give him the maximum flexibility while arguing with Eisenhower against the Broad Front policy. As far as the Canadian Army was concerned, this resulted in a most unrealistic approach to their tasks. On 13 September Montgomery asked the Canadian Army whether it could capture Boulogne, Dunkirk and Calais and simultaneously start opening Antwerp! With the very limited transport and the troops strung out along the 200 miles from Le Havre to near Antwerp this was an utterly impracticable suggestion. On 14 September, that is before the sieges of Boulogne and Calais had been started, Montgomery instructed Crerar that 'the whole energies of the Canadian Army will be directed towards operations designed to enable full use to be made of the port of Antwerp' Montgomery refused to transfer the British 53rd Division, then in the Antwerp area, to the Canadians; it was earmarked for flank protection for 'Market Garden' The dramatic and tragic effects of this operation dominated the Twenty-first Army Group's policy-making to the exclusion of all else until 27 September. Even then, in a major directive, Montgomery still insisted that the Twenty-first Army Group had two main objectives: one was the capture of the Ruhr and the other the opening of Antwerp. Only on 16 October did Montgomery issue the uncompromising order that 'operations designed to open the port [Antwerp] will therefore be given complete priority over all other offensive operations by the Twenty-first Army Group, without any qualification whatsoever' This prolonged lack of a sense of urgency over the opening of Antwerp is now almost incomprehensible.

Even discounting the plentiful evidence of German activity, a glance at the map should have been sufficient to convince anyone that the Scheldt Estuary was ideally suited to defensive operations. The longer therefore that Antwerp's conquest was postponed, the more formidable would be the Allied task, particularly with winter approaching.

The clearance of the approaches to Antwerp was a Canadian responsibility. As the Corps Commander in this area, Simonds had, by mid-September, begun to examine the problems involved in this very extensive operation; Canadian Army H.Q. was also involved in the planning and as Crerar had to go back to hospital in England, Simonds took over command of the Army at this time. Although no detailed planning could start until the end of September, some important preliminary studies had been undertaken beforehand. These soon revealed serious differences of opinion as to the type and the scale of the forces needed. Simonds concluded that, if this highly complex operation was to succeed without undue losses or delays, continuous and substantial support would be required from all three Services, and that this should be granted top-level priority. Such widespread claims on resources soon met with vigorous opposition, and three particularly contentious issues emerged. The first was Simonds's proposal to employ some airborne troops. These, he declared, would provide the extra support essential in speedily securing the two places which control access on to and off the narrow South Beveland isthmus; this is the sole land link between the island of Walcheren and the Netherlands mainland. Although by 1 October the very experienced 6th British Airborne Division was again ready for action, repeated Canadian requests for airborne assistance were rejected by Lieut.-Gen. Brereton, Commander of the Allied Airborne Army, and Eisenhower would not overrule his objections. Probably fear of another Arnhem-style disaster was responsible for the withholding of this valuable assistance. Secondly, Simonds asked that he should be given the right to call for uninterrupted support from both British and American heavy bombers to be used against the numerous well-sited and heavily fortified German defences, many of which could only be attacked head-on and by amphibious landings. This plea was turned down as tending to divert these bombers for too long from their proper role which was seen as the bombing of targets in Germany. Thus the Canadians could rely only on some relatively weak and intermittent backing from R.A.F. Bomber Command and on nothing at all from the American heavy bombers. Finally Simonds wanted the sea defences of Walcheren breached and the island flooded. This was as much a political as a military issue, and on 1 October Eisenhower agreed to this proposal.

As a combined operation, the battle for the opening of the approaches to Antwerp developed into an undertaking second only in scope to the Normandy landings. At one time, the Canadian Army consisted of five infantry and two armoured divisions, two Commando brigades, as well as several smaller formations; a large proportion of the medium and heavy regiments of the Twenty-first Army Group were involved as were a monitor and two battleships, mounting altogether ten 15-inch guns; in addition there were scores of naval amphibious craft, and finally hundreds of aircraft of all types were engaged in bombing and strafing. Despite these massive forces, this highly complex operation proved a costly affair and lasted seven weeks. The terrible weather and the waterlogged terrain made it a very messy business.

In its opening stages, this battle was fought in two entirely separate sectors. In the eastern sector, to be described first, the main object was to advance northwards from Antwerp to the South Beveland isthmus to enable an attack to be made along there upon the island of Walcheren. A secondary but important objective was to sweep forward on a broad front of about thirty miles to the line of the River Maas from north of Breda to the coast, thereby eliminating the narrow Nijmegen salient. Such a movement would safeguard the western flank of the British Second Army, from which it had been attacked on several occasions during the latter part of September. Montgomery also hoped that success here might yet lead to the British being able to resume their advance on the Ruhr that autumn. This large sector was given to Lieut.-Gen. Crocker's British I Corps, whose multi-national force consisted of British, American, Canadian and Polish formations. Facing I Corps was the LXVII German Corps, which was almost entirely composed of troops who had earlier escaped along the South Beveland isthmus.

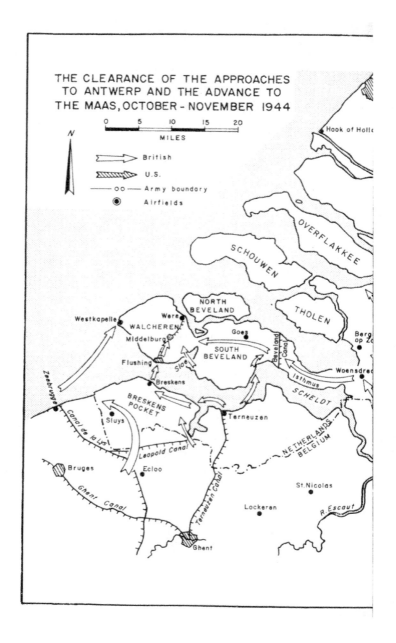

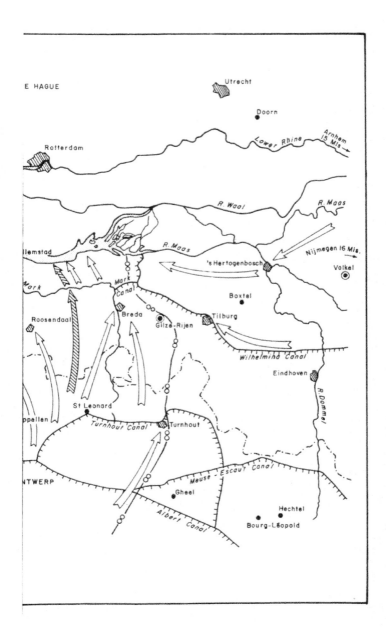

Some fighting began on 23 September, when the Canadians tried to break out from Antwerp on the east and swing round to outflank it; but their attempts were contained by strong German resistance. The full offensive began on 2 October. During the rest of October and on into early November, there ensued, in north-western Belgium and the southern Netherlands, some of the dreariest campaigning of the war.

In order to stress the gravity of this forthcoming battle, General von Zangen, the Commander of the German Fifteenth Army, had circulated a message to all his units, emphasizing that 'the German people is watching us. In this hour, the fortifications along the Scheldt occupy a role which is decisive for the future of our people. Each additional day that you deny the port of Antwerp to the enemy and all its resources will be vital.' On the right wing of the Canadian Army, the Germans had made the fullest use of the low-lying terrain to impose upon the Allies the greatest delay and the heaviest casualties possible. Mines had been plentifully distributed, especially in the tracts of forest and heathland, while many of the isolated farmhouses had been converted into strongpoints; these were best eliminated by the Churchill 'Crocodile' flame-throwing tanks (I remember watching from the air the large ball of flame being spewed out of the tank to bounce slowly to the building and then a pause, as if nothing was happening, before a sheet of flame enveloped the whole structure). The most troublesome and punishing obstacles were the roads which were often built up on exposed embankments. With the surrounding fields too marshy to bear the weight of tracked or armoured vehicles, the infantry had, time and again, to edge forward yard by yard, protected as far as possible by machine-gun, artillery and mortar fire. Starting early in October, this offensive by a

Canadian, a British, an American and a Polish division took a month to cover about twenty-five miles. By then the leading formations had reached the soggy banks of the Maas Estuary, where the front remained static for the rest of the war. Although generally unspectacular, this sort of laborious fighting was typical of the little-publicized, but essential, campaigning that characterized the war during the late autumn and winter of 1944–5.

On each flank of this right wing, two very hard-fought but little-known battles took place. At the eastern extremity, in the process of linking up with the British Second Army, the Polish Armoured Division was ordered to take Breda, one of the largest towns in this region and occupying a vital strategic position. The Germans had compelled the Dutch civilians to dig, at some distance outside the town, a large anti-tank ditch. This almost encircled Breda, and the Germans had constructed strong defences based on this extensive line. In conjunction with the Second Army's 7th Armoured Division and the newly-arrived 104th U.S. Division, the Poles managed, partly by a surprise enveloping movement, to capture the town in four days. The citizens of Breda were particularly grateful that their liberation had been achieved without recourse to heavy aerial or artillery bombardments. The Poles, who spent most of the rest of the winter in Breda, were made very welcome and came to regard the town as a little Poland. Their losses of nearly 1000 men killed, wounded and missing, were similar to those of the other divisions in this offensive.

On the extreme left edge of this flank of the conflict, the Germans resisted even more desperately, throwing in the Battle Group Chill, one of their toughest formations that had been originally formed to stem the British advance beyond Brussels.

The key position here was the small village of Woensdrecht that commanded the mainland approach to the South Beveland isthmus. Although the 2nd Canadian Division soon obtained a foothold on the base of the isthmus, it was held up there from 7 to 16 October, losing very heavily in a series of unsuccessful frontal attacks, there being no possible way here of outflanking the German defences. The stalemate was ended only when the 4th Canadian Armoured and the 49th British Division pressed forward farther inland to capture Bergen op Zoom and Roosendaal, thus sealing off the South Beveland isthmus. By 24 October, the Germans had begun to retreat and had flooded part of this narrow neck of land. It was to help in this battle that Simonds had originally asked for an airborne brigade to be dropped.

It is now necessary to switch over to the other, the western, sector of the Canadian Army, where they were confronted with the daunting obstacle of the Breskens Pocket, also known as the Scheldt Fortress South. From east to west, it measured about twenty-five miles; from north to south about twelve miles. The Belgian-Dutch coast and the Scheldt Estuary formed its western and northern sides, while the other two, the landward, flanks had been almost sealed off by the very widespread flooding of this low-lying region. Within its boundaries, the small towns and villages, as well as some old forts, had been turned into strongpoints. The defence was in the hands of Gen. Eberling's 64th Division which, though just formed, was composed of 14,000 experienced troops on leave from other fronts. It was supported by heavy guns on Walcheren Island and had over 500 machine-guns and mortars, in addition to 300 other guns. Two Allied divisions were employed, the 3rd Canadian and 52nd (Lowland); paradoxically the newly arrived

Scottish Lowland Division had been trained for mountain warfare but went into action for the first time on ground which was mainly below sea-level – it was, however, the last major reserve formation in the British Army. Indeed, on both sides, there was a growing difficulty in finding trained infantrymen; in one under-strength Canadian regiment, less than half of its 379 combatant soldiers had had more than three months' training, while 174 of its most recent recruits had had one month's training or less.

On 6 October, an attack was made against one of the very few dry places on the perimeter of the Breskens Pocket. But even here the wide Leopold Canal, running between high banks, had first to be crossed. Although the Canadians managed this, a week's fighting saw little further progress, and the cost to the brigade involved was 533 casualties, of whom 111 were killed. The stalemate here gave added importance to the success of what had originally been conceived of as a subsidiary thrust by another brigade. On the night of 9 October, its vanguard embarked on 96 amphibious vehicles at Terneuzen. They moved off in two columns into the waters of the Scheldt Estuary and two hours later came ashore on the north-eastern corner of the Pocket. The Germans did not realize their presence before the morning, and by then reinforcements were already being ferried in under cover of a smoke-screen. Nevertheless German opposition was far from ended, and it was not until 3 November that all resistance in the Pocket was finally subdued. Sluys (where Edward III's fleet had defeated the French in the Hundred Years War) and Zeebrugge (famous for the raid in the First World War) were almost the last places taken. The scale of the fighting is evident from a few statistics. The prisoners numbered 12,707, but the 3rd

Canadian Division's losses were 2077, of whom 500 were killed, the Germans probably suffered an equal mortality rate.

By the end of October, the battle for the control of the Scheldt Estuary was entering its last stages, these centred on the capture of Walcheren where it was certain that the Germans would resist tenaciously. Before this offensive could be started, it was essential to gain control of South Beveland. It will be recalled that the 2nd Canadian Division was last mentioned when it had reached the mile-wide neck of the South Beveland isthmus. On 24 October, it resumed its advance and by the 28th it had covered the eleven miles to the large ship canal that severs South Beveland from the isthmus. The Canadians were greatly assisted in dislodging the Germans here by the outflanking movement of the Lowland Division who had sent troops from Terneuzen to land on the south part of South Beveland. By 31 October, South Beveland had been cleared of the enemy.

The clearance of the Breskens Pocket and the capture of the isthmus and South Beveland had removed three out of the four major obstacles blocking the approaches to the port of Antwerp. The final and most formidable, Walcheren, still remained to be tackled. Nearly square in shape, this island extends about twelve miles from north to south and about ten miles from east to west, and dominates the seaward entrance to the Scheldt Estuary. In configuration it resembles a big saucer. Most of its interior is below sea-level and massive sea-walls, up to 30 feet in height and 300 yards in width, protect its shores. After a series of raids, in which over 2500 tons of bombs were dropped, R.A.F. heavy bombers had breached these walls in four separate places and thus, by the middle of October, most of Walcheren had been inundated. Protruding from these watery wastes were the port of Flushing, the town of Middelburg and some land to the east of it, as well as long stretches of the great sea-walls and the dunes that stretch behind them. Cooped up, chiefly in the towns, were 8000 experienced German troops of the 70th Division. Known as the 'white bread' division, they had been invalided from the other fronts with gastric disorders; yet, despite their internal ailments, men from this division had already fought very tenaciously and skilfully in South Beveland. In addition to anti-aircraft guns, there were some fifty guns in fortified sites scattered around the perimeter of Walcheren, these guns, some of them very large, were served by special crews.

The invasion of Walcheren concluded the amphibious assaults in this campaign. Unlike the Normandy landings, complete surprise could not be achieved, but as in the Invasion, the two major determining factors were still the weather, unlikely to improve as the winter days drew in, and the tides, which were favourable only from 1 to 4 or from 14 to 17 November With the Allied supply crisis worsening, there was naturally considerable inducement to risk the earlier dates, even if the weather looked unpromising both at sea and in the air. The preliminary bombing had been given much lower priority than had been asked for, and accordingly, the four massive concreted gun emplacements commanding the sea lanes were largely intact. D-Day experience, further confirmed during the Channel Port sieges, had proved that nothing less than prolonged heavy bombing could destroy such fortifications; even the largest naval and land guns made little impression on such structures.

It was decided to attack Walcheren in three separate places, and on 31 October the Canadians opened the offensive from the east. Here the island is linked to South Beveland by an exposed road and rail causeway 1200 yards long and 40 yards wide. Half-way along it, the Germans had scooped out a broad ditch which was filled with water, at the Walcheren end, they had built a substantial road block, and from the raised dike walls on either side of it they could rake the flanks of the bare causeway with anti-tank and machine-gun fire and bring down artillery concentrations anywhere along its length. The adjacent shores of both South Beveland and Walcheren were almost impassable mud flats ending in tidal creeks. Tanks could not hope to survive on this narrow raised platform, no airborne troops were available to be dropped on the defenders, and so the hard-pressed infantry had to be used once again. An attack on the first day made little progress and had to be abandoned. On 1 November, despite intense direct and indirect German fire, a few troops succeeded in getting on to Walcheren, only to be repelled by a fierce counter-attack. On 2 November, under cover of an artillery barrage, another small body of Canadians crossed the causeway but were too weak to enlarge their tenuous bridgehead, and on the following day were relieved by Scottish troops from the 52nd Division who took over this front from them. The main attack was now switched two miles south, where assault boats had been assembled, and on 3 November a night-crossing of the creek was made, followed by a hazardous approach march of nearly a mile over the soft, sinking sands and mud before terra firma could be reached. No opposition was encountered until daylight, but the link-up with troops across the causeway took another two days of fighting, by which time the German resistance had begun to collapse everywhere.

The second place chosen for attack was Flushing, at the southern end of Walcheren. As the Dutch population had not been evacuated no heavy bombing was permitted, and it was with difficulty that authority was obtained even for fighter bombers to be employed against targets in the dock area in this strongly fortified town. The attack was launched from Breskens, where over 300 guns had been concentrated to give massive artillery backing. The assault was led by an Army (as opposed to a Marine) Commando who fought its way ashore in the early morning of 1 November, with few casualties. It was soon joined by a brigade of the 52nd Division, and these troops spent the next three days in harsh street-fighting, winkling the Germans out of their innumerable strongpoints.

The third attack, the most hazardous, dramatic and costly, was directed at Westkapelle on the western tip of Walcheren, where the great sea-wall had earlier been breached by the R.A.F. On the night of 31 October, despite uncertain weather reports, the Marine Commando under Brigadier Leicester, and the attendant naval force, under Captain Pugsley, R.N., sailed from Ostend on their 30-mile voyage. The brigade was transported in a variety of landing-craft, 150 in all, and was supported by twenty-seven gun and rocket-firing vessels. With Westkapelle beyond the range of all but a handful of the biggest guns on the mainland, three warships, H.M.S. *Warspite, Erebus* and *Roberts*, were attached to provide support from their 15-inch guns; it was known that most of the heavy German gun positions were undamaged. Although the weather at sea improved, low cloud had prevented any heavy attacks that night and stopped most flying in the morning, and so the R.A.F. did not provide spotter aircraft for the warships' guns, which had to rely on visual corrections; Air Observation Post aircraft could not be used effectively as their wireless sets were too feeble. Nevertheless during the critical morning hours of 1 November the 15-inch guns gave invaluable support.

Just before 0800 hours, the 27-strong naval support squadron, under Commander Sellar, split into groups as they made the final run in towards Westkapelle. To reduce losses in the more vulnerable landing-craft that were carrying the troops, they intended to draw the German fire on themselves and this they did. With unarmoured vessels and guns often firing over lowered ramps, they presented excellent targets, but they continued until 1230 hours when only seven vessels still remained fit for action. Out of a complement of about 1000 men (over half of them Marines), 170 had then been killed and 200 wounded. R.A.F. rocket-carrying Typhoons joined in this maelstrom, and the main force began to arrive at about 1000 hours. Getting their amphibious vehicles ashore was not easy and most of the tanks were lost, but by the afternoon the Commandos had firmly established themselves in and around Westkapelle. The heaviest German battery had now run out of ammunition and the German positions, isolated by floods, began to surrender. By the evening the Marines had fanned out in both directions from Westkapelle and were moving around the rim of the island; their 'mopping up' operation continued for the next two days. On 3 November, an enterprising force in amphibious vehicles sailed from Flushing to Middelburg where the commander of the 2000-strong garrison was persuaded to surrender. Flushing's commander capitulated on 4 November and the few outlying strongpoints had abandoned the fight by the 6th. Minesweeping began on the 4th, on the 26th a channel had been cleared, and on the 28th the first convoy reached the port of Antwerp, which soon became the main supply port for the Allied forces in North-West Europe.

From 1 October to 8 November, the fighting to open up Antwerp had cost the Allies 12,800 casualties, half of whom were Canadians. The prisoners totalled 41,000. Taking the period from D-Day (6 June) to 30 June, the larger British and Canadian forces had suffered 24,698 casualties and this included the airborne units. Thus by any standards, the opening of Antwerp had been not only a lengthy but a costly affair.

Chapter 9
The November Offensive Geilenkirchen–
The little-known battle
SIR BRIAN HORROCKS

Eisenhower was still hoping to finish the war in 1944. On 18 October he arrived in Brussels with Tedder and Bradley to explain to Montgomery his plans for the further conduct of the campaign. In view of the parlous Allied administrative situation, Montgomery had already given the opening of Antwerp an unequivocal priority over all other operations by the Twenty-first Army Group – a decision enthusiastically approved by the other three Commanders.

Eisenhower then explained precisely what his Broad Front policy involved. Using U.S. First Army as the main effort, Bradley's Twelfth Army Group would attack early in November to gain a footing across the Rhine south of Cologne. On its left Simpson's Ninth Army would also drive towards the Rhine, protecting the First Army's left flank. Later it would turn north, between the Rhine and the Maas, in conjunction with a thrust from Nijmegen by the Twenty-first Army Group. Having thus closed with the Rhine, Eisenhower proposed to encircle the Ruhr with Ninth Army in the north and First Army in the south. Montgomery was thus left in no doubt that he would no longer be responsible for the main part of the northern thrust into Germany. If logistics permitted, Patton's Third Army was to advance in a north-easterly direction on the

Saar. Those who knew Patton had no doubt that logistics would permit.

Sixth Army was to resume its advance towards Strasbourg, with the First French Army on its southern flank. To make cooperation easier between Patton and Hodges, Bradley was ordered to locate his own Headquarters at Luxembourg: this was soon to place him in a most embarrassing position south of the Ardennes. 'We were certain', wrote Eisenhower in *Crusade in Europe*, 'that by continuing an unremitting offensive we would, in spite of hardship and privation, gain additional advantage over the enemy. Specifically we were convinced that this policy would result in shortening the war and therefore in the saving of thousands of Allied lives.' Finally, the thought that Hitler might still have it in his power to stage a counter-offensive does not seem to have entered anyone's calculations.

For Twelfth Army Group Headquarters the immediate situation on their front, north and south of Aachen, was not reassuring. Although the northern outskirts of the Hürtgen Forest had been reached in September, little progress had been made since then, and Aachen itself did not fall until 21 October. Throughout October the revitalized German formations exploited to the full the difficulties of the terrain. Thick woods hemmed in the few roads; the fire-breaks and all the tracks in the forest were knee-deep in mud from the abnormally heavy October rain. Surprisingly, there was a shortage of ammunition, arising from the failure of American industry to keep pace with the expenditure in Normandy. In planning his offensive, Bradley aimed initially at securing crossings over the River Rur (Roer) which traversed his front seven miles ahead. To reach it, First Army, attacking on III Corps' front, would have to fight its way through the Hürtgen Forest three miles deep. On its flanks stretched heavily built up industrial areas. Immediately east of the River Wurm, however, the country was more open, with large villages surrounded by big unharvested fields. Facing the Americans, Model had both the Fifth Panzer Army and the reconstituted Seventh Army. Unknown to the Americans, behind them he had already started to form another Panzer Army – the Sixth – particularly strong in artillery; his infantry losses, too, had been made up with some troops, admittedly of low category, but well qualified to give a good account of themselves in fixed and well-concealed offensives. Finally, he had ready to hand, as a 'Fire Brigade', XLVII Panzer Corps, consisting of two first-class divisions, well up to strength in infantry, tanks and self-propelled guns.

During September, Montgomery had thrust towards Arnhem, and Bradley towards Aachen. A huge gap had then developed between their Army Groups in the Peel marshes, a large forlorn area west of the Maas, and about ten miles east of Eindhoven. In this unattractive area, at the end of September, the Americans had committed a small and oddly constituted force, which failed to make progress towards the Maas, and quiet descended on this dismal front. Late in October, hoping to take the pressure off his troops in the South Beveland peninsula and the rest of Holland, Model had ordered XLVII Panzer Corps to investigate the area about Meijel. To the surprise of both sides, the Germans drove the Americans back ten miles in a three-day offensive, and in so doing threatened the rear areas of British Second Army. Montgomery took immediate steps to plug the gap with two divisions sent from west Holland. Although Model was tempted to try a large-scale raid behind the British lines, of the type with which Rommel had familiarized them in North Africa, von Rundstedt refused, wanting to use his XLVII Panzer Corps elsewhere. The German force had achieved its aim with the loss of thirty tanks.

In accordance with Eisenhower's plan, Montgomery on 2 November ordered a complete re-deployment of his Army Group. First Canadian Army now assumed responsibility for the front, from the sea to the Reichswald. This would take time to carry out, but in the meanwhile Second Army was ordered, without delay, to clear the Germans west of the Maas from the huge pocket between Venray and Roermond. As soon as possible they would take over the American front north of Geilenkirchen, known as the Heinsberg Salient.

In this redistribution of forces, XXX Corps was switched from the Nijmegen area to the American front north of Geilenkirchen. These changes made it even more apparent that the British were once again sadly short of infantry. In September Montgomery had had to disband 59th Division to make good the losses in Normandy. The famous 50th Northumbrian Division, which had fought all the way from Alamein, had been one of the first divisions to land on D-Day and had been in the forefront of the battle ever since, now had to be broken up, to provide manpower elsewhere. Very soon their famous Tyne/Tees sign disappeared from the battlefield, except on the divisional R.A.S.C. vehicles. Montgomery could see no justification whatever for dissipating his dwindling infantry resources in Bradley's coming offensive south of Geilenkirchen and the Hürtgen Forest; in the short, damp and dark days of November, he had no illusions as to its likely outcome: memories of Passchendaele in similar circumstances had burnt deep.

The boundary between the British and American armies ran along the sluggish River Wurm that flowed north-eastwards through the town of Geilenkirchen, to join the River Rur seven miles further on. The town itself was surrounded with clusters of pillboxes which also flanked the south-east bank of the river, as part of the Siegfried defence system, and ran right up to the Rur. Gently undulating slopes, pock-marked with small but strongly built villages and several thick woods, rose gradually on each side of the Wurm. From Geilenkirchen radiated six main roads, which Ninth Army urgently needed to enable it to deploy. The Geilenkirchen Salient thus formed a wedge between the British XXX Corps and Ninth Army which it was vital to eliminate. The proposed two-pronged attack, with the British on one flank and the Americans on the other, dictated that one H.Q. should be in control of the operation. The British were known to have greater ammunition stocks than the Americans and in the 79th Armoured Division they possessed assault equipment of more advanced design. Fortunately, the personal relations between British Second Army, XXX Corps and the American Ninth Army, despite the fact that the Americans had only recently arrived in the theatre, were already cordial.

My own relations with General Simpson, the Ninth Army Commander, were particularly good. Although XXX Corps had not been assigned an attacking role in the forthcoming offensive, Simpson proposed to me that we should support the Ninth Army's drive by taking the town of Geilenkirchen. To capture it himself, he argued, would mean overextending his front. Much as I wanted to help I had only one division, the 43rd (Wessex), at my disposal, and this was clearly a task for which two would be needed. As neither the Twenty-first Army

Group nor the Second Army could be persuaded to lend me extra troops, I did not see how we could overcome this problem.

Soon afterwards, however, I had dinner at Simpson's H.Q. with Eisenhower, who was visiting the area. The question of Geilenkirchen came up again, and I explained my difficulties to Eisenhower. His immediate response was to offer me the newly arrived American 84th Division.

This of course was highly gratifying, but I had considerable misgivings. For one thing, in order to take Geilenkirchen we would have to break through the heavily defended Siegfried Line, and I felt this was asking a lot from troops who had no previous battle experience. Also it seemed to me that for reasons of morale they would be better led by an American. But these objections were simply brushed aside by Eisenhower and Simpson, and I soon found myself agreeing to attack Geilenkirchen with my two divisions.

The 84th was an impressive product of American training methods which turned out division after division complete, fully equipped and trained for war. Their staff work, however, was not yet geared to battle conditions. Each morning Simpson held a conference, at which someone from each branch of his staff had to stand up and 'say his bit' I attended one of these and found it a complete waste of time – a commodity which is always in short supply in war. In an experienced corps like the one I was privileged to command, ten minutes with my Chief of Staff each morning before setting off to 'smell the battlefield' was quite sufficient.

As soon as the 84th U.S. Division came under my command and was positioned in the line prior to their attack, I went forward, as was my normal practice, to 'smell this new

American battlefield' and have a look at their objectives. On arrival in the area I was halted abruptly by a U.S. sentry who, in the best style of the normal U.S. Western film, leaped out from behind a tree, pointing his rifle menacingly at my stomach, and shouted 'Who the hell are you?' I got out of my jeep somewhat gingerly and replied, 'I am a Britisher – and what's more, your Division has just been placed under my command.' Looking at me most incredulously, he asked my rank, and when I said, 'A three-star General', he said, 'Holy Moses! We don't see many of them up here.' He then became very friendly and I was able to meet and chat to a number of these fine-looking young soldiers. It soon became obvious that, with the exception of the U.S. Paratroop Divisions, whose commanders literally lived with their forward troops (and, of course, with the exception of Patton) the normal U.S. Corps and Divisional Commanders rarely, if ever, visited their forward troops, who hardly knew what they looked like. This was something I had to put right without delay, because of the appalling wintry conditions which the 84th were likely to meet in this their first experience of battle, opposed by experienced, battle-hardened German troops. This situation in many ways brought back to me vivid memories of the First World War, when we, the forward troops, had little use for our superior commanders, who lived in large chateaux behind the lines, while we inhabited muddy trenches. I remembered suddenly the famous story of a young officer who was posted to Corps H.Q. the day before the launching of a massive offensive in which his unit was taking part. That evening the rain came down in bucketfuls, and while sitting at the Corps H.Q. dinner table, complete with white tablecloth, etc., he gazed out of the window, and during a pause in the conversation was heard to say, 'I feel dreadful sitting here in comfort when all my friends are crouched in muddy trenches in the pouring rain, waiting to go over the top tomorrow.' The Corps Commander looked up, snorted, and said, 'Don't be stupid, they have got their groundsheets – pass the port.' This story went straight round the army and showed only too clearly what we thought of our superior commanders. On the rare occasions when they did visit us they were much too brave to take the normal precautions, but stood up, wearing their red hats which where visible to the Boche over the parapet. After their departure the Germans invariably brought down a heavy artillery concentration on our unfortunate heads. In view of this, we always displayed a large notice at the entrance to our trenches, which read: 'Please remember that we LIVE here.'

Most of the senior commanders in the Second World War had served in the First World War and had thus learnt their lesson, and now lived in caravans in the forward area, visiting the front frequently. I won't say for one moment that the U.S. troops hated their senior officers as we had done. They simply did not know them, so their Divisional and Corps Commanders had very little influence on the actual battle after it had begun. Oddly enough, the senior officers did not seem to worry much about the welfare of their troops, and regimental *esprit de corps* was largely absent, or at least not obvious. This was something that we British officers had learnt the hard way as junior commanders. I remember in August 1914 having, at the age of 18, brought out 95 reinforcements to join the 1st Battalion of the Middlesex Regiment, during the battle of Le Cateau. I was then given command of No. 16 Platoon, and we set off on that famous race for the Channel Ports, which meant endless, exhausting marching day after day and bivouacking for the night in wet fields, which had usually been overpopulated by cows. My Company Commander, Gibbons, was a wonderful example. Although he had a horse, never once during those gruelling days did he ride. Usually, he marched in the rear of the company, carrying at least two rifles which were too heavy for smaller men of his company. On one occasion the Adjutant offered the officers accommodation in a house where Battalion H.Q. was billeted. Gibbons was furious. 'If the men sleep out, we sleep out!' he shouted. He held me entirely responsible for the welfare of my platoon. Woe betide me if I attempted to have my meal before reporting to him, 'No. 16 Platoon fed and settled in for the night as comfortably as possible, sir.' There was nothing unusual in this. It was the splendid family spirit which pervaded all the regiments in the old British Regular Army.

Curiously enough, except in certain specialized units, such as the airborne troops and the Marines, this 'family spirit' did not seem to exist to the same extent in the U.S. Army.

Early in the Second World War, during the withdrawal to Dunkirk, I had learnt the value of Commanders 'smelling the battlefield' Montgomery was an adept at this. He would suddenly appear at an H.Q. which was having a difficult time, and while sympathizing with the Company, Battalion or Brigade staff, all the while he would be slipping into the conversation little pieces of good news – the arrival of fresh reserves, a successful air strike, and so forth – and one could feel the atmosphere lightening almost visibly. When we emerged I could just imagine the Adjutant, Brigade-Major or Chief of Staff concerned, who probably hadn't slept for the last twenty-four hours, looking revitalized, and saying to the others, 'Well, well, things are not so bad after all.' Montgomery once told me, 'If you go in, slap everybody on the back and show no awareness of their difficulties, you will have the reverse effect to the one you hope to achieve.' He was also very good at gathering a group of soldiers round him, handing out packets of cigarettes and explaining the situation on a large map which he always carried in his car.

Now the 84th U.S. Division, though completely raw, was composed of splendid, very brave, tough young men. I knew from past bitter experience that they were faced by a very, very unpleasant introduction to war. After capturing the heavily defended Siegfried Line they would have to stand up to vicious counter-attacks by two first-class German Divisions, the 15th Panzer and the 10th SS. Moreover, according to the experts, we were about to experience the worst possible weather conditions, rain pouring down until the ground turned into a soggy, glutinous marsh. Unfortunately, for once they were only too correct.

I was determined that the 84th should have every possible assistance, so for tank support I gave them my most experienced armoured regiment, the Sherwood Rangers Yeomanry, commanded by Stanley Christopherson, some flails and flame tanks from the 79th Division and, above all, the support of my superb Corps Artillery.

This was a very hard-fought battle, as the 84th U.S. Division on the right and the 43rd Wessex on the left launched their attacks on 18 November against the Geilenkirchen Salient. The raw U.S. troops met tough opposition, but they gradually captured the town, house by house, with the help of our tanks, flame-throwers and, of course, artillery concentration. Now we began to experience winter public enemy No. 1 – rain. After continuous rain the ground became so sodden that even the tanks were bogged, and the Germans as usual began launching the vicious counter-attacks which I had expected. Realizing that the situation was becoming confused, I went forward on the night of the 20th, a particularly unpleasant drive in pitch darkness, made worse by torrential rain, and eventually found Advanced Headquarters, 214 Brigade, of the 43rd Division, almost in the front line. There I met Brigadier Essame, who as usual had spent most of the day with the leading troops of his brigade. He warned me not to go farther, as this was what he laconically described as 'Jeep Head', with the enemy very active and only a few hundred yards away.

I gave him permission to withdraw his leading battalion, the Duke of Cornwall's Light Infantry, from the village of Hoven, the sharp point of our advance which now resembled a triangle. He declined, however, on the grounds that they had suffered heavy casualties in capturing the village and it would be bad for morale to withdraw them now. He was confident that they could beat off the counter-attacks which were now being launched by the battle-experienced 15th Panzer and 10th SS Divisions. I agreed and promised to try to get the 84th U.S. Division farther forward on his right. This was now warfare at its most beastly, with continuous cold, driving rain turning the ground into a sea of mud and constant counter-attacks from experienced German troops.

I spent most of my time, however, smelling the 84th battlefield, using the Montgomery technique. I was greatly concerned to find that the troops in the front line were not getting hot meals. My own experience had shown me that this was a matter of the utmost importance, for troops cannot go on fighting at their best in winter without hot food, and whatever the difficulties it must be got to them. In spite of ever-worsening conditions, each day the forward units of the 43rd

Division received not only a hot meal, but also a dry pair of socks, in order to prevent the spread of that winter scourge, 'trench feet.' The inexperienced U.S. Commanders soon learnt the value of my 'smelling the battlefield' technique, and in the following days I was glad to see a rapid improvement in the administration of supplies.

The 84th eventually secured their objectives. Ideally they should then have been rested, but the circumstances of war dictated otherwise, and they could not be spared from what had now become a static front. On 23 November the 84th reverted to U.S. control.

The Battle of Geilenkirchen is barely mentioned in most military histories, yet it was one of the hardest-fought actions of the whole war at the Battalion, Company and Platoon level. I was filled with admiration for the extreme gallantry displayed by the raw G.I.s of the 84th Division. If only their administration and staff arrangements had been up to the level of their courage, the veteran German troops might well have had a bloody nose. Although it was no business of mine, I was very annoyed by the patronizing attitude of the First and Third U.S. Armies towards the newcomer, the Ninth U.S. Army, which in this, its first action, had proved that it could fight just as well as, if not better than, some of the so-called veteran U.S. divisions had in Normandy.

In the short hours of daylight of late November and early December in almost incessant rain and sleet the Ninth, First, Third and Sixth American Armies continued this nightmare battle. South of Aachen the main effort cost 24,000 casualties plus a further 9000 sick who succumbed to the misery of the Hürtgen Forest with trench foot, respiratory diseases and battle exhaustion. By the time they reached the Rur, in mid-

December, they were still twenty-five miles from the Rhine. Farther south, Patton's progress had been more spectacular and less costly: by early December he had substantial bridgeheads over the Saar and had penetrated the Siegfried Line.

Chapter 10
The Ardennes Battle

I. Introduction
SIR BRIAN HORROCKS

Early in December 1944 Montgomery gave me the outlines of our next operation, a massive affair which came to be known as the Battle of the Reichswald. In order to start planning, XXX Corps very quietly began to pull out of the line on 13 December, while Corps H.Q. moved to Boxtel. Incidentally, it was the first time that the Corps had not been responsible for part of the front line since landing in Normandy. It was a wonderful relief, and leave was granted liberally. Thanks to the kindness and hospitality of the Belgian people, Brussels and the surrounding villages became the most popular leave centre in Europe.

I myself took up a standing invitation from Queen Elisabeth of the Belgians to visit the Palace of Laeken on the outskirts of Brussels, where the Queen Mother lived alone, with one lady-in-waiting, La Baronne Carton de Wiart. With its own golf course and indoor swimming pool, it was the perfect place for a rest, and the clamour of battle seemed miles and miles away.

I had hardly been there a day when, in the evening of 16 December, I was rung up by a Senior Staff Officer from Second British Army, who said, 'The Germans have launched a large-scale offensive on a frontage of some eighty miles against the U.S. forces on our flank in the Ardennes. The situation is very confused, but the front affected seems to stretch from approximately Monschau in the north to Echternach in the south. Some of the senior U.S. Generals think this is only a holding attack, to delay our assault on the River Rur, but that old war horse, Monty, does not like the smell of it at all. He wants you to return tonight and move your Corps, which is the only reserve readily available, to occupy a lay-back position to protect Brussels. Can you return immediately?'

As it happened, the night was so foggy that I could hardly see a yard in front of my face, and it would have been futile to attempt the long journey back to my Corps. It would merely have been an exhausting and frustrating drive for nothing. Moreover, there is no point in keeping a dog and then barking yourself; once I had indicated where the different formations were to go, the actual movement orders would have been issued anyhow, by my extremely competent B.G.S. Brigadier Jones. So I decided to wait until morning before rejoining my Corps.

This offensive was the last thing which I had expected, and it seemed incredible that the German Army, whom we all regarded as a beaten force, should have been able to concentrate what was obviously a very large contingent opposite the Ardennes, without U.S. Intelligence becoming aware of it. I did not think for one moment that the Germans were capable of launching a counter-offensive on this scale [ILLEGIBLE] particularly after the virtual destruction of their Air Force.

At first sight this new move by the Germans was deeply disturbing, for a number of reasons. For one thing the Ardennes were relatively unprotected; the Americans were using the area as a rest-cum-training sector and the whole ninety-mile front was manned by four divisions at the most. At the same time Eisenhower's Broad Front policy, with its constant deployment in the line of almost all available forces, inevitably meant a shortage of reserves. True, the wooded and hilly terrain presented enormous difficulties to an attacking force, but this had not prevented the Germans from breaking through with their Panzers in 1940. Then the French had been caught off their guard, with disastrous results; could the same thing now happen to the Americans?

Then, as I studied the map, I realized that it was really an act of madness, probably inspired by Hitler (we heard afterwards that poor old Rundstedt had thought so all the time but had been ordered by the Fuhrer to carry it out). The Germans were doing us a favour by saving us the trouble of a winter offensive across flooded rivers like the Rur, on the other side of which we would be vulnerable to counter-attacks by Panzer divisions. Instead it was they who would now be vulnerable, and I concluded that the farther they came the fewer would get back, and that we had a good chance of eliminating much of their remaining armoured forces.

It seems that Patton rapidly came to the same conclusion. 'Fine!' he is reported to have said, 'We should open up and let them get all the way to Paris. Then we'll saw 'em off at the base!'

At any rate I was in a much more optimistic mood when I went in to dinner. My poor hosts were badly in need of reassurance, for wild rumours were spreading everywhere, but I think I succeeded in cheering them up – particularly by arguing that there might now be a quicker end to the war. Nevertheless it was sad to see the gloom which now settled over Brussels at the prospect of another German occupation.

Next day, XXX Corps began to arrive in their positions. With the Guards Armoured, the 43rd, the 53rd Divisions, plus a little later the 51st Highland and the 29th Armoured Brigade, under the orders of the 53rd Division, north of the Rivers Meuse and Dyle, we were almost occupying the battlefield of Waterloo (subsequently, the 6th Airborne Division also arrived from the U.K. and was placed under XXX Corps). The Household Cavalry and Reconnaissance Units were dispatched to the far side of the River Meuse, while all the bridges were prepared for demolition and defence. We were holding an almost perfect defensive position, and from now on the Germans had no hope whatever of even approaching Brussels, let alone Antwerp, which we learned afterwards was one of their objectives. At the time I could only hope that the Germans would come our way, for with the forces at our disposal we were sure to inflict very heavy losses, and the idea of a second Battle of Waterloo was understandably appealing.

Confusion reigned supreme throughout the battle area, largely owing to the activities of German Commandos under their famous leader, Major Otto Skorzeny, the man who had rescued Mussolini from his hotel prison in the Italian mountains. He had been given command of all the Germans who spoke American and knew America; they were concentrated in a special training camp, were clothed in captured U.S. uniforms and taught to handle American jeeps. Their role was to spread alarm and despondency in the rear areas and do what damage they could. Although, when the time came, only a relatively small number were able to operate behind our lines – certainly no more than fifty jeep loads – their presence had a disproportionate effect, and the atmosphere of suspicion they created greatly hampered the movements of our own personnel. I was once asked by an American sentry to establish my credentials by naming 'the second largest town in

Texas' As I did not know the answer, I had some difficulty in avoiding arrest. In general communications were very bad and few of the higher commanders were completely in the picture as to what was going on, even in their own sectors. Montgomery's 'gallopers' did valuable work in this respect, but ran into problems with the Americans, who regarded them as Montgomery's spies. The Americans disliked Montgomery – particularly so after Eisenhower had placed Hodges's First U.S. Army under his command. It consisted of all the U.S. forces north of the Bulge which developed in the centre of the German attack where the Fifth Panzer Army reached Celles (the farthest point of the German advance). The First Army had previously been under Bradley's command, but he was finding it increasingly difficult to communicate with them as his H.Q. was south of the Bulge. This was the obvious thing to do, and Bradley admitted afterwards that had the First Army been placed under an American he would have had no objection, but he strongly resented part of his command going to Montgomery. It showed great moral courage on Eisenhower's part that, in spite of Bradley's furious protest, he gave him his orders personally by telephone and ended a long, obviously heated, conversation by saying abruptly, 'Well, those are my orders, Brad' and slamming the instrument down.

Montgomery was, of course, delighted and, in the words of one of his staff officers, 'The Field-Marshal strode into Hodges's H.Q. like Christ come to cleanse the Temple.' The First U.S. Army was on too wide a front, and Montgomery, in spite of Hodges's protests, concentrated his forces by handing over sectors to the British. This enabled him to launch an offensive from the north, in depth and on a comparatively narrow front. In fact, he showed all his old mastery of the tactical battle, but, in addition to military skill, great tact was required at this particular moment, and this was not one of his strong qualities. So, although the U.S. simply had to admit that his handling of the consequent battle was supremely skilful, they resented the fact that a large proportion of their troops were put under his command in this very difficult battle.

As I have already said, this was a very confused battle, and the only way I could keep in touch was to send my Intelligence Officer daily to study Montgomery's map, which was always completely up to date, thanks to the daily visits of his 'gallopers' to the various sectors of the battle. Each evening, on their return, they would report to Montgomery personally, with the result that he was probably the only man in the American, German or British Armies who knew exactly what was going on from moment to moment.

My own role in this battle was very small. After spending Christmas Day in the Dinant–Givet sector with the 1st Brigade of the newly-arrived 6th British Airborne Division, I heard that Montgomery wanted to speak to me, so I rang him up. To my astonishment he ordered me to fly home the next day. When I asked the reason for what I took to be my dismissal, Montgomery exploded: 'Don't be a fool!' he said, 'You are not being sacked – I want you to go home and have a rest before the big battle I have in store for you as soon as we have cleared up this mess here.' I protested that the Germans were still advancing and that I was very reluctant to leave my troops at such a critical moment, but all to no avail. 'This battle is finished,' Montgomery said. 'You will fly home tomorrow.'

The battle was indeed all but finished. On 29 December, von Manteuffel was already begging the Fuhrer for leave to start a withdrawal before it was too late. Quite apart from the splendid resistance put up by many isolated detachments of relatively young and inexperienced U.S. troops, as soon as the weather cleared, our Air Forces turned the narrow Ardennes road into a shambles of bombed-out German vehicles and tanks.

I heard afterwards of the magnificent work carried out by our own Royal Electrical and Mechanical Engineers (R.E.M.E.) because the icy roads took their toll of our vehicles as well and it was thanks to the skilled work carried out day and night by our workshops that our forward movement was possible. R.E.M.E. does not often get mentioned in accounts of battles, but there is no doubt at all that they played a major role in the shattering defeat suffered by the Germans in the Ardennes.

Back in England I dropped in at the War Office and gave Archie Nye, the Vice-Chief of the General Staff, a nasty shock. His first thought was that there had been some terrible disaster; failing that the only plausible reason for my sudden return was that I had been sacked. I had great difficulty is convincing him that neither was the case, that the Ardennes battle was over and we had reached a turning point in the war.

II. The Battle
SIR BRIAN HORROCKS

Having been 'in on the start' of the Battle of the Ardennes, it was only natural, on my return from leave in the U.K., for me to discuss its progress with those who had been closely involved throughout.

First of all I have never yet understood how the Germans achieved complete surprise.

It seems incredible that Hitler and Goebbels, to whom almost dictatorial powers were assigned, should have managed to raise three armies two armoured and one infantry approximately 200,000 strong, and then have succeeded in moving this vast force, complete with all its guns and warlike stores of every kind, secretly into positions in the Eifel, facing the Ardennes, on an 85-mile front, stretching from Monschau to Echternach, without our Allied Intelligence having any inkling whatever of the vast counter-offensive about to strike them. During the war we always prided ourselves on the accuracy of our information about the enemy. The Battle of the Ardennes proved the great exception.

The Germans knew very well that this sector of the front was regarded by the Allies as a 'hospital area' where exhausted divisions could be resting and fresh ones introduced gradually to active service conditions. At this time they were faced by the American VIII Corps, with its H.Q. in Bastogne, consisting of four divisions. Opposing this thinly held stretch of front was Army Group 'B', as the German Assault Corps was called, commanded by Field-Marshal Walter Model, an extremely able and experienced General (who had commanded the forces opposed to us during the battle of Arnhem) with three German Armies under his command.

Working from north to south, there was the Sixth SS Panzer Army under Joseph Sepp Dietrich, who had once been in charge of the Fuhrer's bodyguard. In the centre was the Fifth Panzer Army under Gen. von Manteuffel, who had earned a high reputation when fighting against the Russians on the Eastern Front, and the exposed southern flank was to be protected by the Seventh Army, consisting of four newly raised infantry divisions called Volksgrenadieren.

The plan was simplicity itself. After a tremendous opening barrage from some 2000 guns of all calibres, picked assault troops would breach the thinly held U.S. lines in some dozen places, through which the armoured divisions would pour, and race for the bridges over the Meuse between Liege and Namur. With these in their possession they would then capture Brussels and Antwerp, thus cutting in two the Allied Armies in Europe. Subsequently, in conjunction with the German forces in the Netherlands they would destroy the U.S. First and Ninth, the British Second, and the Canadian First Armies.

It was certainly a grandiose project, but without complete air supremacy it stood little chance of success. Moreover, the Germans would be advancing against the 'grain of the country' as nearly all the main roads ran north-east and south-west, with only second- or third-class roads (in some cases almost tracks) winding their way over the rugged, hilly country in between. The Ardennes was easier country to defend than to attack. The vital objectives were therefore the villages or small towns, which constituted the road centres and the bridges in the valleys – places like Malmédy, St-Vith, Houffalize and, in particular, Bastogne.

To describe this battle in detail would require a book in itself as, in my opinion, it proved to be the turning point of the war in the west. So I propose to concentrate on a few vital incidents which changed the whole shape of the battle.

To start with, fortune favoured the Germans. When the vast barrage opened at 0530 hours on 16 December, it was a foggy, wet day, which precluded all air operations. Oddly enough, although all the guns had been 'surveyed in', this intense artillery bombardment did very little material damage and caused a minimum number of casualties; but it succeeded in destroying the communications, which meant that

Commanders above Brigade level were often completely out of touch with what was happening to their forward troops.

What saved the U.S. forces from a complete débâcle was the great courage and initiative shown by the young, inexperienced officers and men of the forward units; not just infantry but also small groups of gunners who, when they ran out of ammunition, continued to fight from trenches round their battery positions; the same applied to the Sappers, who fought to the last before blowing their bridges. Administrative personnel, including cooks, fitters and so on, also played their part, and fought like infantry in this battle. This unexpected resistance caused the Germans delays, particularly on their northern front; this was led by the vanguard of the 1st SS Division, Battle Group 'Peiper', which, approaching Malmédy, succeeded in capturing some 160 Americans, but as these prisoners might prove an embarrassment, the German tank crews lined them up and shot at least 142. Word of this 'Malmédy Massacre', as it was called, got round, and from then on the U.S. forces showed no mercy and were always prepared to fight to the last.

Late in the afternoon of the 16th, when news of the enemy attack reached Versailles (H.Q. of S.H.A.E.F.), Eisenhower and Bradley were discussing plans for future offensives. Eisenhower was at once convinced that this was no local attack; Bradley at first thought that it was merely a spoiling attack to hold up Patton's advance in the Saar, and, what is more, he continued to be of the same opinion for several days. He does not, I am afraid, emerge from this battle with an enhanced reputation. Eisenhower instructed him to reinforce the Ardennes with two armoured divisions, one from the Ninth Army in the north and the 10th from Patton's Third Army in the south. Their arrival did much to blunt the enemy advance. When planning this operation, the Germans underestimated not only the fighting capabilities of the U.S. troops but, more important still, their astonishing mobility. Let me give just two examples.

Before dawn on the 17th, the 7th Armoured Division, led by Brigadier General R. W. Hasbrouck, one of the heroes of this battle, had covered the fifty miles to St-Vith and by the early afternoon they succeeded in halting the advance of the northern German column. By that night he had also organized service units and some retreating combat troops into fighting formations, and had established a loose, horseshoe defensive position around St-Vith, against which the advancing enemy column beat in vain.

Later on in the battle, when, owing to numerous casualties, his force became too thin on the ground to withstand further assaults, Hasbrouck requested permission from his Army Commander, Hodges, to withdraw to a stronger position in the rear. When Hodges refused, he replied, 'This means the end of the 7th Armoured Division.' Hodges at once removed him from command. Fortunately, however, by this time Montgomery had taken over command of the northern front, which included Hodges's Army, and hearing what had happened from one of his 'gallopers' he immediately reinstated Hasbrouck, and permitted him to withdraw to a stronger defensive position in the rear, where once again he halted the northern prong of the German advance. Montgomery thus saved the lives of the St-Vith garrison.

The most extraordinary miscalculation of the battle was that for forty-eight hours Eisenhower failed to order his two reserve divisions, the 101st and 82nd Airborne, to move to the

Ardennes. Once again, however, the astonishing American mobility saved the day. The 101st were on leave in the Rheims area, 100 miles away, and their Divisional Commander was in the U.K., but the second-in-command Brigadier McAuliffe, got the Division, 11,000-strong, on the move at once, and travelling flat out with headlights blazing throughout the night, they covered the hundred miles in well under twenty-four hours, and reached Bastogne just in the nick of time. It was absolutely vital for the Germans to capture this important road centre, and the task was handed over to General von Luttwitz, Panzer Corps, which contained one of Germany's most famous armoured divisions, Panzer Lehr. His first attack failed, but eventually the town was encircled by German divisions – attack after attack was repulsed, though on one occasion, when his infantry had penetrated the suburbs, von Luttwitz demanded 'unconditional surrender, in order to save the needless slaughter of U.S. troops' To which McAuliffe replied, with one word, 'Nuts', – which has now become one of the most famous words in military history; the 'Nuts' museum in Bastogne is visited by thousands of sightseers every year.

At one stage no fewer than five German divisions were involved at and around Bastogne, where the situation was becoming very serious, as the gallant garrison was running desperately short of ammunition of all sorts. Suddenly, the gods intervened, and the skies cleared. For the first time in the battle Allied aircraft were able not only to fly in what supplies were required, but also to bomb and shoot up the German columns besieging the town. At the start of the battle Patton had been about to launch a large-scale offensive with his Third Army towards the Rhine, and had been very reluctant to release an armoured division to advance towards Bastogne, but as soon as he realized the seriousness of the Ardennes offensive, he turned the direction of his Army's advance from the east with incredible speed and skill and started to advance in a northerly direction.

The German advance had been delayed to such an extent that all elements of surprise had been lost. The northern SS thrust had been held up, and the southern attack was heavily involved with Bastogne. Only in the centre had von Manteuffel's army succeeded in penetrating to within striking distance of the Meuse, thus creating a bulge (from which the 'Battle of the Bulge' derived its name). Unfortunately, Bradley's H.Q. was south of the Bulge in Luxembourg, and it was almost impossible for him to control the U.S. forces, which included Hodges's Army north of the Bulge, so, as I have already described, on 20 December, Eisenhower placed all the troops north of the Bulge, including the First and Ninth U.S. Armies, under Montgomery's command. Strategically, this was the obvious thing to do, but Bradley was furious and the relationship between Montgomery and Hodges was never a happy one. Montgomery's handling of the battle was scientific, while Bradley's and Hodges's was emotional. Even a short withdrawal, to straighten the line, was considered a disgrace to American arms.

After considerable argument Montgomery succeeded in shortening Hodges's front by handing over sections to the British, and prepared to assault the German north flank on a narrow front. He so positioned his command that when the 2nd Panzer Division reached a ridge near Dinant from where they could look down on the Meuse – short of petrol and impatiently awaiting reinforcements which were not forthcoming they suddenly found the 2nd U.S. Armoured

Division bearing down on their northern flank in overwhelming force. For two days the battle raged, as the trapped German force struggled to avoid annihilation, but by the evening of the 27th the spearhead of von Manteuffel's army lay broken in the snow. The Germans had looked down upon the Meuse for the last time. Hitler's final bid to save the Reich had failed.

I must end this account with my own personal opinion. If Bastogne had fallen, and the Germans had succeeded in crossing the Meuse, the British could have halted any advance towards Brussels, while the U.S. Army to the north and south of the Bulge would have advanced in an invincible pincer movement across the German lines of communication. Few, if any, of their forces would ever have got back to Germany and the war might have ended several months earlier.

III. The Air in the Ardennes
EVERSLEY BELFIELD

The Ardennes offensive demonstrated the decisive importance of air power. Immediately prior to the attack and for the first day after it had begun, bad weather severely restricted flying and it was partly owing to this Allied blindness that the Germans were able to gain such initial surprise. Most of the roads through the Ardennes are narrow and twisting, with steep gradients. The German failure to capture both Bastogne and Malmédy, two important road junctions, compelled many of their columns to make long detours on smaller roads and also helped to concentrate their traffic on other communication centres such as St-Vith, Houffalize and Laroche.

When the weather improved, the Allied tactical air forces came out in strength. Not since the latter part of the Normandy battle had the pilots found such targets, and the closely packed armoured and transport vehicles were relentlessly attacked with bombs, rockets and cannonfire, causing huge traffic jams. Despite some breaks caused by bad weather, these attacks continued until the end of the offensive on 16 January. Altogether over 63,000 sorties of all kinds were flown and 72,000 tons of bombs dropped, over half being on supply depots further back and on the Rhine bridges. The Ardennes counter-offensive from the airmen's point of view was a closely co-ordinated series of night and day operations, in which both R.A.F. and U.S. Air Force heavy and medium bombers and fighter-bombers all took part. Altogether the Allied air forces lost 647 aircraft, mainly from anti-aircraft fire, which was particularly intense over the railway network along which supplies were moved to support this offensive. In the early stages of the battle, the Luftwaffe made considerable efforts to intervene, but though they flew about 500 sorties per day, they were overwhelmed by the Allies who mounted up to 3000 sorties in a 24-hour period. The German losses were, nevertheless, high, being estimated at 750 machines destroyed up to 27 December, when the Luftwaffe was largely withdrawn in preparation for the great Raid of 1 January.

IV. Göring's Last Fling
EVERSLEY BELFIELD

Stung by Hitler's taunts about the conspicuous absence of the Luftwaffe during this campaign, Göring decided to retrieve its prestige by a single ambitious raid which he code-named

'Bodenplatte' (Baseplate). By 15 December all was ready. Göring had intended that this great aerial strike should coincide with the opening of the Ardennes offensive and should deal a crippling blow to the Allied tactical air forces, but no flying was possible during the opening days of that offensive. The attack therefore had to be called off, but later the Luftwaffe did make strenuous efforts to support their ground forces.

After their heavy losses and with the Ardennes offensive conclusively repulsed, the local German Air Force commanders had naturally supposed that 'Bodenplatte' was cancelled. They were as astonished as the Allies were to be when, on the afternoon of 31 December, they were summoned to briefing conferences and told that it was to take place after all. They were flabbergasted when they heard that, the weather conditions being favourable, the very next morning, 1 January 1945, had been chosen for 'Bodenplatte' Although based on the very detailed planning carried out during November and early December, the Luftwaffe's last major attack was an undeniable gamble. This very complex plan of operations demanded that ten fighter Groups, consisting of nearly 1000 aircraft distributed over thirty-eight different aerodromes, should converge on sixteen of the most forward Allied airfields in Belgium, Holland and France at 0920 hours precisely. Using cannon and rocket fire, the Luftwaffe was meant to destroy, on the ground, the bulk of the unsuspecting American and British tactical aircraft. The essential element of surprise could be achieved only by keeping the strictest wireless silence, once airborne, and by maintaining very close formation at very low altitudes throughout the approach flights, which were up to 200 miles long. Such technical expertise would tax even very experienced pilots, but the Luftwaffe had been so run down that some of those taking part had only just completed their training. Finally to make matters worse, all those participating were forbidden to take any alcohol during their New Year's Eve parties – which they were also ordered to leave before midnight!

In some groups, JU 88 night fighters helped to assemble the masses of aircraft and set them on their correct courses. The security arrangements had been so efficient that German anti-aircraft batteries had not been notified and, being unaccustomed to seeing the Luftwaffe in any strength, they assumed that these large formations of ME 109s and FW 190s must be Allied planes and they opened fire. On their way to their targets, the Luftwaffe are known to have lost at least sixteen aircraft from their own flak defences.

The most southerly of the ten Groups set out for an American airfield near Metz, but about a third of these planes never joined the main force. Spotted by an American Thunderbolt patrol, these Luftwaffe pilots had immediately to jettison their long-range fuel tanks and in the subsequent fight lost nine planes and were broken up. The rest of the Group did considerable damage to the Thunderbolts on the ground at Metz, but lost fourteen planes. Three other Groups were ordered to attack three American airfields in southern Belgium. One Group never found its airfield (Le Calot) and some of the pilots took on ground targets of their own choice, whilst the rest tagged on to other Groups, some even getting as far as Brussels. A second Group reached St-Trond, where it did little damage to the aircraft, which were well dispersed. Already alerted, the anti-aircraft batteries in the area were largely responsible for shooting down about 40 per cent of the attackers. The third Group surprised Asch airfield, which was close to the front and, as a result of the Ardennes offensive, was packed with Mustangs, Thunderbolts and four squadrons of visiting Spitfires. The morning being misty, only a few planes were aloft, but more managed to take off during the ensuing melée, which lasted three quarters of an hour and cost the Allies a considerable number of planes damaged and destroyed on the ground. Altogether these four Groups which attacked American airfields lost over 100 planes out of some 350.

Twelve R.A.F. airfields were assigned to six Groups and over 600 aircraft took part in these attacks. After having flown a long dog-leg course which took them over the sea, one of the Groups came in from the west. With little loss to themselves, fifty FW 190s destroyed about thirty aircraft on two airfields near Bruges. The rest went on to Ghent airfield itself (St-Denijs-Westrem), where they jumped an incoming Polish Spitfire squadron, knocking down nine planes. But the other two Polish squadrons soon returned and in a fierce dogfight shot down nineteen German fighters round their airfield. Two other Groups, totalling about 170 planes, concentrated on the three airfields in or near Brussels where they encountered little opposition and did considerable damage, especially at Brussels-Evèrt, which was the main aerodrome for the Twenty-first Army Group and packed with assorted aircraft. Here the single runway had just been cleared of ice and a Canadian Spitfire squadron, about to take off, was caught by the Luftwaffe. The anti-aircraft guns soon exhausted their ammunition and a hundred or so German planes spent the next half-hour undisturbed shooting up the hangars and the planes, destroying Montgomery's personal Dakota and Prince Bernhardt's private Beechcraft; nevertheless out of sixty Spitfires there, only eleven were destroyed and twelve damaged. In these raids one low-flying German pilot was brought down by a partridge getting jammed in his air-intake! Finally with Luftwaffe planes milling all round Brussels at roof-top level, a Dakota-load of senior officers of the Twenty-first Army Group approached the aerodrome, but the pilot was warned off just in time and slipped away, which, one cynic observed, spoilt many people's chances of quick promotion.

The eighth Group fared very differently. Its 100 aircraft were briefed to attack two airfields near Antwerp, one of which was almost deserted. Most of the rest of the planes spent some time trying to find the other airfield on the outskirts of Antwerp and some eventually did so, destroying one machine and damaging fourteen others. Out of the four pilots lost, the lowest of any Group, three had been shot down by German anti-aircraft guns *en route* to their targets. The ninth Group, 70-strong, were allocated two airfields in southern Holland but their JU 88 guide plane left them on a wrong course; only three planes found Volkel airfield and these were all shot down. Most of the rest attacked the other airfield (Heesch), where the Canadian Spitfire squadrons were ready for them and claimed twenty-four victims. The pilots in the tenth Group were the most successful but had the advantage of a direct course to the airfields which were very close to the front line. They swooped on Eindhoven unexpectedly from the south-west and in twenty minutes reduced the place to chaos, destroying dozens of Typhoons and Spitfires, as well as knocking out buildings and blowing up ammunition dumps. At the other airfield (Gilze-Rijen) they encountered greater opposition, but also did considerable damage. Most of their sixteen losses happened when they were returning and were intercepted by R.A.F. fighters.

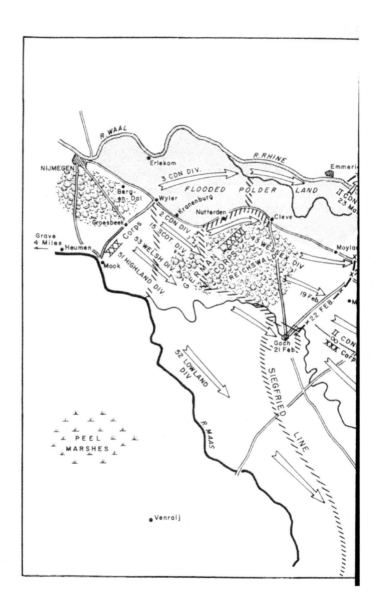

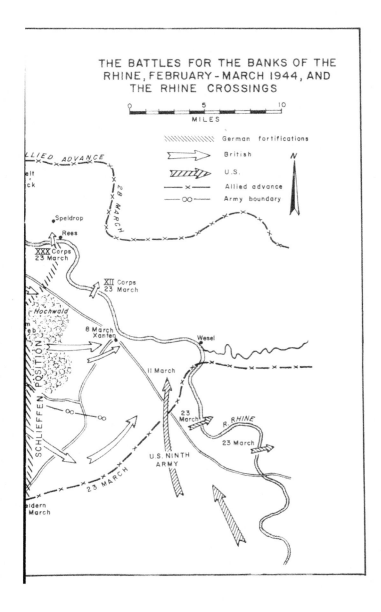

The total Allied losses were 130 aircraft destroyed and 111 damaged, with forty-six airmen killed. The Luftwaffe had, however, gained this partial victory at the cost of over 200 machines and pilots, many of whom were their most experienced leaders. Just as the Ardennes offensive had quickly demonstrated the decline in the power of the once all-conquering Panzer forces, so this ambitious attack exposed the feeble condition into which the formerly invincible Luftwaffe had now sunk. The New Year's Day Raid of 1945 was the Luftwaffe's swan-song.

Chapter 11
The Battle for the Lower Rhine Bridgehead

I.   Operation 'Veritable'
SIR BRIAN HORROCKS

On my return from leave I plunged into the preparations for the Battle of the Reichswald (given the code-name of 'Veritable'), the largest operation I had ever carried out.

The object was to clear the Germans from the west bank of the Rhine, preparatory to crossing the river and penetrating the heart of the Reich itself. The overall strategic plan, as explained by Montgomery, was simplicity itself. XXX Corps, under command of the First Canadian Army, was to launch an attack in a southerly direction from the Nijmegen area, with its right on the Maas, and its left on the Rhine. Forty-eight hours later our old friends, General Simpson's Ninth U.S. Army, were to cross the River Rur and advance north to meet us. The German forces would thus be caught in a vice and faced with the alternatives, either to fight it out west of the Rhine or to withdraw over the Rhine and then be prepared to launch counter-attacks when we ourselves subsequently attempted to cross. We hoped that they would adopt the first course, as fewer troops would then be available to counter our thrust into the interior of Germany. Considering Hitler's passionate objection to giving up ground anywhere, it was almost a certainty that he would order every inch of his precious Reich to be defended to the last man. And so it turned out.

In theory, this looked like a comparatively simple operation, but all battles have their problems, and in this case the initial assault would have to smash through a bottleneck well suited to defence and consisting in part of the famous Siegfried Line. Our Intelligence services, as always, were right up to date. Their information was that the front line was held by two infantry regiments of the German 84th Division plus one parachute regiment – about 8000 men all told, while a third infantry regiment, some 3000 strong, guarded the German right flank. This was part of the LXXXVI Corps – the right-hand formation of the First Parachute Army which was commanded by General Schlemm, a veteran from the Eastern Front. It was estimated that the enemy also had three infantry and two Panzer divisions in reserve available to intervene rapidly in the battle.

Our existing front line, along the wooded hills, south-east of Nijmegen, which had played such a vital role in the Battle of Arnhem, was held by the 2nd Canadian Division, so the first thing I did was to study the battlefield from one of their observation posts. In front of me lay a gentle valley, with small farms rising up on the far side, and merging into the sinister blackness of the Reichswald (i.e. the 'German forest'), which was intersected by narrow rides, but with only one metal road running through it. North of the forest was the main road from the Netherlands into Germany (from Nijmegen to Cleve). On the north-west corner of the Reichswald was the Nutterden feature, the highest ground on the front, which dominated Cleve and the main road. North of the road lay the flooded Polderland, running down to the broad expanse of the Rhine itself, and the Germans were holding the far bank.

South of the Reichswald was more low-lying ground, which was obviously dominated by the forest running down to the River Maas, with the British Second Army holding the far bank. We were therefore faced by a bottleneck between the Polderland and the forest, some 5000 yards in width. This had been heavily fortified in depth by the Germans and was really the outpost position of the Siegfried Line; it consisted of an anti-tank ditch, concreted emplacements and pillboxes, barbed wire entanglements and, as I learnt afterwards, the whole area was sown with mines. Furthermore, the small Rhineland towns – Cleve, Goch, and so on – had been turned into fortresses prepared for all-round defence. I was told that the houses of all these German frontier towns had been specially constructed for battle; with loopholed concrete basements they were capable of all-round defence. In war, as in most other things, the Germans certainly are thorough. Further east, some ten miles back, was yet another defensive position called the Hochwald.

We had to smash through this bottleneck before breaking out into the German plain beyond, which consisted of open country, well suited to armoured warfare. The hinge to this open country was the Nutterden feature and the first essential was to seize this high ground and debouch beyond it before the Germans could bring up their reserves. So it was obviously a race for Nutterden, but at the same time we had to clear the forest, or the Germans could have concentrated here and struck at our flank. Moreover, I badly wanted that one metalled road which ran through it because I knew from experience how difficult it was to maintain a large force, with all its manifold requirements, by a single road.

So I determined to use the maximum force possible from the outset and to attack with five divisions in line: from right to left,

51st Highland, 53rd Welsh, 15th Scottish, 2nd and 3rd Canadian. Behind, I kept the 43rd Wessex and Guards Armoured, prepared to pass through and sweep down the Rhineland. The artillery support was very carefully worked out and was on the most massive scale I ever remember.

Since the war I have often paid tribute to the part that our artillery played. The core of the Royal Artillery was the fantastic accuracy of their Survey Units. The one I knew best was a pre-war Territorial Unit, 4th (Durham) Survey Regiment from Gateshead. I first met them in the Middle East and we were then together until the end of the war and I came to rely on them completely, as will be seen from the account of the forthcoming battle. Neither the Germans nor the Russians, nor even the French, who were always supposed to be the masters of artillery fire systems, could approach the accuracy or the weight of concentrated fire power which, on my Corps front, I had at my disposal in a matter of minutes. To simplify and speed up the call for a concentration of artillery fire, only code-names were necessary. Thus, if I wanted the fire of all the seventy-two 25-pounder field guns of any division to be concentrated on one target, my Gunner Brigadier (C.C.R.A.) would merely have to get in touch with Brigadier R.A. at the division concerned and ask for an 'Uncle' target to be fired. If a target was sufficiently important to warrant all, or most, of the Corps Artillery being employed, this was called a 'Victor' target; this might involve 216 field guns from three divisions, and perhaps 128 medium and heavy (5·5-inch, 7·2-inch and 155-mm. calibres) guns of two Army Groups R.A., with four regiments each with sixteen guns; in addition there would usually be on call at least forty-eight guns from two or more regiments of 3·7-inch heavy anti-aircraft guns firing high explosive shells in a field role. In a matter of minutes, therefore, about 400 guns could be brought into action where I wanted them. This system of predicted fire, not controlled by an observer, was made possible by a combination of excellent surveying, good communications and a high degree of flexibility at the guns. Finally these concentrations could be fired in any weather by day or by night and were thus far more reliable than any air strikes, which were always very dependent on the weather.

The Germans were expecting a large-scale Allied offensive, and the first essential was to prevent them discovering on which part of the front this would be launched. Fortunately, our Air Force now dominated the skies, but, even so, it seemed almost impossible to concentrate such a vast force in the woods round Nijmegen without the Germans finding out.

Our build-up was awesome in its magnitude, involving intricate staff work of the highest order on the part of both the Canadian Army and XXX Corps. Just to give some idea of what was involved, XXX Corps consisted of 200,000 men for this operation. To bring forward these men and their supplies, 25,000 vehicles were used; 1,300,000 gallons of petrol were required. Five special bridges were constructed over the Maas; one hundred miles of road had to be improved, and in places remade, in order to take all these vehicles. This involved fifty Companies of Royal Engineers, twenty-nine Companies of Pioneers and three special Road Construction Units, all working round the clock. An intricate traffic control system was set up, involving 1600 Military Police (Provost), and each unit was given the most exact timing.

When it came to the question of the supplies required for this mammoth force it was estimated that half a million rounds of

350 different types of ammunition were required, 8000 miles of four different kinds of cables, 10,000 smoke generators, 10,000 gallons of fog oil, 750,000 maps and 500,000 aerial photographs.

As the troops moved forward into their concealment areas, all of which had been carefully reconnoitred beforehand, nearly two-and-a-third million rations were required.

I have deliberately given these figures as a reminder of the many different ingredients required in a modern battle on this scale.

By day the normal amount of transport for the two Canadian divisions already in the area used the roads freely and no change was made, so that the Germans would not become suspicious, but from dusk to dawn the roads were packed with transport, moving nose to tail, and before it became light, almost like magic the units would disappear into their concealment areas. When this concentration was complete it would have been almost impossible to drop even a pea into the woods round Nijmegen without hitting some part of XXX Corps.

There were two other important aspects of this cover plan. Wireless communication had to be kept at the same level which had existed before the concentration started, but, more important than anything else was the control of reconnaissance: literally thousands of officers and N.C.O.s had to be given a chance to study the ground over which they were to attack. The Germans, who had become used to seeing very little movement on the wooded hills held by the Canadians in front of them, would suddenly have seen these same hills almost covered by figures wearing a different-coloured khaki battledress (the Canadian battledress was darker than ours), studying maps, using field glasses, and so on. There is an old Army saying,

'Time spent in reconnaissance is seldom wasted', and this unusual amount of movement could only mean one thing – an impending attack. We therefore had to impose the most rigorous control on any movement in the area occupied by the 2nd Canadian Division, and a reconnaissance report centre was established in the Dutch barracks at Grave, where everyone wishing to view the battlefield had to report. The staff at this centre would then control the number of people entering any particular area, by a system of passes, allowing them access to a certain view-point, for a definite period. They were then fitted out in a suit of the darker Canadian battledress. A series of sentries were posted at intervals, to whom the passes had to be shown. At the same time that all this was going on, bogus activity west of Nijmegen along the Waal, and on the Lower Maas, was set in motion, designed to confuse the Germans.

This completely deceived the higher German staffs. On 5 February the Chief Intelligence Officer at von Rundstedt's (C.-in-C.) H.Q. sent a memorandum to all the Chief Staff Officers of Army Group 'H', which was holding this area, saying that the activities opposite the Reichswald were intended as a bluff, and, although a limited offensive might be launched in this area, its object was to draw the German attention away from the main event which would be launched from the big bend of the Maas. Incidentally, on the Commander-in-Chief's map, XXX Corps was labelled 'Whereabouts unknown'

In spite of this warning, that experienced old war dog, General Schlemm, commanding the troops opposite us from the First Parachute Army, was far from certain that a large-scale attack would not be launched from the Reichswald area, and quietly, without informing his Higher Command, he moved part of the 7th Parachute Division away from their position opposite the Second British Army to Geldern at the southern end of the 2nd Defence Line east of the Reichswald.

I have deliberately described our deception plan in some detail, as this vital aspect of all battles is often overlooked.

During the build-up period I had little to do, except to go around visiting troops. I had so far not come in contact with the Canadians, so I set out to try and get to know them better. I also saw quite a lot of their Commander, General Crerar, who, in my opinion, has always been much underrated, largely because he was the exact opposite to Montgomery. He hated publicity, but was full of common sense and always prepared to listen to the views of his subordinate commanders. Every day after the battle started he would fly over the front (a somewhat dangerous operation) in a small aircraft, and then came to see me wherever I might be. I grew to like him very much, though I am afraid I must have been a terrible pain in his neck, for during part of this long-drawn-out battle I was feeling very unwell (a recurrence of the attack I had developed before crossing the Seine), though this time I managed to conceal it from everyone other than my A.D.C.s and senior members of my staff. The outward and visible sign was that I became extremely irritable and bad-tempered, yet Crerar bore with me very patiently.

The Canadian troops, with the exception of the Vingt-Deuxième (22nd), which was composed entirely of French Canadians, seemed bigger than our men. After intensive training in the U.K., they had been involved in some hard fighting on the left flank of the Twenty-first Army Group from Normandy to the Scheldt and were therefore by now tough, battle-experienced troops.

But to return to the battle:

So far, all had gone very well, and I was beginning to be optimistic about the forthcoming offensive. Then suddenly it seemed as though the 'gods who control battles' must have thought that we had been given too many advantages, and decided for a change to give the enemy a chance. I had chosen 8 February as D-Day for the attack. Throughout January there was a severe frost and the ground in front was frozen hard. If only this frost would last until, say, the middle of February, there could be no doubt about the result of our attack. Within a couple of days we could have burst out into the German plain beyond the Hochwald, and I secretly hoped to be able to bounce at least one bridge over the Rhine. But it was not to be; at the beginning of February a heavy thaw set in and, instead of hard ground suitable for our many armoured formations, we were faced by a soggy valley. Fortunately for my peace of mind, I did not realize just how soggy it could become.

One day Crerar visited me and said that, in addition to the whole of the Tactical Air Force being available to support our attack, the 'Heavies' from Bomber Command were all at my disposal. He then said, 'Do you want Cleve taking out?' By 'taking out' he meant, of course, 'totally destroyed' This is the sort of problem with which a General in war is constantly faced and from which there is no escape. I knew that Cleve was a lovely old historic Rhineland town. Anne of Cleves, Henry VIII's fourth wife, came from there. No doubt, a lot of civilians, plus women and children, were still living there. Their fate depended on how I answered Crerar's question, and I simply hated the thought of Cleve being 'taken out' All the same, if we were going to break out of the bottleneck into the German plain it was a race between the German reserves and the 15th Scottish Division for the Nutterden feature, and the German reserves would have to come through Cleve. If I could delay them by bombing it might make all the difference to the battle, and, after all, the lives of my own troops must come first. So I said, 'Yes' – the most terrible decision I had ever had to take in my life, and I can assure you that I felt almost physically sick when, on the night before the attack, I saw the bombers flying overhead on their deadly mission. And yet people sometimes say to me, 'As a General, surely you must like war.' But then possibly I have too much imagination, and it was fortunate for the British Army that I never rose above Corps Commander.

After the war, I used to suffer from nightmares and literally for years these always concerned Cleve. Unfortunately, it was even worse than I had imagined. I had specifically asked for 'incendiaries' to be used, but through some error 1,384 tons of high explosive had been dropped, and the huge craters in Cleve not only held up the German reserves but our own troops as well.

In the early hours of 8 February I climbed into my Command Post for the battle; it had been constructed for me by the Royal Engineers and consisted of a platform half-way up a large tree. From here I could see most of the valley in front, and I was connected by line with a group of small scout cars below me at the bottom of the tree, each of which was tuned in on the same wireless link with a similar vehicle at the advance H.Q. of each of the divisions taking part. From my viewpoint I could follow the progress of the attack by the lifts in the barrage. Everything seemed to be going according to plan, though units began to complain (over the air) more and more about the state of the going, and late in the afternoon it appeared that almost every tank was bogged down and the infantry had to fight their way forward without armoured support.

We were supported by 1400 guns. It was a cold and grey, miserable dawn, raining steadily as it did without cease for five days, thus making life even more unpleasant, if possible, for the unfortunate infantrymen and preventing any support from the air. At 0500 hours the barrage opened, and the noise was unbelievable. With 1000 field medium and anti-aircraft guns, it was the heaviest barrage employed by the British Army during the whole of the war in Europe, and the artillery support had been most carefully worked out. After two-and-a-half hours every gun suddenly stopped firing. The silence seemed somewhat unreal. Smoke was then fired across the whole front; this was done deliberately to make the Germans think that the infantry attack had been launched. The German gunners who had survived the first bombardment now rushed to man and fire their guns. The position of these batteries had previously been very accurately surveyed by our flash spotters and sound rangers of the Survey Regiment. Then, after ten minutes, the original barrage started again, concentrating particularly on the German guns which had been located. In addition to the artillery, each division employed also what we called the 'pepper pot' Every weapon not actually in the assault opened up on the German positions. The effect was so devastating that, when the attack really went in later on, the German gunners remained crouched in their trenches.

The enemy was completely bemused and very little resistance was encountered; our worst enemies that day were mines and mud. The continual rain turned the terrain into a quagmire. Mud and still more mud must be the chief memory of anyone who fought in this battle. After the first hour almost every tank was bogged down and the infantry had to struggle forward on their own. The chief enemy resistance came from the cellars in the villages. It has been said that no two attacks are ever the same, and that was exemplified by this battle.

On the left, the 2nd Canadian Division cut the main Nijmegen–Cleve road and then half of their force turned back to attack and capture Wyler from the rear (where incidentally they encountered very stiff resistance), while the other half moved to support the 15th Scottish advancing on their right, carrying out an entirely different type of operation. The role of the 44th Brigade of the 15th Scottish was to break the northern extension of the Siegfried Line. Not one single man was on his feet: the officers controlling the artillery fire were in tanks, the leading wave consisted of tanks with flails, beating and marking a passage through the minefields; then came more tanks, with bridges and fascines to form bridges over the anti-tank ditch; the next echelon was flame-firing tanks to deal with the concrete pillboxes, and finally infantry in 'Kangaroos'

On their right were the 53rd Welsh Division, who disappeared into the Reichswald itself, where they were to spend one of the most unpleasant weeks of the whole war owing to the difficulty of movement up the narrow boggy rides; they fought their way steadily forward against increasing German opposition. This was the Division which, in my opinion, suffered most. For nine days without ceasing they edged their way steadily forward. The narrow rides made tank support almost impossible, and they were constantly being faced by fresh German reserves. They never faltered, and on 18 February they reached their objective, the east edge of the forest, having suffered 5000 casualties – 50 per cent of the total lost by this Division during all their operations in Europe. The 18th of February is a day of which Wales has every right to be proud.

One day when visiting the 53rd Welsh Division in the Reichswald, I almost stumbled over two young soldiers crouching in a very muddy trench. They were all alone and could see none of their comrades, who were also concealed in foxholes nearby. Here, I thought, is the cutting edge of this vast military machine, whose tentacles stretch way back to factories and training establishments in the U.K. or the U.S.A.

These two young men were desperately lonely; how much harder is the lot of the infantryman today, compared with, say, his great-great-grandfather on the battlefield of Waterloo, where the infantry would be formed up into squares with their officers and N.C.O.s all around them. There would then be shouting, noise and excitement in the air. From time to time they would see their Commander, the Duke of Wellington, riding along the slope in front of them on his famous charger, Copenhagen. Moreover, as soon as it grew dark, the armies of both sides slept round their camp fires. In the morning, when they were all formed up, the Generals said, 'Let battle commence', and off they went again. Now, owing to the power of modern weapons, more and more fighting takes place at night. Yet nothing in their previous life had prepared these young soldiers for their loneliness and the darkness, as the greater proportion of them lived in large, well-lit towns or, at any rate, in villages. This was bad enough for them during the last great war, but since then has come the development of nuclear weapons, which will mean even emptier battlefields than ever.

The 51st Highland Division, who were the right-hand formation, were dealing with the southern part of the forest, where they encountered and overcame strong German opposition.

Nor was this all. As soon as it was dark the 3rd Canadian Division would climb into amphibious vehicles (Buffaloes) provided by the 79th Division, and set out on what were almost maritime operations, to capture one or more of the villages in the Polderland on the left flank, which was entirely flooded, thanks to the Germans having destroyed the banks of the Rhine. The villages stood out above the floods like small islands.

When the attack was launched, 50,000 troops were on the start line, supported by 500 tanks and some 500 specially adapted tracked vehicles. In addition there were another 10,000 waiting to advance north-east, in order to secure the left flank, and another 15,000 front-line troops in reserve with over 500 tanks.

That night the Germans made a further breach in the banks of the Rhine upstream, and the floods started to rise; some water was lapping over our one road. In spite of all these difficulties the 44th Brigade of the 15th Scottish continued to advance, and succeeded in breaching the northerly end of the Siegfried Line. I received a message that they had captured the Nutterden feature and were moving into the outskirts of Cleve. This was the information for which I had been eagerly waiting, because speed in capturing Cleve before the German reserves got established there was essential. So I unleashed my first reserve, the 43rd Wessex Division, which was to pass through the 15th Scottish, to burst out into the plain beyond and advance towards Goch.

This, however, turned out to be one of the worst mistakes I made in the war. The 15th Scottish had not reached as far as had been reported and one of their brigades had not yet been employed at all. The chief enemy at this time was not the

Germans but the congestion caused by the flooding which almost precluded cross-country movement. The arrival of this fresh Division, bursting for the fray, caused one of the worst traffic jams in the war – equalled only, I believe, by the scenes in the Liri Valley in Italy after the Battle of Cassino. My only excuse is that all too often during the war I had witnessed a pause in the battle when one division was ordered to pass through another, which allowed the enemy time to recover. In this case, speed was absolutely vital, and I was determined that our attack should flow on. Nevertheless, in spite of their Corps Commander's interference which very nearly snarled up everything, the 15th Scottish, who had put up a magnificent performance under the most difficult conditions, forced their way into the shattered ruins of what once had been Cleve – they were followed by the 43rd, and after some very hard, almost hand-to-hand fighting, they succeeded in capturing the town. Meanwhile, the 53rd Welsh and 51st Highland were making steady progress in the Reichswald.

It was now that I heard the second really bad piece of news – namely, that on 9 February the Germans had blown the dam over the Rur, which meant that the Ninth U.S. Army was faced by a wide strip of surging water which was quite unbridgeable. So their attack from the south had to be postponed. It was estimated that the floods would continue for at least two weeks. In fact, it was not until 23 February that Simpson's leading troops were able to start crossing the Rur.

Up to this point, the German High Command had still not been convinced that the Battle of the Reichswald was anything more than a holding attack. After the capture of Cleve, however, they realized that ours was the main offensive for which they had been waiting. With their south flank now secure, they ordered all available reserves to move up to the area of Operation 'Veritable'

At the start of our attack we had been faced by one division approximately. Now, nine divisions had been drawn into the battle against us and Operation 'Veritable' developed into a slogging match under the worst possible weather conditions, when air support was rarely possible. It became a soldier's battle, and the men who really influenced it were the Battalion Commanders who, for twenty-eight horrible days, never gave up the struggle which continued by day and by night, against some of the best and most experienced German Panzer and Parachute troops.

I was almost powerless to influence the battle one way or the other, so I spent my days 'smelling the battlefield' I always made a point of visiting Brigade and Battalion H.Q. which had been having a particularly gruelling time.

It would be quite impossible to describe the many small, extremely fierce, battles which were going on right across the front. The floods rose continuously and at one stage our only road to the front was submerged to a depth of several feet; in order to reach the front line and, incidentally, to evacuate casualties, it was essential to use amphibious vehicles and I don't really know what we should have done without the 79th Division, with its many different types of armoured vehicle – the 'Funnies'

As I have said, we attacked every day and every night for five long weeks, and it was the staunchness of the British infantry, supported as always by our superb artillery, which gradually wore the enemy down. When all did so well, it seems unfair to pick out any particular division for special praise, but I must mention the 43rd Wessex Division, who, having fought their way through Cleve on 16 February, carried out a brilliant 8000-yard advance, which enabled them to occupy the escarpment overlooking the fortified town of Goch. This proved the turning point in the battle.

Goch was subsequently captured by the Jocks of the 51st and 15th Scottish Divisions, after some very bitter fighting indeed. At this time my right flank was very much a Scottish army, since south of Goch, protecting my right flank, was the 52nd Lowland Division (which had joined the Corps after the battle started), and the attack on the town was supported by that magnificent medium artillery regiment 'The Scottish Horse' – in addition, of course, to their divisional artillery.

Clearing these frontier towns was a costly business in casualties, because almost each house had to be dealt with separately. The Germans were almost immune to artillery fire and could sweep the road with fire through the loopholes in the reinforced cellars.

II. The Canadian Corps in the Second Stage of the Battle
EVERSLEY BELFIELD

After a week's fighting XXX Corps was through the bottleneck, and the front widened sufficiently for Crerar to bring in the II Canadian Corps, commanded by General Simonds, on our left, or northern, flank. It was his Corps which now bore the brunt of the assault on the strongly-held Hochwald position. Its left flank was almost completely masked by the widespread flooding of the land between the Rhine and Cleve to the Calcar road which was also under water in places. Here only very limited amphibious operations were possible, but some small detachments managed to reach the banks of the Rhine opposite Emmerich.

The Canadians' first major objectives were the two villages of Calcar and Üdem together with the road that joins them. This part of the front was now considered by Hitler to be the most seriously menaced, and reinforcements had been sent by First Parachute Army to von Luttwitz's XVII Panzer Corps whose high-grade troops were motivated by the knowledge that they were fighting on their own soil to prevent a crossing of the Rhine. Well dispersed and concealed, the German defences were always in great depth, while the country, with its marshy fields and thick woods, further aided the defenders. Poor weather conditions throughout the period usually deprived the Allies of the support of their tactical aircraft whose 'cab rank' system of rocket-firing Typhoons was particularly valuable in dealing with enemy strongpoints. Although advancing on a narrow front, rarely more than ten miles across, heavy saturation bombing was impracticable as this would have reduced the soft going to an absolute quagmire that would have bogged down all vehicles.

In this phase of 'Veritable', the Canadian infantry divisions employed were soon confronted by two centres of German resistance. On the northern flank, a wood near Moyland blocked their advance to Calcar. It took six days of harsh fighting to clear the Germans from this small, dense and dark forest. About three miles to the south-east an equally bloody struggle developed over the control of the important road that links Calcar with Goch. Although they soon got astride this road, the Canadian hold over it became most precarious when the Germans mounted a series of fierce counter-attacks for two days, including a night thrust supported by tanks. In less than a week, the Canadians had suffered 885 casualties, nearly all in their infantry. This was more than equivalent to the complement of a full battalion, but as all the six battalions in the two brigades involved were seriously below strength, it amounted to about one-fifth of their total fighting strength. The German losses were probably higher and by now 'Veritable' had become increasingly a battle of attrition.

After a brief pause, and reinforced by the 11th British and 4th Canadian Armoured Divisions, as well as by the 43rd Wessex Division, II Canadian Corps was ready to resume 'Veritable' by 25 February. With Wesel and its bridges across the Rhine only fifteen miles away, the German resistance became fanatical as more and more fresh troops were sent in and new defences were hurriedly prepared. These were concentrated around the small town of Üdem (still uncaptured) which had been turned into a strongpoint, with an anti-tank ditch completely encircling it. Other and even more formidable lines had also been constructed to the east of Üdem, and were known as the Schlieffen Position. This sector of the German front was shared between von Luttwitz's LXXXVI Corps, and the much weaker II Parachute Corps holding Üdem itself. Von Luttwitz followed the delaying tactics so effectively used on the Eastern Front and in Normandy, by having relatively weak forward outposts and keeping his main force in reserve, to be thrown in only when the direction of the Allied thrust had been established.

Although from 26 February to 10 March, II Canadian Corps and the German forces were locked in almost continuous conflict, the intensity of the battle fluctuated considerably. On the opening day of their offensive the Canadians met considerable resistance to the north of Üdem, but the town itself was taken without much difficulty on 27 February, the anti-tank ditch proving only a minor obstacle. On the following day, 11th Armoured Division moved forward beyond Üdem and reached the Schlieffen Position (this was about twenty miles long, but nearly all the German forces were in the northern half).

On the northernmost flank, progress was also satisfactory with the 43rd Division taking Calcar, which had been abandoned, and advancing towards Xanten across the flat fields that bordered the Rhine. The strongest German resistance was in the centre. Starting from the northern part of the Calcar–Goch road, the Canadians were forced to make direct assaults on to rising open ground within a very narrow front. To obtain some protection, many of the attacks were made at night with the infantry being brought as far forward as possible in armoured carriers, but these and some of the supporting tanks often got bogged down during the approach march; also massive artillery support was given. Nevertheless, it took two days of very hard fighting for the infantry of the 2nd and 3rd Canadian Divisions to reach the outer defences of the Schlieffen Position where on 27 February a small break-in was achieved – into the only clearing between the two forests that lay just behind the Schlieffen Position. Despite repeated and costly attempts to smash through what became known as the 'Hochwald Gap', the Canadians could get no further for five days. All along the Schlieffen Position, their progress was terribly slow and expensive, with the Germans employing tanks, 88-mm. anti-tank guns and extensive mining to augment their delaying tactics. In addition hundreds of mortars and hundreds of guns (the larger ones firing from across the Rhine) produced what Montgomery regarded as the heaviest volume of fire from enemy weapons encountered by British troops in the whole campaign; especially lethal was the shrapnel air burst effect in the forests where the trees exploded the shells before they reached the ground.

It was not until 4 March that the Germans pulled back here. By then the Ninth U.S. Army had already broken through on the River Rur and they linked up with XXX Corps on 3 March near Geldern, thereby outflanking the Schlieffen Position in the south. One of the most valuable consequences of 'Veritable' had been the way in which it had sucked German troops away from the Ninth Army, so assisting the Americans to make rapid advances from the south and achieve a pincer movement with the First Canadian Army.

On 6 March, the German High Command ordered a withdrawal across the Rhine which was to be completed by the 10th. To protect their bridgehead at Wesel, it was essential for the Germans to prevent the Canadians and Americans from taking a few key places. Of these the mined town of Xanten was the most important. With troops from the 43rd Wessex Division, the Canadians had a costly struggle, losing 400 men, before the German Parachutists were driven from the town and its immediate neighbourhood. Two small but strategically vital villages were the scenes of similar bloody rearguard actions.

In 'Veritable', a comparatively unknown offensive, the 'butcher's bill' had been tragically high on both sides. From 8 February to 10 March, the First Canadian Army had suffered 15,634 casualties, of which nearly two-thirds were from the British troops of XXX Corps. Of the 5414 Canadian losses nearly all were in the 2nd and 3rd Infantry Divisions, and 3600 of these were incurred during the short period from 26 February to 10 March. The German losses were estimated at about 22,000, with a further 22,000 taken prisoner.

By 10 March, British, American and Canadian troops had reached the Rhine from just below Emmerich in the north to just above Strasbourg in the south, and Patton's troops were already across the river at the Remagen bridge, seized on the 7th. Thus, not only were the Allies poised for the last phase of the campaign, but they had also cut the main German supply artery; the bombings of the railways and roads made the Germans rely increasingly on the Rhine for the movement of their heavier equipment and stores.

During this battle, the Canadian forces gained two out of the four Victoria Crosses awarded to them in the whole campaign. The first of these was won on 26 February by Sergeant Cosens (Queen's Own Rifles of Canada). The description in *The Official History of the Canadian Army in the Second World War* gives a vivid picture of the conditions during this very terrible battle:

> Sergeant Aubrey Cosens took command of the other survivors of his platoon, only four in number. Through the thick of the enemy fire which was sweeping the area from all sides he ran twenty-five yards across an open space to a tank of the 1st Hussars which had now come up in support. Seating himself in front of the turret he calmly directed the gunner's fire against the German positions, and then broke up a second counter-attack by plunging the tank into the midst of the startled paratroopers. Next, taking the offensive, he reorganized his little group and, still crouched on top of the Sherman, ordered the driver to ram the first of the three buildings. While his men gave covering fire he went inside, killed several of the defenders and captured the rest. When he entered the second house he found that the occupants had not awaited his coming. Covered by the tank's fire he then crossed the road alone to clear the third strongpoint – a two-storey building held by several Germans. 'We followed him from building to building gathering the prisoners', one of his

comrades later reported. Having thus broken the hard core of resistance in Mooshof, Cosens gave orders for consolidating the position, and set off to report to his company commander. On the way he was killed by a sniper's bullet. This very gallant non-commissioned officer had himself killed at least twenty of the enemy and captured as many more, and had gained an objective vital to the success of the 8th Brigade's operations.

On 1 March, the outstanding bravery and leadership of Major Tilston (Essex Scottish Regiment) also earned him the very rare distinction of the Victoria Cross; he was so seriously wounded in the fighting that both his legs had to be amputated. *The Official History of the Canadian Army in the Second World War* records:

> The fighting was fiercest on the left, where the Essex 'C' Company, led by Major F. A. Tilston, had to cross 500 yards of open ground and ten feet of barbed wire to reach the foremost trenches. That they succeeded in their task was largely due to the inspired leadership of their commander. Although wounded in the head during the advance, Major Tilston was the first into the enemy trenches, silencing with a grenade a machine-gun post that was holding up one of his platoons. As he pressed on with his main force to the second line of defences he was again severely wounded in the thigh but remained in command. In vicious hand-to-hand fighting the Essex cleared the trenches; but before there was time to consolidate the Germans launched a counter-attack heavily supported by mortars and machine-guns. Through this hail of fire Tilston calmly moved in the open among his depleted forces (now one-quarter of their original strength), organizing his defences platoon by platoon. Six times he crossed bullet-swept ground to the flanking Essex company to carry grenades and ammunition to his hard-pressed men. Though hit a third time he refused medical aid until, lying in a shellhole, he had

ordered his one remaining officer to take over and had briefed him concerning the plan of defence and the absolute necessity of holding the position.

III. Summary
SIR BRIAN HORROCKS

This was the grimmest battle in which I took part during the war. No one in their senses would choose to fight a winter campaign in the flooded plains and dense pinewoods of Northern Europe, but there was no alternative. We had to clear the western bank of the Rhine if we were to enter Germany in strength and finish off the war. Although our losses seemed very high, I kept on reminding myself that there had been 50,000 casualties during the first morning of the Battle of the Somme in the First World War. Eisenhower summed up the situation when he wrote in a letter to Crerar, 'Probably no assault in this war has been conducted in more appalling conditions than was this one.'

To end this chapter on a cheerful note, I recall that we were visited by the Prime Minister. I am glad to say that my final memory of seeing him on the battlefield was of a happy Churchill. It was in March 1944 during the Battle of the Reichswald, when we were driving down the west bank of the Rhine and fighting for the first time on German soil. What made it so dramatic was the 51st Highland Division's massed bands and pipes marching and counter-marching before the old warrior. He was visibly moved, as he stood for the first time with his feet firmly planted on the territory of the enemy which he had been fighting for so long. And, as a fitting background to the skirl of the pipes, he could hear the thunder of the guns of my Corps continuing the battle only a few miles away.

Chapter 12
The Rhine Crossing and the Advance to the Elbe
SIR BRIAN HORROCKS

The final Rhine bridge on the near bank which had been held so tenaciously by the German paratroopers was finally evacuated on the night of 9–10 March and XXX Corps reverted to the command of the Second British Army. By 10 March 1944 there was no more organized German resistance west of the Rhine.

During the Battle of the Reichswald, General Dempsey and his Second Army H.Q. had been planning the crossing of the Rhine and the establishment of a bridgehead on the far bank. His plan was to force an initial crossing over the Rhine by two Corps – XII Corps on the right and XXX Corps on the left, between the two small towns of Wesel and Emmerich. On this occasion, however, the main thrust, or *Schwerpunkt* as the Germans call it, was to be made by XII Corps, so the airborne operations to be carried out by the XVIII Airborne Corps, consisting of the 6th British and 17th U.S. Airborne Divisions, would be developed in depth on their front, with the primary object of seizing the bridges over the River Ijssel.

This was the first time since Normandy that the 'Old Pig', as we were called because our Corps sign was a wild boar, would not be in the lead; after our gruelling battle in the Reichswald, this came as a welcome relief. Towards the end of that battle, I had pulled back into reserve the 51st Highland Division, in order that they might practise river-crossing operations over the River Maas.

The idea of breaching the famous Rhine appealed to me enormously. Nevertheless, I realized that this was not going to be quite such a simple operation as many people seemed to think. The river was 1500 feet across, and according to my Intelligence staff, whose reports were always extremely accurate, on our particular front we were faced by the 8th Parachute Division in and around the town of Rees, with part of the 6th and 7th Parachute Divisions on their flanks, and supported by approximately 150 guns. Behind them, in reserve, were the 15th and 116th Panzer Divisions, all of whom we knew only too well from previous battles. Although they had suffered heavy casualties, these had been made up from within Germany. The bulk of their reinforcements of course were callow youths, since by this time the Germans really were scraping the bottom of the barrel to make up losses. But many of these youngsters were dedicated Nazis, and under the guidance of the extremely tough and experienced Parachute and Panzer officers and N.C.O.s they had been soon moulded into a formidable fighting force: It was bad luck that once more we should be faced by these diehard Nazis; after the crossing we heard stories, from the U.S. and our flanking corps, of German soldiers surrendering in their thousands, and of villages with white sheets hanging from every window, but this did not happen on our front. We had still to fight, and fight hard, right up to the end. I could not resist a feeling of admiration for the sterling qualities displayed by these German paratroopers and Panzers, when the bulk of them must have known that the war was irretrievably lost.

Crossing a river of this size presented the Royal Engineers with many highly technical problems, but experiments and preparations for bridging the Rhine and other wide water obstacles had been going on in the U.K. since early in 1943 on the Yorkshire Ouse at Goole. For the Rhine Crossing no less than 8000 Royal Engineers came under command of C.E. XXX Corps. Fortunately, orders for the necessary specialized equipment had been placed with the Ministry of Supply in good time. On the Rhine alone 22,000 tons of assault bridging had to come forward, including 25,000 wooden pontoons, very vulnerable to shell-fire and ice, 2000 assault boats, 650 storm boats and 120 river tugs, together with 80 miles of balloon cable and 260 miles of steel wire rope. Although this was primarily a Royal Engineers affair, it developed into a combined operation. For instance, the ferries and rafts had to be winched across by cable and there were not sufficient Royal Engineers for this purpose, as they were all required for other technical jobs, so we asked the R.A.F. – 159 Wing – whether they could spare us some of the men who operated their balloons. They produced fifty specialists in twelve hours, from a distance of 150 miles, and said that another 300 volunteers were available, if required. This was typical of the assistance which we always got from the R.A.F. The Navy were equally helpful, and produced a Royal Naval team which, under Bos'n Lescombe, established anti-mine booms upstream to prevent the Germans floating down demolitions and destroying the bridges when they were constructed.

In addition to the specialist Royal Engineers stores, a vast concentration of troops, assault boats, Buffaloes, guns, etc., had to be got into position. Unfortunately, the far bank of the Rhine was slightly higher than ours, so that German observers could see all that was going on on the flat ground on our side. To deceive the enemy about our crossing-place was a difficult problem, involving some intricate staff work under the direction of my B.G.S. Brigadier Jones (subsequently Major-General C. B. Jones, Vice-Adjutant General at the War Office). He took the whole thing in his stride. One of his first problems, just as in the Reichswald, was to control reconnaissance. Before an attack of this sort a large number of people must go forward and reconnoitre the position they are to occupy. This applies particularly to the Gunners, who have many mysterious rites of their own to perform before they can bring down accurate concentrations of fire.

Nobody was allowed forward on to the flat Polderland stretching back from the banks of the Rhine without reporting to a special branch of XXX Corps H.Q., where a very large-scale map of the forward area was maintained. This was known as 'The Pig Hotel' After examining the accommodation which they had been allocated, the reconnaissance parties were allowed to go forward a few at a time to see their 'rooms', which, if satisfactory, were then marked up on the plan as 'booked' I was particularly angry one day to hear that a certain Major-General, who was much too brave to take the normal precautions, had walked along the near bank of the Rhine, wearing his red hat. He subsequently left our area, with a monumental flea in his car

The final move forward on to the flat ground was under cover of darkness, and from the first night I had arranged for a continuous smoke-screen to be put down right along the river bank. This proved most effective, though when the wind blew towards us the smoke was apt to make everyone feel sick.

Just to show how regiments have to be prepared to turn their hands to almost anything, the Royal Dragoons, with 2000 men under command, were detailed to act as 'bank control troops'. This was no easy task, as units had to be marshalled into their correct areas and/or lanes in the dark, while all moves were co-ordinated with extreme accuracy. These alien tasks were handled skilfully and accurately by this highly-trained Cavalry Unit.

Thanks to Jones and his excellent team of officers, by 23 March all was ready, and at 5 p.m. our artillery opened fire. The 51st Highland Division had been earmarked to carry out the first crossing and just before 9 p.m. I climbed into an observation post on some high ground overlooking the Rhine. All around me were the usual noises of battle and, though I could see very little except the flicker of the guns, I had a mental picture of what was going on in front of me in the hazy darkness of that warm spring evening. I could imagine the leading Buffaloes carrying infantry of the 153rd and 154th Infantry Brigades lumbering along their routes which had been taped out and lit beforehand, and then lurching down into the dark waters of the Rhine. Upstream near Wesel, I could hear the aircraft of Bomber Command preparing the way for XII Corps, which was to assault later that night.

Then, at four minutes past nine precisely, I received the message for which I had been waiting – in its way a historical message, because it was from the first British troops across the Rhine: 'The Black Watch has landed safely on the far bank.'

The initial crossings went very smoothly, opposition was not as heavy as might have been expected, and our casualties were comparatively light. The enemy, however, soon recovered from their first shock and particularly bitter resistance was encountered in Rees by the 1st Gordons, who were under command of a very famous character, Lieut.-Col. Martin Lindsay, D.S.O., who had already distinguished himself in the Reichswald and usually made a habit of leading all attacks in person. Their real C.O., Grant-Peterkin, was acting Brigade Commander. For forty-eight hours it was hand-to-hand fighting before Rees was finally cleared of the enemy. This was very important, since the enemy in this town had good observation of the vast activities being carried out by the Royal Engineers on the far side of the river. It is bad enough to advance under heavy enemy shell-fire; it is far worse being engaged in static activities while being steadily shelled by the enemy. But the Royal Engineers never flinched. The Germans were not going to give up their famous river without a bitter struggle, and on the evening of the 24th, the 15th Panzer Grenadiers launched a vicious counter-attack, which was driven back by the 51st Highland Division.

In spite of the hard fighting on the far bank and under considerable shell-fire, the Sappers went steadily on with their vital task of building ferries and bridges so that tanks and self-propelled guns, etc., could be ferried across to help the infantry. In spite of the hostile artillery fire, by 1900 hours on 24 March three rafts started their ferrying operations opposite Rees. The other ferry site farther down the river was not under direct enemy observation and many tanks and other vehicles were ferried across from there. But, of course, ferrying is a comparatively slow business compared to crossing by bridge. The first bridge (Class 9) was completed at 0100 hours on 26 March and christened Waterloo Bridge; the next (Class 15), named Lambeth Bridge, was opened at 0830 hours that same day; meanwhile work on the larger Class 40 bridges proceeded apace – the first, London Bridge, was completed by midnight of 26–27 March, then Blackfriars at noon on the 28th. The last to come into operation was Westminster, in the evening of the 29th. I have always felt that the Rhine crossing was probably the Sappers' finest hour of the whole war. There were 155 killed or wounded on the banks of the Rhine.

The enlargement of the bridgehead was a slow business, far too slow for my liking, and I was determined as soon as possible to get the divisions on to narrow fronts, so that pressure on the enemy could be maintained by day and night. It would be tedious if I were to attempt to describe each action in detail. The German operations were nearly all of a similar pattern. Every possible road junction or bridge was systematically cratered, and the demolitions were then covered by fire from skilfully chosen defensive positions. Each developed as a little battle on its own. During the morning of the 24th I received a wireless message which caused me great grief, to the effect that Thomas Rennie, the Commander of the 51st Highland Division, had been killed by a mortar bomb when visiting one of his brigades on the far side of the river. I have always felt that Rennie had some foreboding about this battle. He and I had fought many times together, and I had never seen him so worried as over this Rhine project – he hated everything about it, and I couldn't understand why, because the actual crossing was fairly plain sailing compared with other operations which he had undertaken quite cheerfully. Like so many Highlanders I believe he was 'fey'. As all three brigades of 51st Highland Division were now engaged in battle, I appointed James Oliver, Commander of the 154th Brigade, to take over temporarily. Rennie's ultimate successor was MacMillan of the Argylls, a most able and popular officer, known throughout the army as

'Babe'. It was a fortunate choice, because, as Commander of the 152nd Brigade in Sicily, he was a familiar figure to all the Jocks.

Before leaving this battle I must mention two acts of extreme gallantry, which affected the whole battle, and indicated the bitter nature of the fighting concerned. The first one occurred just on the far bank of the Rhine. Speldrop was captured by 'C' Company of the 1st Black Watch, but it was violently counter-attacked by German infantry, supported by self-propelled guns. The situation became very confused, and as one platoon could not be located, 19-year-old Lieut. J. R. Henderson volunteered to take out a patrol to try and find how far the Germans had penetrated. After going a few hundred yards he came under intense fire, so, ordering the rest of the men to take cover, he went forward, accompanied by only one man carrying a Bren gun. Almost immediately an enemy machine-gunner opened fire at very close range. The Bren-gunner was killed and Henderson's revolver was knocked out of his hand. Undaunted, he charged the machine-gun position alone and killed the gunner with his shovel. He then went back to the patrol, which was cut off from the rest of the Battalion; realizing that it would be difficult to hold out without a machine-gun, Henderson crawled back several hundred yards under very heavy fire to the place where the Bren-gunner had been killed, collected the gun and with great difficulty made his way back to his men. By now, the house where he had left them was blazing, so he led his men across the open into another one, where they established themselves in a defensive position. During the next twelve hours enemy attacks against this house never relaxed and it was not until the following evening that the Highland Light Infantry of Canada, attacking with considerable artillery support, cleared the village after stiff fighting, and so relieved Henderson and his men, who were still holding out most gallantly. He was subsequently awarded the D.S.O. I had hoped that he might be given the Victoria Cross.

With the Rhine behind us, the drive into the heart of Germany began – Ninth U.S. Army, VIII, XII and XXX British, and II Canadian Corps from right to left. Owing to the stubborn resistance of the German Parachute troops we found ourselves echeloned back behind VIII and XII Corps – a somewhat unusual experience for The 'Old Pig', as up to now we had usually led the hunt through north-west Europe.

The next obstacle on which the Germans obviously intended to make a stand was the River Ems. The Household Cavalry reported that all bridges had been blown, with the exception of one at Lingen, and this one was prepared for demolition and strongly held. Had it not been for the second gallant action which I mentioned, we might well have been delayed there for several days, while arrangements were made for an opposed river crossing.

The Coldstream Guards (1st and 5th) Battalions, under Lieut.-Col. Gooch, decided that their only hope was to capture it by a *coup de main*. From a wooded hill some 400 yards away they reconnoitred the position. The road leading up to the bridge was on an embankment and the actual approach was barred by a solid timber road block. Six 500-lb aerial bombs were wired together on the bridge, ready to blow it up; on the far side were numerous trenches, and at least three of the deadly 88-mm. guns could be seen. If the bridge was to be captured intact, split-second timings were required.

The attack opened with an intense artillery concentration, while our tanks moved into position on the wooded hill and opened up on the enemy positions with every weapon they had. Under cover of this, No. 3 Company, commanded by Capt. Liddell, moved forward on either side of the embankment. As Liddell did not want his Company blown up on the bridge, he halted them just short of it and, going forward by himself, climbed over the road block which was 10 feet high. He then ran on to the bridge, in full view of the enemy, most of whom were firing at him, and cut the wires leading to the bombs. He then climbed back on to the top of the road block, waved his Company on, and at their head charged over the bridge, followed by a troop of tanks which smashed down the road block. The German positions were overrun – forty were killed, ten wounded, and forty-two taken prisoner, while the bridge had been captured intact. The slightest hesitation, and the whole thing might have been a disaster. This action saved at least two days in our advance, and I was so impressed that next day I went to the site and Liddell took me round, explaining how his battle had developed. Eighteen days later he was killed by a stray bullet. His death was a great tragedy which we all felt deeply, but then it is always the best who die in war.

The V.C., of course, is in a class of its own as regards decorations; not only has the recipient to carry out some almost suicidal act of gallantry, but that act must also have a definite effect on the outcome of the battle as a whole. Although I made several applications for this award to be granted to people serving in XXX Corps during the course of the war, the only time I succeeded was in Liddell's case, and he was killed before realizing that he had been awarded it.

Generally speaking, however, the awards of what might be called the normal decorations for gallantry involved the most cumbersome process imaginable. After the recommendation had been initiated by the Commanding Officer it had to obtain the approval of the Brigadier, Divisional, Corps and Army Commanders before being forwarded by the Commander-in-Chief to some mysterious committee in the U.K., whose composition I never discovered, but which almost certainly must have consisted of ancient warriors who had little, if any, experience of the conditions prevailing on the modern battlefield.

This process literally took months, so that when the award, with the committee's approval, arrived back at its source of origin, the odds were that the recipient had either been killed, or was wounded and in hospital, or had been posted elsewhere. Consequently, it was quite rare to see anyone in the front line wearing the ribbon of a medal awarded for gallantry. I complained many times about this laborious process, which did more harm than good, as the only soldiers with medal ribbons were almost certain to belong to non-combatant units. For instance, a cook at Army H.Q. was much more likely to be wearing a decoration than an N.C.O. leading a platoon or section in a fighting unit.

Decorations for the higher ranks arrived almost automatically – like the rations, in fact. If someone described to me the career of a Colonel or General, I could tell them pretty accurately what orders or decorations he wore. I remember on one occasion, when visiting a forward battalion, I asked a young Lance-Corporal commanding a section, with no medal ribbon on his breast at all, how many attacks he had taken part in. He replied, 'Seven or eight.' Yet there was I, living in comparative safety at Corps H.Q., with a chest shining like morning glory. For this reason I often felt quite ashamed when visiting forward units.

In the U.S. Army the system of awarding decorations was quite different, and much better. When the 101st and 82nd Airborne Divisions were under my command, the Divisional Commander would invite me to accompany him and present decorations to G.I.s of a unit just coming out of the line. The Battalion, tired and dirty, would be halted, and the Divisional Commander would call out, 'G.I. Jones!'; Jones would then step forward and, as he stood in front of his comrades, I would be asked to pin the particular decoration which he had earned on his chest. You could almost feel the morale of the unit rising, and that, after all, is the object of awarding decorations in war.

Returning to the events of the last few weeks of the war, slowly but steadily the advance from the bridgehead continued. The Guards Armoured, 3rd Division, 43rd Wessex and 51st Highland all took a hand. But the order of battle was constantly changing; at one time the 3rd Canadian Division held the sector on our left flank and distinguished themselves by some very hard fighting in the capture of Dornick and Frasselt. But on the 29th they passed back to the command of II Canadian Corps on our left. We were now advancing with, from right to left, 3rd Division, 51st Highland Division and 43rd Division: subsequently 3rd Division also passed temporarily to the command of XII Corps and the Guards Armoured took their place. During the whole of this advance we had wonderful support from the air – time after time the Typhoons smashed enemy counter-attacks.

On 14 April we suffered an irreparable loss, when Brigadier George Webb, C.B.E., D.S.O., was killed when his jeep hit a pothole and he then ran into a tree. He was known to everyone in the Corps and spent more of his time in the front line than he did at Rear H.Q.: he was, in my opinion, the best Administrative Staff Officer in the Army.

The primary task of XXX Corps was to protect the left flank of XII Corps, and towards the middle of April it became obvious that we should have to capture Bremen. Because a large town simply eats up troops, I had been doing my best to 'sell' this task to Neil Ritchie, commanding XII Corps. In a message to him I quoted from Joshua, pointing out to him how successfully the Israelites had dealt with the walls of Jericho. He cornily replied, 'Go ye and do likewise.' As by now his Corps was on the Elbe, there was nothing for it; Bremen was on my plate.

The more I studied the problem the less I liked it; without going into technical details, we were not properly balanced for this task. While I was thinking it over, the telephone rang and a Staff Officer from the Twenty-first Army Group said that Field-Marshal Montgomery was on his way down to see me. A few minutes later he entered my caravan and said, 'Jorrocks, I am not happy about Bremen.' 'Nor am I, sir', I replied. 'Tell me about it', he said. So, sitting in my map lorry I described the problem to him and made certain suggestions. He said not a word until I had finished. After a short pause while he considered the problem on the map, he said, 'We will do A, B, C and D.' These four decisions were vital – and Bremen was finished.

I have deliberately mentioned this because it was typical. Montgomery was not my immediate Commander, but he always kept in such close touch with the battle that he knew when and where 'the shoe pinched' He then went down to see the Commander on the spot – in this case, me – and listened to what he had to say. He then made up his mind immediately. As he drove away I knew that already he had probably forgotten all about Bremen and would be considering the next problem. This was what made him such a superb battle commander.

By now the 52nd Lowland Division and the 3rd British were back under my command. At this stage of the war the 52nd was one of the best divisions in the Twenty-first Army Group, because it still retained a high proportion of its original personnel. It had undergone a long period of the most rigorous training in the U.K. to prepare it for mountain warfare, but its first major battle had taken place below sea-level, at Walcheren – such is fate. They had fought magnificently on my right flank in the Reichswald battle, and I was delighted to have them in my Corps again. The plan for the capture of Bremen was that the 43rd Division and 52nd Division should attack from the east, north of the River Weser, and the 3rd Division south of it, while the 51st Highland Division carried out a feint from the south-west to draw the enemy defences in that direction.

The main assault on Bremen commenced on 24 April, and after some very hard fighting the 52nd Division fought their way into Arbedgen, then broke through the main eastern defences and on the following day penetrated right into the city centre; meanwhile, 43rd Division reached the autobahn. South of the Weser, 3rd Division captured Kattenturn and then, advancing over the flooded area south-west of the town in Buffaloes provided by the 4th Royal Tank Regiment and supported by the flame-throwers from the 5th Royal Tank Regiment, they passed over the ruins of the Focke Wulf factory and penetrated deep into the southern part of the city. This came as a complete surprise to the German garrison. In fact, Gen. Becker, the German C.-in-C., considered that we had cheated. 'You put your soldiers into the Verdammte

Schwimmen Panzer and came up behind us – it is not fair!' he said.

This was the last battle fought by 3rd Division. An assault division on the Normandy Beaches, they had subsequently fought a series of brilliant battles, culminating in this particularly successful operation. I was delighted and sent them the following message: 'As I started the war commanding a battalion in the 3rd Division, nothing could give me greater pleasure than to see it in such fine fettle at the end. Well done, 3rd Division!'

On that same evening men of the 4th/7th Dragoon Guards were sitting by their tanks, having the inevitable brew-up of tea, right in the centre of the city, when an immaculate jeep, driven by an equally immaculate British Military Policeman, drove up. He got out and, unconcernedly, nailed up a sign on an adjacent air-raid shelter. The sign read, 'Club Route Up' One driver was heard to remark, 'I reckon Clubs are trumps today.'

By midnight of 26–27 April it could be said that Bremen, the first big German port on the North Sea to fall into Allied hands, had been captured by XXX Corps. In four days we had taken 6000 prisoners (including two Generals and one Admiral).

Up to now I had been fighting the war as a professional soldier, without any particular hate for the enemy, but just short of Bremen we uncovered Sand-bostel, one of those horror camps which are now common knowledge, but which at that time came to us as a great shock. When General Adair and I entered we came across the most ghastly picture I have ever seen. The floor of the first hut we visited was covered with emaciated figures, clad in the most horrible striped pyjamas. Many were too weak to walk, but on seeing us they heaved themselves up and gave a pathetic cheer. Most of them had some form of chronic dysentery and the stench was so bad that I disgraced myself by being sick in the corner I was so angry that I ordered the Burgomaster of every one of the surrounding towns and villages to supply a quota of German women to clean up the camp and look after these unfortunate prisoners who were dying daily at an alarming rate. When the women arrived we expected some indication of horror or remorse when they saw what their fellow countrymen had been doing. Not a bit of it – I never saw a tear or heard one expression of pity from any of them. I also brought one of our own hospitals into the camp, and when I found some of our sisters looking very distressed – one was actually weeping – I apologized for having given them such an unpleasant task. 'Goodness me,' they said, 'it's not that. We are only worried because we can do so little for the poor things. Many of them have gone too far.' A somewhat different approach to the problem by the women of two countries.

But to turn to a more pleasant subject: we discovered a collection of sailing yachts of all sizes, tucked away in odd creeks and on hards along the River Weser near Bremen. As the war was nearly over I thought these would come in handy for our troops in the Army of Occupation, so I ordered a couple of soldiers to be placed on each, just to make certain they didn't disappear. A few weeks later I received a signal from the Senior British Admiral in the area, asking for these boats to be handed over forthwith to the Royal Navy. I flatly refused, and added in my message, 'Who captured Bremen – the Army or the Navy?' Back came a terse message, 'Everything that floats belongs to the Navy', to which I replied, 'Rather than hand them over, I'll sink the lot.' The quarrel ended peacefully when we shared the spoils between us, and when the war was over many soldiers spent profitable hours learning to sail.

After the capture of Bremen, XXX Corps was ordered to clear the peninsula which lies between the estuaries of the Elbe and the Weser. For the final phase of the war in Europe the Corps consisted of, from right to left, the Guards Armoured Division, 51st Highland Division, 43rd Division and 52nd Division. The German resistance was intermittent – some ardent Nazis preferred to die rather than surrender, but the chief difficulty we encountered was the nature of the country, which was low-lying, easily flooded and containing few roads, all of which had been, as usual, systematically cratered by the Germans. However, our advance went on.

On 3 May I was told confidentially that the Germans were negotiating surrender, but this was not to be communicated to anyone else. I was determined that, with the war so nearly over, no lives should be lost unnecessarily. So, as I went round the different formations, instead of urging them on, as was my normal practice, I invented all sorts of excuses to make them postpone the next day's offensive operations. I could see them looking at me with astonishment, and no doubt after I had departed they must have shaken their heads sadly and said, 'The old man has lost his nerve at last.'

I had often wondered how the war would end. When it came it could hardly have been more of an anti-climax. I happened to be sitting in the military equivalent of the smallest room, when I heard a voice on the wireless saying, 'All hostilities will cease at 0800 hours tomorrow morning, 5 May.'

It was a wonderful moment – the sense of relief was extraordinary; for the first time for five years I would no longer be responsible for other men's lives. The surrender on our front took place at 1430 hours on 5 May, when the German General who commanded the Corps Ems and his Chief of Staff arrived at our H.Q. Elaborate arrangements had been made for their reception. Our military police, looking very smart, escorted them to a table in the centre of the room: all round the wall was a ring of interested Staff Officers and other ranks of XXX Corps. When all was ready I came in and seated myself all alone opposite the two Germans. After issuing my Orders for the Surrender, I finished with these words: These Orders must be obeyed scrupulously. I warn you we will show no mercy if they are not. Having seen one of your horror camps, my whole attitude towards Germany has changed.'

The Chief of Staff jumped up and said, 'The Army had nothing to do with those camps.' 'Sit down!' I replied, 'There were German soldiers on sentry duty outside, and you cannot escape responsibility. The world will never forgive Germany for those camps.'

The German forces, who were concentrated in the north-west corner of the Cuxhaven peninsula, were ordered to stack all their weapons at certain points. A couple of days later, with an escort of armoured cars from the Household Cavalry which had been specially cleaned and burnished for the occasion, I drove round the enemy lines just to see that our orders were being obeyed, and how the disarmament was proceeding. I found the remnants of the parachute army concentrated on an airfield. When I saw the miserable equipment – just a few old patched up self-propelled guns and tanks – with which they had managed to delay our advance for so long, I turned to their Divisional Commander and said, 'I must congratulate you on the fighting qualities of your Division', but then I added, 'Your officers and N.C.O.s will be placed in a concentration camp for the time being, under our guards. This is really a compliment. They look much too tough and dangerous to have them knocking about just at the present moment.'

We celebrated the final victory by holding a parade, where I took the salute, and all the formations of XXX Corps marched past. As I saw the smart men, well-polished tanks, guns and vehicles passing by, it was incredible to think that only a week before they had been covered with the grime of battle.

So ended the active war of XXX Corps. It had been a long journey through many lands, starting in the Western Desert some three years before, it had now ended deep in the heart of Germany.

Chapter 13
The Final Liberation of the Netherlands
EVERSLEY BELFIELD

Introduction by *Sir Brian Horrocks*

The airborne battle for Arnhem had marked only the partial liberation of Holland. This chapter deals with the final freeing of the Dutch from the iron grip of the Germans. I followed this liberation as closely as possible. I have always felt that the Dutch suffered more from the German occupation than any other western country. I have therefore found this last chapter intensely moving.

*   *   *

By April 1945, First Canadian Army had been reinforced by the transfer of their I Corps from Italy, which meant that nearly all their troops were now under one command. In the concluding weeks of the war, the Canadian forces remained on the westernmost Allied flank. They liberated most of Holland north of the Rhine and the part of Germany that lies between the Ems and Weser estuaries. For the seven divisions involved, five Canadian, one British and one Polish, this was often an exhilarating and rewarding period as they were welcomed by the Dutch who were overjoyed to be at last freed from Nazi rule.

The larger II Corps played the more active role, and its progress will be traced first. On 24 March, 2nd and 3rd Canadian Infantry Divisions crossed the Rhine near Rees and spent the next week clearing the northern bank of the river down to Emmerich, meeting some unpleasant pockets of resistance on the way. With Emmerich under their control, the Canadians could construct three bridges across the Rhine and, starting on 1 April, they began an advance in a northerly direction that continued until the fighting ceased on 4 May.

By 10 April, the Canadians had taken both Zutphen and Deventer Although occasionally German units stood and fought brief delaying actions, their main concern was to retreat as quickly as possible. Throughout their progress the Canadians were frequently assisted by up-to-date and vital information passed to them by the Dutch underground movement. In the final stage of the liberation of the northern Netherlands, the main objective was the large old town of Groningen. To create confusion behind the German lines, it was decided to drop a mixed French and Belgian brigade of the Special Air Service (S.A.S.). During the night of 7–8 April, these troops were scattered over a wide rural area to the south of Groningen and probably helped to demoralize the Germans further. Groningen was reached on 13 April, but it took the Canadians three days of hard fighting before the town fell. The opposition here came largely from Dutch SS soldiers, who, knowing that their days were numbered, often sold their lives dearly; the Canadian task was also made more difficult by the decision not to bomb any part of Groningen. In the next few days detachments fanned out to reach the coast and almost all the northern Netherlands was liberated by 20 April. In less than four weeks the 2nd and 3rd Canadian Infantry Divisions had covered nearly 120 miles on an increasingly broad front, they had taken about 10,800 prisoners and to sustain their advance had had to build some fifty bridges.

The fighting had not, however, ended for the 2nd and 3rd Canadian Divisions who had to be switched to the other flank of II Corps. At first the advance had been much swifter here, meeting only sporadic opposition, but by 15 April, 4th Canadian Armoured Division had penetrated deeply into Germany, coming up against the strongly defended Küsten Canal. This wide waterway, which links the Ems to the Weser, blocks the path both to Oldenburg, an important communications centre, and also to the Ostfriesland peninsula on which is the large naval base of Wilhelmshaven. In their approach to the western end of the Küsten Canal, the Polish Armoured Division had had to move through the peat bogs of the broad and desolate Ems valley and there they came on two large hutted camps in which they were amazed and delighted to discover 1700 Polish women fighters who had been taken prisoner by the Germans after the Warsaw Rising the previous August.

In some unco-ordinated last-ditch stands, the Canadians now had some of their fiercest fighting since they had crossed the Rhine. Their problems were complicated by an almost complete dearth of intelligence about the sizeable German forces who were composed of *ad hoc* groups of parachutists and others, as well as marines and sailors from the naval garrisons of Wilhelmshaven and Emden. Although the Küsten Canal had been breached by 20 April, the German resistance did not lessen and the terrain now proved to be a major obstacle. The Polish Divisional Commander claimed that he had never encountered more glutinous mud, even in the marshes of

Poland. The going was made even harder, as the Germans had methodically blown up the innumerable small bridges that carried the few roads across the network of streams and culverts. They had also liberally strewn the area with mines and craters. Nevertheless when the ceasefire was ordered on 4 May, both Leer and Oldenburg had been taken, and the Canadians and Poles had advanced well into the peninsula, being less than fifteen miles from Wilhelmshaven. When a war is obviously almost finished, casualties become particularly hard to accept and troops naturally tend to be cautious. It is therefore a measure both of the intensity of the German resistance, and also of the Canadian determination, that in one of their brigades the losses, from 17 to 25 April, amounted to 402 men. The Germans suffered even more severely in this last cruel spasm of the war.

Most of the western Netherlands lies below sea-level, and it is one of the most densely populated regions in the world. The humanitarian constraints of keeping to the minimum casualties amongst about five million civilians, as well as avoiding the wholesale destruction of property, meant that liberation had become, by April, more a political rather than a purely military affair. The result of this was that plans had to be continually changed to try to mitigate both the horrors of an ever-increasing food shortage and the threat by the notorious Seyss-Inquart, the Nazi High Commissioner, to blow up the great dikes and flood huge tracts of Dutch soil with sea-water. In this section, therefore, the events of April 1945 took on a dreamlike quality in which a growing sense of elation, inspired by the knowledge that the war was almost finished, was tempered by a fearful foreboding that the Nazis might yet unleash an overwhelming act of brutality against the near-starving Dutch people.

The first move here was the clearance of the 'Island', the widely-flooded chunk of land stretching between Nijmegen and Arnhem. This was now quickly occupied, on 3 April, by the formations of the newly-arrived I Canadian Corps. After a pause to regroup, Arnhem was taken on 13 April by 49th British Division (attached to I Canadian Corps throughout this last phase). At this time, I noted in my diary that

> ... the vast smoke-screens, a feature of all the river crossings, made observation often very difficult. The unhappy town of Arnhem was burning hard, with smoke towering up to several thousand feet, but the wind was blowing it away from me. To the right was the smaller town of Velp where I saw people running as smoke shells burst above it, sending down their streamers and sometimes starting a fire; I wondered whether they were civilians, one cannot distinguish from the air. The process of liberation is often a most unpleasant one; if we were conquering the Germans, I should not care much, but the unfortunate Holland had suffered enough already.

Inevitably Arnhem had come to occupy a particularly emotional place in the minds of tens of thousands of British soldiers. So near, yet so elusively distant, perched on a gentle hill on the far bank of the Lower Rhine, this town had almost come to be the symbol of the unattainable. For nearly seven months troops had gazed into its dim shape, wondering when it would be liberated. This had now at last happened and I wrote:

> It was a stirring thought to realize, as we gently switchbacked our way in a jeep over the seemingly fragile floating bridge, that it was

the Rhine that was below us and Arnhem in front of us. I passed into the area where the Airborne Division made their final stand. It is a terrifying sight with wrecked houses, the trees still damaged, being torn and slivered by the mortaring and shelling, with broken branches with their brown autumn leaves attached. Piles of equipment lie around, burnt and abandoned. It is the complete lack of any attempt to clear up the place which gives it this air of macabre unreality. Some men had found a Stirling aircraft that had gone in nose first; the crew still in the machine, the Germans had merely taken their parachutes from them. The whole area, almost devoid of civilians as it is, breathes an air of tragedy. One always gets this eerie feeling when taking over a place directly after it has been vacated by the retreating Germans.

A few days later, the advance had reached the open moorland country beyond Arnhem where most of the Airborne Division had landed. I found,

> … everywhere along both sides of the Ede road there are graves [I was trying to find the grave of a friend killed at Arnhem], little rough wooden crosses made of two sticks or the cross-piece merely a part of a wooden box, seldom a name, though a few have one, most just proclaim 'ein Engleesch soldar' or 'ein Duitch soldar', nearly all have some token of the soldier, a red beret, a steel helmet or a parachute helmet, or perhaps only a gas mask at the foot of the grave. The burials must have been done in the main by the Dutch people; often one sees a larger airborne troop's grave and nearby a similar German grave, both marked by their respective type of steel helmet. By the road are several charred jeeps and on the heath itself are the parachute packs of a regiment or perhaps a brigade. In other fields the grass is dead in the shape of gliders, perhaps 40 in all, whether they were burnt before or after the landing I cannot tell. I inspected two wrecked gliders, one that contained a jeep and six-pounder anti-tank gun,

the other a jeep and trailer, the vehicles were rusted up. All around are split cartridge cases, anti-tank ammunition, small arms containers, etc. One can only realize vaguely the heroism with which the Airborne Division fought.

Meanwhile, farther north, the 1st Canadian Division had reached Apeldoorn. The Germans were determined to make a stand here along the canal which runs through the eastern edge of this pleasant city. To avoid damaging Apeldoorn, the Canadians surrounded the town by sending the 5th Armoured Division up from Arnhem. On 17 April the Apeldoorn garrison capitulated. Two days later, after some sharp skirmishes with retreating units, the Canadians had taken Barneveld and had come to the outskirts of Amersfoort which was on the Grebbe Line. These formidable fortifications ran from Grebbe, on the Lower Rhine, to a flooded area on the IJsselmeer, and the Germans clearly intended to hold them at all costs. By this time the other formations of I Corps had also moved up to or nearly reached the Grebbe Line and to all intents and purposes the fighting ceased on 19 April. It was stopped because the risks of any further advances into the western Netherlands far outweighed any conceivable advantages. Some food began to be sent in to help the starving Dutch, and supplies of all kinds were accumulated to alleviate the worst hardships when the war ended.

The meeting that led to the German surrender at Wageningen on 5 May took place in a half-ruined hotel whose lounge had been filled with chairs and tables and whose windows had been boarded up for the occasion. When I arrived there,

> ... there were a large number of jeeps, staff cars, motor bicycles as well as press and film-crew cars parked in the little open square

opposite the building, and white and pink chestnut trees were in bloom. The Germans had been ordered to turn up at 1600 hours, and as the time approached the feeling of tension grew. The first to arrive was Prince Bernhardt in a vast open Mercedes, once the property of Seyss-Inquart, which had been stolen (as had his other car) by some youths in the Dutch underground movement who had presented it to the Prince. A pause of about ten minutes occurred before a large Buick arrived, flying the Corps Commander's flag, out of which stepped the General [Lieut.-General Foulkes, I Canadian Corps Commander] and his brigadier with some other staff officers. A few minutes later an open German staff car, driven by a black-coated driver, came rushing round the corner, stopped with a jerk and the Germans piled out, literally like the Marx Brothers in a hurry; General Blaskowitz did not register much with me since I saw him so briefly, but he was apparently somewhat taken aback by the roomful of pressmen and photographers; following his machine was a Volkswagen with more Germans, who also entered the building.

I listened over the microphone in the BBC recording room as

> ... the Corps Commander started telling, in a very firm tone, the Germans exactly what was expected of them, and giving them the terms which he read out. It was good to hear him say that 'I am in charge of the Netherlands and mine are the only orders you will obey and I hold you personally responsible for seeing that they are carried out.'

Amongst other orders were that all explosives should be removed from the dikes and that the Dutch SS criminals should be locked up, which Blaskowitz said he had already done. I wrote in my diary:

By this time there was quite a crowd of drivers and various lesser officers listening to the microphone, everyone was smiling as the terms were read out and feeling that this was the day that they had been waiting for, for five and a half years. A dozen yards away, the three Germans not attending the conference stood sullenly around, although Blaskowitz's SS driver still looked arrogant. The Germans came out as precipitately as they had gone in and drove off to their lines at full speed. The whole business had lasted just over an hour.

Two days later we moved into the newly-liberated Netherlands.

The enthusiasm is such as I have never seen before [I had missed the liberation of France and Belgium]. I walked into Doorn, where the ex-Kaiser had spent his exile, and the little town looked like an ant-heap that had been disturbed, in the park a band was playing, watched by crowds, whilst others danced. Some people sat in their gardens and others by the roadside watching columns of food lorries passing through with white flags flying. In other parts, young people and old were waving orange flags and cheering, coming out on to the road with arms outstretched to touch hands with the passing soldiery, streamers were stretched across the road, flowers were thrown into the cabs of lorries. All this was still happening at least twenty-four hours after the first troops had been through.

That evening a friend and I took a jeep into Utrecht. The road was still lined with some orange-bedecked, waving, cheering crowds. Occasionally a car with German officers went by and the crowd fell silent. In Utrecht there were scenes of wild rejoicing, the whole population seemed to be walking through the main streets. Now and again they would coalesce into a large procession, headed perhaps by a drummer, and they would all start singing English and Dutch songs. I saw three Marines caught up by some people, they all held hands and pranced around in a circle for a few minutes. Once a ragged collection of German soldiery, with their horse-drawn vehicles, went down the street and a sudden silence descended on the scene.

Behind these festivities there were unseen tragedies. I had flown low over Utrecht that morning and had been horrified at the number of hearses to be seen in the streets. A day later in The Hague, I visited a Dutch family where the old grandparents were so enfeebled by starvation that they could not stand. Unfortunately here the first food supplies had had to be dropped from the air and were hard-style rations with biscuits, and these were unsuitable for the elderly whose digestion had been so weakened by food shortages. The official Canadian report stated that

> ... while a state of such acute general starvation as feared had not been reached at the time of the entry of our troops, the state of food supplies would indicate that this catastrophe had only been avoided by a matter of two or three weeks.... It is probable that there are many cases of people suffering from starvation in their houses. Reports would indicate that death from starvation has been confined to the very old, the very young and the very poor.

Later on in Germany, I never witnessed anything comparable to the conditions then prevailing in the Netherlands.

I was privileged to round off this period with a memorable experience. Before we left our kind landlady in Nijmegen, we had promised that as soon as possible we would try to get her some news of her husband. He had been visiting one of his firm's factories near Leiden when the Airborne Division landed at Arnhem in September and she had heard nothing from him since then. Two of us set off in a jeep, but got lost in a very rural part near Leiden where some bridges had been blown up. When we asked the way we were directed down a road with a house at the end of it. In my diary I wrote:

> There were swarms of people who greeted us and asked us to go down to the local Resistance Headquarters and there officially liberate the village because no Allied troops had yet entered and the village had been waiting two days for this ceremony. We drew the jeep into the small yard near the pub, where a big crowd had gathered to look at the jeep which was one of the first they had seen. The mayor, a stout little man, spoke good English after years in Singapore and Hong Kong. He asked us to inspect the local Resistance, who were lined up and included two girls who were carrying flags of Britain and the U.S.A. Having strapped on our full military equipment, we went round the assembled ranks and then made short speeches to say how glad we were that the Dutch were free and might they never suffer the same horrors again. This was translated by the mayor and was received with cheers and finally by three cheers. The main officials then invited us into the pub, where the grave landlord, an ex-seaman, produced a bottle of luncheon port to toast the liberation; all the other wine saved for the liberation had been prematurely consumed at the time of the Arnhem landing. We then talked to those who spoke English of their recent experiences. They told us that 60 per cent of the young men between 18 and 40 had been taken off to forced labour in Germany. The rest had had to live in circumstances similar to those of recusant priests in Elizabethan England, with special chambers in cellars and attics where these young men were hidden. They had to spend the nights in these poky spots since the Gestapo and the local traitors usually came at night; the latter were the more dangerous as they knew the people and the country better. They had cornered and killed the mayor's son only three weeks before. The village had hidden two men from the Airborne forces and had buried two

airmen who had been killed when a Mosquito plane had crashed, this had been done at night since the Germans had earlier refused permission for the burial. I asked how the Germans had behaved, and they said, as I had expected, that the Wehrmacht on the whole behaved well, but that the SS were vile and liable to shoot on the slightest provocation. Just before we left an excited messenger came in to report that the last of the uncaptured traitors had been found dressed as a woman in a neighbouring farm. The final ceremony had now been arranged. We stepped out of the double doors of the bar parlour to where the villagers had all assembled. Two little girls gave us bouquets of flowers, tulips, lilies of the valley, roses and lilac. While a little boy handed us a large round cheese, we kissed the children to the accompaniment of cheers and set off in the jeep over the bridge. The crowd grasped at my waving hand and almost pulled me out of the machine. Thus ended our liberation of the little beflagged village of W———brugge [I never knew its exact name].

In conclusion, 126,500 German soldiers were taken prisoner during April and May in the western Netherlands; of these 117,629 laid down their arms at the surrender. To the north, II Canadian Corps collected another 30,000 prisoners after the end of the fighting. Nevertheless since crossing the Rhine, the Canadian Army's losses had been 6300, of which 1482 were fatal; thus this last victorious phase had been far from a 'walk-over.'

Postscript
Germany after V-E Day
SIR BRIAN HORROCKS

It was almost unbelievable that the war was over at last. At our next morning conference, instead of laying down objectives and arranging for artillery concentrations to destroy German positions, etc., we had to switch our minds 180 degrees, because the problem which confronted us now was to preserve life in Germany during the next year. Everything was in short supply, and there was a distinct possibility that large numbers of Germans would starve unless we came to their help. Nearly all the roads and important rail junctions had been smashed by our bombers, and cities like Hanover, Bremen and Hamburg were just a shambles, where the bulk of the hollow-eyed shabby population eked out a troglodyte existence under the ruins of what had once been their homes.

In the country districts things were better, though what struck us most was the complete absence of all able-bodied men. The farms were run by women and very old, or badly wounded men, plus, of course, slave labourers who had been compulsorily brought in from countries which the German armies had overrun, but who were now naturally turning on their German masters and demanding to be sent home. All the men were either dead, in hospital, or in prisoner-of-war camps, mainly in the east.

Montgomery divided up the British Zone among the corps, and I found myself responsible for an area north-west of Hanover, about the size of Wales. Luckily I had a very able staff. XXX Corps had been together for a long time, and the weaker brethren had long since fallen by the wayside. The post-war problems with which we were faced were right up our street. Montgomery laid down priorities food and housing – but then did not attempt to interfere in any way. Our first task was to open up communications, to repair broken bridges and get the railways running again. To start with, a great deal of this work had to be carried out by the British troops and this very naturally caused some resentment. So I arranged for officers to go around and explain that it was in the interests of Britain to start trading as soon as possible with the Germans. This could not be done until communications had been repaired. Moreover, if large numbers of Germans starved to death that winter, the world would blame us.

This was the second time that I had occupied Germany after a war, so I knew what to expect. It is one of the most difficult things in the world to occupy a defeated country without causing bitterness and hatred which can only lead to trouble in the future. As a young officer in Cologne in 1919 I had seen for myself the horrors of raging inflation. Only the 'spivs' with their flaxen-haired mistresses in large Mercedes cars seemed to flourish. The rest of the population suffered terribly. I got to know a German professor and his family who could never afford meat, and had potatoes only three times a week, while we used to draw the pay for our troops in sacks of them. It was a horrible situation, which has always remained in my mind, and I was determined to do my best to prevent it happening again in my zone of Germany. But we had to work fast as winter was not far away. It was the only time in my life when, to all intents and purposes, I was a dictator in my district – though, I hope, a benevolent one. To give just one example, reports began to come in that there was a grave shortage of coal – the output was getting worse because the miners were short of clothes. I immediately ordered a levy to be carried out in the nearby towns to provide adequate clothing for the miners, and, sure enough, a few weeks later the graph showing coal production began to rise. I could not help smiling when I thought of what would have happened in dear old democratic Britain if the Government had ordered clothes to be removed forcibly from, say, Cardiff, to clothe the miners in the Welsh valleys.

Apart from the horror camps which, to this day, I cannot understand, as such barbarism is alien to the German nature, I had always had a considerable admiration for the German Army which, with the exception of certain SS units, and of course the Gestapo, had always fought cleanly. We had fought them twice and I was determined to do my best to see that, in the event of a third war breaking out, we should both be on the same side.

For some astonishing reason which I have never understood, strict orders were issued that there was to be no fraternization between the British troops and the German people. I could imagine no better way of breeding permanent hostility. So I ordered all the C.O.s in XXX Corps to organize clubs for German children. I felt that nobody could blame the children for this war – some of them had never even seen a bar of chocolate. The British soldier likes children, and very soon, in many of the villages, you would see a tall, khaki-clad figure walking along hand in hand with a couple of flaxen-haired children. German parents were coming up to our men and thanking them for all that they were doing to help their children. In fact, the scheme was working well.

Then one day I gave a party at my H.Q. for 150 German children: we had saved up our rations and the cooks had worked miracles. Unfortunately, some callow press reporters also came to the party (the senior experienced men whom I knew so well had all left us when the fighting ceased). They were obviously hostile, and next day there were headlines in the British press: 'General gives party for German children' The fat was now in the fire. 'Nobody was giving parties for the British children', etc. Letters poured in, and the kindest comment was that I must obviously be mad. Montgomery was furious, and I was ordered to 'stop this nonsense', an order which, of course, I officially obeyed. But I also let it be known quietly that Nelson was not the only Commander with a blind eye.

So much for our relations with the Germans, but my first problem, as always, was the welfare of our own troops. Although demobilization was working smoothly, it would be months before some of the men could expect to be back in civilian life. We decided to do two things. Firstly, I had a particularly brilliant welfare staff, and they took over completely Bad Harzburg, a German holiday resort in the Harz Mountains. This proved very popular with the troops. In addition, there were hundreds of canteens and clubs, and one particularly popular resort on a large inland lake called Steinhuder Meer, where the yachts came in very handy and many soldiers learned to sail.

Arrangements had also been made for manufacturers in neutral countries to supply XXX Corps with toys and suitable gifts to send to families in the U.K. Lorries containing these presents called in at all the units, and their contents were eagerly snapped up.

Secondly, and still more important, was the question how to keep the men occupied. It was no good training them to be soldiers as the war was over, so we collected machinery, tools, etc., from factories which we had overrun, and started courses for men in their civilian trades. We arranged for union officials to come out from the U.K. to explain the new regulations and developments which had taken place during the war. The enthusiasm shown on these courses was most encouraging. Men were so delighted to get back to their old civilian trades that they would often forgo their dinner hour.

Although the war was over, I and my Staff were kept very busy. Then in the late autumn I was posted to the U.K. to take over the appointment of G.O.C. Western Command, with H.Q. in Chester. My last social engagement in Germany was to dine with my old friends, the 51st Highland Division, whom I had first met just before the Battle of Alamein, and I was very moved when they drank my health, with Highland Honours.

On the last night I was sitting down to a farewell dinner with my Staff when an orderly rushed in to say that the house was on fire. Fire engines arrived from all over the place but owing to lack of water they fought a losing battle with the flames, and we had to evacuate the house. My last night with XXX Corps was therefore spent in my caravan and when I flew off next day the house was still burning merrily. The fire was started in my study by a smouldering beam under the floor, but no one has ever believed this. I shall go down in history as the Commander who burned down his house during some fantastic orgy on the night before he left.

British and German Artillery

British

The 25-pounder gun had a maximum range of 13,400 yards and a normal rate of fire of three rounds per minute. First line ammunition carried was 144 high-explosive rounds, sixteen rounds of smoke and twelve rounds of armour-piercing shells.

Thu 5·5-inch medium gun fired either a 100-lb high-explosive shell to a maximum range of 16,200 yards or an 80-lb shell to 18,000 yards. The normal rate of fire was one round per minute. Each Medium Regiment had sixteen guns.

Although the Air Observation Post Squadrons were a part of R.A.F. Fighter Command, all the pilots were artillery officers. A squadron had three flights of four Auster aircraft. Each Corps had its own Air O.P. Squadron, as did both the two Armies, their squadrons being primarily employed in directing the fire of the AGRAs.

Note: The Typhoon was a large single-seater aircraft with a 2180 h.p. Napier Sabre engine. It could be armed with four 20-mm. Hispano cannon, two 500-lb or 1000-lb bombs or eight 60-lb rocket projectiles.

German

The Germans relied increasingly on heavy mortars rather than artillery. Their most effective weapons were the five-to ten-barrelled Nebelwerfers which fired rocket-type high-explosive projectiles and had a very rapid rate of fire. These weapons were hard to locate, being extremely mobile, and produced only a small flash. They were nicknamed 'Moaning Minnies' by the British troops. In Normandy there were five of these mortar regiments, each having 60–70 weapons. They came in three sizes:

150-mm.	751-lb projectile	Range 7300 yards
220-mm.	248-lb projectile	Range 8600 yards
300-mm.	277-lb projectile	Range 5000 yards

British and Canadian Divisional Organization

The composition of British and Canadian divisions is set out below. To save space the various headquarters, defence and employment platoons, field security sections and postal units have been omitted

	ARMOURED DIVISION		INFANTRY DIVISION		AIRBORNE DIVISION	
Brigades and their Main Units	Armoured Brigade	1	Infantry Brigades	3	Parachute Brigades	2
	Armoured Regiments	3	Infantry Battalions each of about 800 soldiers)	9	Parachute Battalions	6
	Motor Battalion	1			Airlanding Brigade	1
	Infantry Brigade	1			Airlanding Battalions	3
	Infantry Battalions	3				
Reconnaissance	Armoured Reconnaissance Regiment	1	Reconnaissance Regiment	1	Airborne Armoured Reconnaissance Regiment	1
Artillery	Field Regiments	2	Field Regiments	3	Airlanding Light Regiment	1
	Anti-Tank Regiment	1	Anti-Tank Regiment	1	Airlanding Anti-Tank Batteries	2
	Light Anti Aircraft Regiment	1	Light Anti Aircraft Regiment	1	Airlanding Light Anti Aircraft Battery	1
Engineers	Field Squadrons	2	Field Companies	3	Parachute Squadrons	2
	Field Park Squadron	1	Field Park Company	1	Airborne Field Company	1

Signals	Bridging Troop		Bridging Platoon		Airborne Field Park Company	
	Armoured Divisional Signals		Infantry Divisional Signals	1	Airborne Divisional Signals	
Machine Guns	Independent Machine-Gun Company		Machine-Gun Battalion			
Special Units					Independent Parachute Company (Pathfinders)	1
Supply and Transport	Brigade Companies	2	Brigade Companies	3	Composite Companies	2
	Divisional Troops Company	1	Divisional Troops Company	1	Light Composite Company	1
	Divisional Transport Company	1				
Medical Services	Field Ambulance	1	Field Ambulances	3	Parachute Field Ambulances	2
	Light Field Ambulance	1	Field Dressing Stations	2	Airlanding Field Ambulance	1
	Field Dressing Station	1	Field Hygiene Section	1		
	Field Hygiene Section	1				
Ordnance Workshops	Ordnance Field Park	1	Ordnance Field Park	1	Ordnance Field Park	
	Brigade Workshops	2	Brigade Workshops	3	Divisional Workshop	1
	Light Anti Aircraft Regiment Workshop		Light Anti Aircraft Regiment Workshop		Airlanding Light Aid Detachment (with units)	7
	Light Aid Detachments with units)	2	Light Aid Detachments with units)			

Provost	Divisional Provost Company 1	Divisional Provost Company	Divisional Provost Company
Strength	Officers 724, Other Ranks 14,240	Officers 870, Other Ranks 17,477	Officers 702, Other Ranks 11,446
TOTAL STRENGTH	14,964 All Ranks	18,347 All Ranks	12,148 All Ranks
Vehicles	3414 vehicles including: cruiser tanks 246; light tanks 44; tracked carriers, armoured 261; scout cars, armoured 100; trucks and lorries 2098	3347 vehicles including; tracked carriers, armoured 595, armoured cars 63; trucks and lorries 1937	708 vehicles including; light tanks 16; cars 5-cwt ('Jeeps') 904; trucks and lorries 567
Weapon	Rifles and pistols 9013, machine carbines 6204; light machine guns 1376; medium machine guns 22; mortars 2-, 3- and 4·2-inch 160; anti-tank projectors (PIATs) 302; field guns, 25-pounder 48, anti-tank guns 6- and 17-pounder 78; anti-aircraft guns 20- and 40-mm 141	Rifles and pistols 2,265 machine carbines 6525; light machine guns 1262; medium machine guns 40; mortars 2-, 3 and 4·2-inch 359; anti-tank projectors (PIATs) 436; field guns, 25-pounder 72; anti-tank guns, 6- and 17-pounder 110; anti-aircraft guns 20- and 40-mm 125	Rifles and pistols 10,113, machine carbines 6504; light machine guns 966; medium machine guns 46; mortars 2-, 3 and 4·2-inch 535; anti-tank projectors (PIATs) 392; pack howitzers, 75-mm 24; anti-tank guns, 6- and 17-pounder, 68; anti aircraft guns 20-mm 23

Note: (i) Although fully mechanized the infantry division required three transport companies (approximately 270 lorries) from corps if it was to move all its infantry battalions in one lift.

(ii) The airborne division had 4502 cycles and motor cycles.

(iii) A German regiment was about the same strength as a brigade.

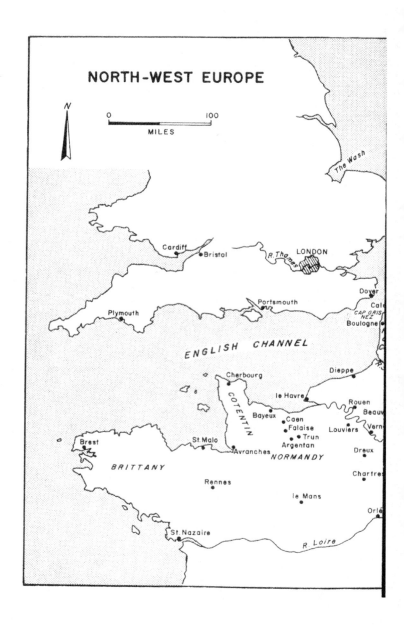

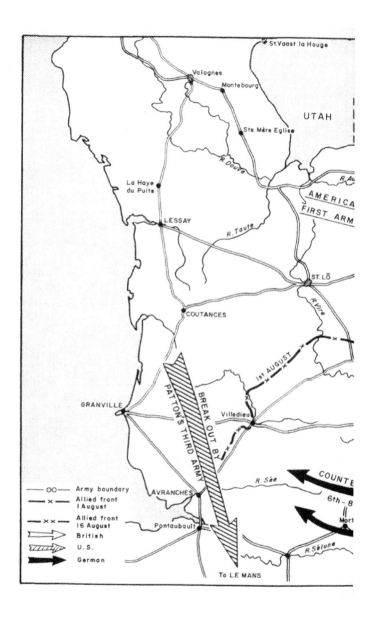

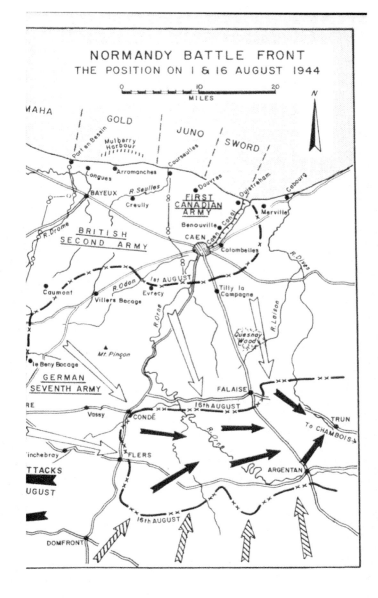

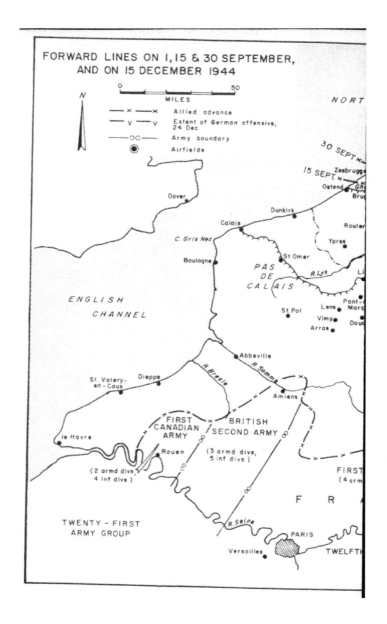

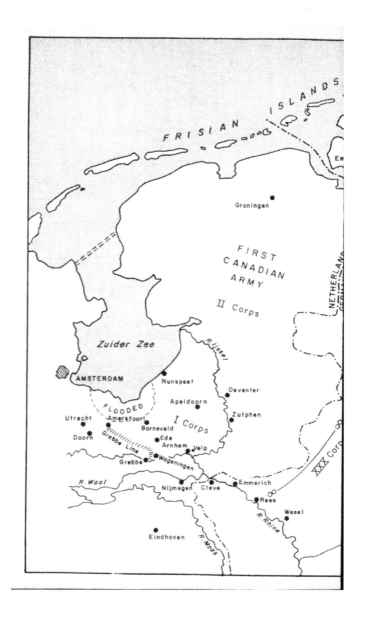

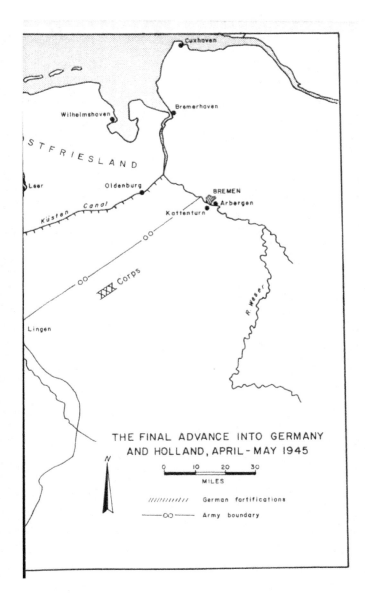

Authors' Acknowledgements

We owe a great debt of gratitude for the encouragement and help given us by our wives Nancy and Felicity during the writing of this book; and also to Felicity for preparing the maps. We are very grateful to Miss 'Billy' Wilson, Sir Brian's secretary, who, in spite of having a full-time job during the week, gave up every Sunday to type the manuscript of this book.

The British and Canadian divisional organization table at the end of this book is taken from volume I of *Victory in the West* by Major L. F. Ellis and is reproduced by courtesy of the Controller of Her Majesty's Stationery Office.

The quotations on pp. 199–201 and the photograph on p. 211 are taken from volume III of the *Official History of the Canadian Army in the Second World War, The Victory Campaign* by Col. C. P. Stacey and are produced by courtesy of the Minister of Supply and Services Canada.

B.G.H. and E.B.

Many of the events in this book have been covered in my autobiography, *A Full Life*, and I am grateful to Leo Cooper for allowing me to draw from this source. However, I have considerably expanded the story of the campaign, particularly in the Arnhem chapter, to which I have added much new and hitherto unpublished information.

I am also grateful to Leo Cooper for permission to draw from his Famous Regiments Series, to which I contributed the

Introductions, to Peter Elstob for allowing me to use information from his book *Bastogne: The Road Block*, the fourth volume in Purnell's series on the History of the Second World War, and to the Colonel of the Regiment for permission to quote from Roden Orde's brilliant history of the 2nd Household Cavalry Regiment, published by Gale and Polden Ltd. in 1953.

B.G.H.

Printed in Great Britain
by Amazon